THE HISTORY OF
THE ENGLISH NOVEL

THE HISTORY OF
THE ENGLISH NOVEL

By Ernest A. Baker, D. Lit., M.A.

THE HISTORY
OF THE
ENGLISH NOVEL

By Ernest A. Baker, D. Lit., M.A.

Volume V

The Novel of Sentiment
and the Gothic Romance

New York
BARNES & NOBLE, INC.

First published 1929

Reprinted 1967 by special arrangement with
H. F. & G. WITHERBY, LTD.
326 High Holborn, London, W. C. 1

27411

PREFACE

An apology is due to my readers for the long delay between the fourth volume of this history and the fifth. From 1930 to 1932 practically all the time that could be spared from the daily demands of teaching had to be devoted to work upon the third edition of my *Guide to the Best Fiction*; and when that was at last finished I found it somewhat difficult to pick up the threads again. I trust that the excuse will be accepted, especially as I think it is safe to promise that there will be no further delay. At the end of this session I shall be retiring from University College, and accordingly hope to have the sixth volume ready very soon and then get on with the volume or volumes necessary to bring the story down to the eve of the present day. It will be noticed that one American writer, Charles Brockden Brown, comes into the present book. I hope this will not arouse any protest. It is not intended to make this a full history of the American as well as the English novel, nor to assert any proprietary rights over all who have written fiction in English. But in the case of such novelists as Poe, Hawthorne, Herman Melville, or Henry James, who have definitely contributed to the development of the English novel, it would be absurd to stand upon ceremony and ignore the logic of facts, as absurd as it would be to omit Conrad, for instance, in a survey of the later English novel.

The later eighteenth century has proved a difficult period, not least because of many confused bibliographical problems and the extreme rarity of existing copies of many important works. Not only for their indefatigable and often unexpectedly successful efforts in running down out-of-the-way books, but also for incidentally helping to solve perplexities of date and authorship through their command of the resources of outlier libraries, are my thanks due first to Colonel Newcombe and Mr Pafford of the National Central Library. One's indebtedness to the British Museum is usually taken for granted; but I must express gratitude for similar bibliographical services, as well as for the mere supply of books, and congratulate the makers of the great catalogue on being right when acknowledged authorities have proved themselves wrong. Upon some obscure points of the same kind I am much indebted to Mr E. Phillips Poole, editor of *Lady Julia Mandeville*.

My thanks are due also to Messrs Macmillan & Co., Ltd., and to Messrs G. Bell & Sons, Ltd., for their ready permission to quote illustrative passages from Austin Dobson's edition of *The Diary and Letters of Madame d'Arblay*, and from *The Early Diary of Frances Burney*, edited by A. R. Ellis. Last of all, I have to thank Dr F. S. Boas and Mr W. E. Doubleday for kindly going through the proof-sheets.

E. A. B.

CONTENTS

7

THE NOVEL OF SENTIMENT
AND THE GOTHIC ROMANCE

CHAPTER I

AFTER THE GREAT FOUR

FIELDING had died in 1754, Richardson in 1761; their novels *The* had come out during the forties and fifties of the century. In *next half-* the next two decades their place was taken by Smollett and *century* Sterne, the younger of whom had been precocious enough to *compara-* publish *Roderick Random* a year before *Tom Jones,* and thus *tively dull* to be regarded by many as Fielding's rival. Before the deaths of Smollett and Sterne, a little earlier indeed than their last and ripest work, appeared *The Vicar of Wakefield,* which affiliates Goldsmith with this epoch-making group as their nearest and still their most popular disciple. And then until the end of the century and the arrival of Maria Edgeworth and Jane Austen comes a period difficult to characterize, which would be called dull if it were judged by purely literary standards, though from other points of view it teems with interest, a period when the production of novels went on with accelerating activity, yet one writer alone, Fanny Burney, achieved anything notably creative on the lines that had now been laid down.

For the impulse given by the four great hands to the art of fiction was curiously slow in taking effect. The proper sequel would have been a general reform in the very idea of fiction and in the way novels were made. What prose fiction is, what it can do and how, had been demonstrated by great examples and by Fielding's discussions of the art and its scope and relation *Failure* to life. Even the writer of moderate ability who thought that *to utilize* the novel had reached finality, and that there were no more *the new* fields to conquer, ought to have done something modest of a *technique* similar kind. The more gifted should have been able to employ the new technique to suit their own proclivities and dramatize their own ideas. But those who had been stumbling in the dark did not at once and with one accord set themselves to relearn

their business. Many, if not most, did not perceive that their
perplexities were ended, the problems that had hampered them
were now defined and solved, and all they had to do now, unless
they were capable of striking out paths of their own, was to
follow in the tracks marked out by the great four. Imitators and
close copyists were fairly numerous of Richardson and Smollett,
the two who had departed least from conventional forms; but
few ventured upon Fielding's broad and comprehensive epical
plan, which had a long time to wait before it was accepted as the
standard type of fiction on the large scale. Sterne was enjoyed,
without being completely understood. If Fanny Burney among
the new generation approached the first rank, the mark of her
contemporaries is that the quality of the next best is so inferior
that little of it deserves even the name of second best. In spite
of a vast and miscellaneous output, this would have been a
barren time had not a number of writers who were poor novelists
but persons of strong views or strong feelings tried out such
special varieties of fiction as the novel of sensibility, the tale of
terror, and the revolutionary or discussion novel, and so bequeathed
a lesson or a warning for those who were to come even a long
time after.[1]

The inability or at any rate the failure of the younger novelists
to avail themselves fully of the new technique was due, however,

[1] In a thesis entitled "The Lesser Novel, 1770-1800," for which she was
awarded the degree of M.A. of the University of London, Miss H. W.
Husbands surveys "more than thirteen hundred novels" of this period, chiefly
such as had not been included in the second edition of my *Guide to the Best
Fiction in English* (1913). That had cited thirty-four novels for the thirty years,
and Miss Husbands does not hint at any serious omission. She gives a most
interesting account of the growth of the reading public, the rise of circulating
libraries, the methods of the publishing booksellers, and the sweated labour
of the Grub Street hacks and the impecunious ladies who, like Smollett's Tim
Cropdale, "made shift to live many years by writing novels, at the rate of
five pounds a volume." Her work entailed a methodical study of the contemporary reviews. The notices in the *Monthly Review*, the *Critical Review*,
and other organs are examined year by year, and ample evidence is provided
of the mistaken and inconsistent standards, the many absurd judgments, and
the dictatorial conceit of the periodical critics. It is a pity that this useful
study has not yet been published.

Another illuminating work on the same period, *The Popular Novel in
England, 1770-1800*, by Dr J. M. S. Tompkins, appeared in 1932. This
handles the subject rather differently, from the point of view of social, or
at least human, rather than merely literary interest. It might perhaps be
described as a critical inventory, though it is far from devoid of historical value.
What may at first seem odd is that two well-informed writers, surveying

not solely to the dearth of talent, though talent of a higher order *Reasons* would have asserted itself in its own way. It was due partly to *for this:—* there being no complete theory of the novel accepted by both *lack of a* authors and critics, and then to the shortsightedness of the *complete* reviewers, who seem to have been unaware that the novel had *theory,* become, or was capable of being, not simply a light form of *wrong-* entertainment, but as legitimate and comprehensive a mode of *headedness* critical, or imaginative, or serio-comic portraiture of human *of the* existence as the play or the narrative poem; in short, that the *reviewers,* potential dramatist who chose to work within its frame could *baneful* provide his own theatre within the pages of a book, and enact *influence* the play on a stage of his own furnishing, securing an illusion *of the* of actuality in the reader's mind, differing psychologically, but *book-* hardly less powerful than that evoked by living actors with *market* scenery mimicking the real world.

But the rapid decline in the quality of fiction so soon after such a series of masterpieces had shown its possibilities was due, more than to anything else, to the very popularity of the novel, which was read chiefly for amusement or for the flattering version that it offered of their own feelings and secret desires by people who

the same wilderness of books, should have coincided much oftener in their comments and generalizations than in the instances singled out to illustrate and exemplify. There was so much of a muchness in the articles manufactured for the trade that superficial variations go for next to nothing.

As students of social conditions and of the vagaries of taste indicated by the efforts of writers to amuse idle readers of their own mental calibre, Miss Husbands and Miss Tompkins have exhumed a mass of suggestive material from these novels rejected by time. The average reader who turned to the novels themselves might well ask how two modern writers were clever enough to extract so much fun out of a subject matter so deadly dull. For these are admittedly the "lesser novels"; as literature they are of no account, and the great bulk of them have no historical importance except for the explorer of the intellectual history of the people. They were affected by literary fashions, but had little influence on the course of literary development, although the demand for certain kinds of literary provender was often an incentive to writers of superior talent. Poor novels may be landmarks when they contain the germs of some tendency or hint at some line of interest that others will pursue much further. But mere plodding efforts in a worn-out genre, timid imitations or copies made to order to compete with best-sellers, need not detain us. All we need to know is that these novels existed, and were produced in large numbers; it would be a waste of the reader's time to pay them much individual attention. Whoso essays to trace the annals of fiction through the period must needs make their acquaintance, even though the results often seem to be purely negative. "Nous avons fait plus de lieues que nous n'en ferons parcourir au lecteur, et nous lui épargnerons la désespérante longueur, le mortel ennui de plus d'une étape" (L. Maigron, *Le Roman historique à l'époque romantique,* préface, xiii.).

had scant appreciation of the more sterling qualities of fiction. Thus it was a saleable article, which could be produced in marketable quantities by writers working under the direction of the booksellers, who were also the publishers. It would be unfair to blame the reviewers. They would have drawn a firm line between this mass of commercial fiction and that which was not produced simply to meet a popular demand. But the reviewers were too schoolmasterly in their standards and too dictatorial in tone to have the confidence of readers or be of much help to the novelist. So the bookseller went on commissioning his base imitations, lifting characters and counterfeiting plots, signing with false names and misdating title-pages, dishing up scandals of the day, and trusting that the farrago would escape the critic's eagle eye or sell to a reasonable extent before the review appeared.[1]

The growing demand for fiction

At the beginning of the century the reading public had been comparatively small, and by no means refined in its preferences. But a new public was at hand, eager to read and not unamenable to tactful direction, in the prosperous and leisured middle class who were now taking their place beside the coteries who had been arbiters of taste since the Restoration. Steele and Addison's small contribution to the art of fiction has been already noted.[2] Still more valuable was the social service rendered by the *Tatler* and *Spectator* and some of the later coffee-house periodicals in spreading the habit of reading, kindling an interest in the little unromantic things of life, and by criticism of the stage and disquisitions on great poetry teaching how literature was to be appreciated. It would have been a service not less important to both readers and writers, a generation later, had some critic as sane as Addison written a set of papers on Richardson and Fielding, in the style of the famous essays on Milton. But the novel was not a subject dignified enough; no critic had the insight to think it worth while. The popularity of these two writers widened the boundaries of the reading world enormously; but most of those who read *Clarissa* with devotion or *Tom Jones*

---

[1] A. S. Collins argues that the reviews were "very influential in raising the standard of literature and taste." Perhaps they did their best; but the effect on the public or on the average novel is not very apparent (*Authorship in the Days of Johnson*, pp. 242-243).

[2] See Volume II., pp. 253-263.

with amusement remained so insensible to their finer qualities
that they gave a cordial welcome to writers glaringly inferior.
Richardson's, more than Fielding's, became a name to conjure
with. It was sometimes appropriated, as in *The History of Sir
William Harrington*, said to be written, or at any rate revised,
by "the late Mr Samuel Richardson," and his characters were
purloined, to pass off crude imitations.[1] Whilst readers of all
kinds were multiplying rapidly, the greatest increase in numbers
was among those who found their favourite pastime in the novel.[2]
Besides the people who bought books of one sort or another
for themselves and their households, reading clubs were formed
up and down the country, and soon circulating libraries were
established in London and other towns for the general public.

Novels being the chosen recreation of an uncritical multitude, *The com-*
there was a market for anything readable; hence competition *mercial*
among booksellers for copy, and on the other hand among writers *novel*
who thought they could provide what the public wanted. Thus
the manufacture of novels speedily became a flourishing trade,[3]
and a supply was forthcoming from a crowd of hacks, in the
regular pay or at the service of the booksellers. Most of them
wrote for a living, like Tim Cropdale,[4] but they had rivals in
the leisured amateur. It looked so easy to set down what passed
as a transcript of experience, or to compose a fanciful version of
life as one would like it to be. Anybody of intelligence, it was
generally assumed and the idea has been maintained in our own
day, has in him the stuff for at least one novel, and if one has

---

[1] See Tompkins, pp. 35-36.

[2] The output of novels went on increasing throughout the latter half of the
eighteenth century, but both Miss Husbands and Dr Tompkins notice a check
in the steady rate of increase during the period 1775-1785, a decline both in
the number published and in the quality. Perhaps the booksellers had gone
too far in underpaying their authors, and the stuff had grown so bad that even
the unfastidious readers revolted (see Tompkins, pp. 13-14).

[3] For concise information on the competitive booksellers, expanding sales,
and the multiplication of presses, even in provincial towns, see Collins,
especially pp. 223-236.

[4] See the satirical portrait of this working-man of letters in J. Melford's
letter of 10th June to Sir Watkin Phillips (*Humphry Clinker*). Clara Reeve has
this relevant observation in *The Progress of Romance* (ii. 7): "They [*i.e.* novels]
did but now begin to increase upon us, but ten years more multiplied them
tenfold. Every work of merit produced a swarm of imitators, till they became
a public evil, and the institution of circulating libraries conveyed them in the
cheapest manner to everybody's hand."

been achieved the writer is likely to go on and do better—or
worse. Fiction was often a hobby when it was not a remunerative
occupation. And yet of all the young women who applied themselves to it for pleasure Fanny Burney and Jane Austen alone
turned out to have genius. Thus it is from the very time, strange
to say, when Richardson and Fielding were before the intellectual
world that must be dated the existence side by side of these
two more or less distinct brands of fiction, novels that are the
fruit of some genuine literary impregnation, and those that are
the products of a commercial industry, meeting a popular demand
which can be gauged and exploited for a certain kind of reading
matter.

Circu-
lating
libraries

The invention of the circulating library was an excellent thing
for the book trade, but an evil for authorship, in that it tended
more than any other circumstance to turn this also into a trade,
and to make authors the hired servants, not merely of the booksellers, but of the crowd of readers. To the bookseller it ensured
a sufficient sale of almost anything he liked to publish to reduce
the risk of loss to a minimum. The system of employing hacks to
write books to order was made a safe business. Some booksellers
not only printed and published books but also ran a circulating
library as an ancillary department. There was even an
author, the Samuel Jackson Pratt who styled himself " Courtney
Melmoth," actor, playwright, popular entertainer and lecturer,
who was partner or proprietor of such a business in Bath, and
himself produced luscious sentimental novels for his own and
other circulating libraries. The first of these institutions of which
there is any record was run for some years by a Dissenting minister
and theological writer, Samuel Fancourt, till 1745, when it was
wound up, to be succeeded shortly after by a more ambitious
venture, the Gentlemen and Ladies' Growing and Circulating
Library, which had a very brief career. Only one-tenth of the
stock consisted of novels; but that proportion was very much
exceeded in the lending libraries that now sprang up in London
and some provincial towns.[1] By 1760, the year when Colman
presented his " dramatic novel," *Polly Honeycombe*, they had

[1] Collins, pp. 245-246; *Cambridge Hist. of Eng. Lit.*, xi., pp. 338-339;
Tompkins, pp. 1-6, 172-173.

grown numerous enough to excite grave apprehensions in those
who interested themselves in the moral welfare of the young.

In *The Female Quixote* Mrs Lennox had made game of readers *Novels*
who drew their ideas of the world from the extravagances of the *and novel-*
old-fashioned romance. It was now the novel, professing to *reading in*
give a true picture of life, that was denounced by critics, often *bad odour:*
with justice, as worthless and often pernicious. The misfortune *Honey-*
was that all of them, good, bad, and indifferent, tended to be *combe"*
lumped together as an inferior kind of literature, and young *and "The*
women addicted to circulating-library fare were warned of the *Rivals"*
dreadful consequences to their minds and morals. Colman bewails
in humorous fashion the passing of the Cassandra strain of romance
and the rise of that dangerous sister the novel, " enchanting,
charming name."   In an oft-quoted bibliographical tirade he
reels off the titles of some hundred and eighty, published, for
the most part, during the previous twenty years, and nearly all
of them now worthily consigned to oblivion. Like Arabella, in
The Female Quixote, Polly has shaped her behaviour on her
unguarded reading of fiction, and fiction to-day is more emotional
and more seductive.

'Tis *Novel* most beguiles the Female Heart.
Miss reads—she melts—she sighs—Love steals upon her—
And then—Alas, poor Girl!—good night, poor Honour.

The conclusion is: " A man might as well turn his Daughter
loose in Covent Garden, as trust the cultivation of her mind to a
CIRCULATING LIBRARY."

Colman's satire sounds crude and exaggerated in comparison
with the irony of Sheridan's *Rivals*, fifteen years later. But
at this earlier date minor novels still had more than a tincture
of the cynical immoralism of pre-Richardsonian fiction; the
sentimental trash that a few years later was to be the chief
stock in trade at the lending library was more harmless, except
perhaps to weak and susceptible brains, though according to
Sir Anthony Absolute Lydia's obstinate refusal to accept the
man chosen for her came of her reading. " Madam," he says
to Mrs Malaprop, " a circulating library in a town is an ever-
green tree of diabolical knowledge! It blossoms through the

year!—And depend upon it, Mrs Malaprop, that they who are so fond of handling the leaves, will long for the fruit at last." Sheridan had doubtless sampled some of the stuff that he gibes at, but evidently not all the novels that Lydia Languish yearned to read, the titles of which were apparently culled from a circulating-library catalogue and thrown together in the manner likeliest to raise merriment.[1] No serious person wants to identify them now. At all events, Lydia is a more plausible character than Polly Honeycombe, even if she does border upon farce.

Obviously, it was not genius or talent but the likes and dislikes of the majority of uncritical readers that dictated what sort of a novel was wanted and what sort would be read. The successful novel was that which put itself at the level of the greatest number and provided the greatest amount of the kind of pleasure that they could enjoy. No wonder that novels and novel-reading fell into disrepute, or that persons who regretted the time so wasted by the frivolous should overlook the fact that there are novels and novels, and consequently, as Jane Austen complained, slight even those which have "genius, wit, and taste to recommend them." But when she railed at the superior persons who railed at the empty-headed and undiscriminating novel-reader, she was a little disingenuous. How many of the works published at the time she was writing these words displayed "the greatest powers of the mind," "the most thorough knowledge of human nature, the happiest delineation of its varieties, the liveliest effusions of wit and humour," in "the best-chosen language"? That she preferred to publish her own work anonymously indicates that she was by no means eager to parade herself in such a disreputable field.

Failure of the reviewers to check the production of bad novels   But what were the reviewers doing not to prevent so much rubbish being flung upon the market? Did they stigmatize it in suitable terms, and give a proper welcome to what was more worthy the name of fiction? They certainly frowned upon the debased products of the circulating-library press; but they were strangely undiscerning in their judgments, and failed too often

---

[1] Thus *The Delicate Distress* and *The Memoirs of Lady Woodfora* stand for two different novels, the one by Mrs Elizabeth Griffith, the other anonymous and published two years later—viz. in 1771; but Sheridan evidently thought them the title and sub-title of one and the same book.

to encourage writers who showed signs of originality and an artistic conscience. Much of the counsel which they dealt out liberally to those brought to the bar before them was thoroughly misleading, for they were themselves misled. Periodicals reviewing books were a power to reckon with in the literary world during the last decades of the eighteenth century. There were a great many of them, though the majority were short-lived. Criticism of current literature was not the object of the group of periodicals, headed by Johnson's *Rambler*, which revived the tradition of the *Tatler* and *Spectator* about the middle of the century. Occasionally these essay-sheets and miscellanies indulged in criticism of a general kind. Richardson, however, was the only novelist who received any serious examination. Smollett and Fielding met with desultory appreciation or condemnation. Sterne was more fortunate, but their treatment of his literary idiosyncrasies was superficial.

The earliest of the more substantial periodicals which were to supplant these miscellanies was the *Gentleman's Magazine*, which first appeared in 1731 and by the middle of the century had attained a circulation of 15,000 copies. It described itself as a miscellany " consisting of News, History, Philosophy, Poetry, Musick, Translations, etc."; which is as much as to say that it proposed to take the place of a crowd of news-sheets and similar organs of information, and its dealings with literary matters were mainly confined to printing short essays, poems, epigrams, and the like, in the section designed to attract the lover of letters. The *Scots Magazine*, which began its career in 1739, was an adaptation of the English miscellany to the wants of readers north of the Tweed. More exclusively literary organs were the *Monthly Review*, which was established in 1749 and maintained existence till 1845, and its rival the *Critical Review*, which lasted from 1756 till 1790; in their heyday, these were substantial publications running to some 120 pages each number. The latter also had a Scottish colouring; it was started by a printer from Edinburgh, and among its most active contributors and for a time its editor was Smollett. Even in these literary periodicals, however, the notices of books were for a long while less reviews than mere abstracts or epitomes with some critical observations. It was about 1783 that reviewing became a regular practice, and might have exercised a very salutary influence on publishers and authors.[1]

Prejudices of the reviewers

But, although a good deal of the criticism was acute and to the point, the influence of the reviews often became thoroughly mischievous through the obstinate prepossessions of the reviewers. Instead of applying canons of imaginative art, they required of these books, which they seemed to think were read only by the ignorant and immature, that they should be didactic in every sense of the term, not merely orthodox in teaching a moral lesson, but infallibly accurate and informative on all the phases of life delineated. Many of their requirements were thoroughly irrelevant, and would only have hampered the unfortunate author who took them to heart. So austere was their attitude and so devastating their gibes that it seemed as if the novel existed as a branch of literature only on sufferance; it is a wonder that some of the female novelists ventured to survive.

Fiction must be didactic : Dr Johnson's view

The reviewers had recognized authority for the view that fiction was not a serious art worth the attention of serious people, and since it was read principally by those who did not think much for themselves it must be made studiously and healthily didactic. Dr Johnson was strongly of this opinion. "These books," he said, "are written chiefly to the young, the ignorant, and the idle." Hence, he continues, "they serve as lectures of conduct, and introductions into life. They are the entertainment of minds unfurnished with ideas, and therefore easily susceptible of impressions; not fixed by principles, and therefore easily following the current of fancy; not informed by experience, and consequently open to every false suggestion and partial account." [2] And so the reviewers insisted that every story must enforce a moral lesson. There was no virtue in a merely truthful representation of life; for Dr Johnson asks, "why it may not be as safe to turn the eye immediately upon mankind as upon a mirror which shows all that presents itself without discrimination." It does not vindicate the legitimacy of a character to prove "that it is drawn as it appears, for many characters ought never to be

[1] The handiest account of these critical and other periodicals is Walter Graham's *English Literary Periodicals*, 1930; especially chapters v.-vii.
[2] *Rambler*, No. 4, 31st March 1750.

drawn." Mixed characters are dangerous, since their amiable qualities may tempt readers to condone their faults. Men in history have been " splendidly wicked," their finer endowments throwing a lustre on their crimes, and " such have been in all ages the great corrupters of the world, and their resemblance ought no more to be preserved, than the art of murdering without pain." But Johnson ignores the perilous consequences of distorting or suppressing truth in the interests of morality, and how much safer as well as wise and honest it is to show Nature going her own way than to falsify the picture. If his reasoning were sound, he ought to have banned realism altogether, including that of his respected friend Samuel Richardson, who had peered into corners of life that ought to have been left in the dark, and in the " splendidly wicked " Lovelace had let loose into the world of admiring readers one of those characters that Johnson regarded as terrible agents of moral corruption.[1]

The *Critical*, the *Monthly*, and the rest of the reviews, when they dealt with fiction, uniformly acted upon these principles, insisting upon the most rigid and indeed the most stilted morality, and implicitly repudiating Fielding's claim that an intelligent study of crucial acts and events and of the unnoticed causes which bring them about is the best mode of instruction in the art of living.[2] Their prudery and censoriousness were in direct opposition to the attitude in these matters of Fielding, Shakespeare, or any of the great imaginative artists. They demanded that in all cases that mechanical and meaningless thing " poetic justice " should be strictly performed, and took the unhappy novelist to task, now because an ill-doer had been let down too lightly, and now for overdoing retribution and not giving an unfortunate sinner the chance of repentance and a happy ending in the long run. Their preference for a happy ending at all costs was, however, partly due to a kindly feeling for the reader, who as

---

[1] Lady Mary Wortley Montagu was not a very level-headed critic, but it is worth while quoting her exaggerated statement of this view: "The circumstances are so laid [in *Clarissa*] as to inspire tenderness, notwithstanding the low style and absurd incidents; and I look upon this and *Pamela* as the two books that will do more general mischief than the works of Lord Rochester " (*Letters*, ed. Lord Wharncliffe, ii. 222).

[2] See Volume IV., pp. 191-196, on the reception accorded to Fielding's own novels.

one of the common herd then as now could not abide tragedy. Dr Johnson's complaint about Mrs Sheridan's pathetic *Memoirs of Miss Sidney Bidulph*, that she had no right to make her readers suffer so much, is well known.[1]

Most of the novelists submit without protest

Most of the novelists cheerfully submitted to this dictation; it was cordially approved by nearly all the women writers, and fiction was becoming the special pursuit of unoccupied and needy women. They willingly accepted even the supererogatory duty of instructing their readers, not only in matters of conduct, but later on in religion, politics, and other dangerous subjects. Hence the theological and evangelical, the revolutionary, and other novels in which the art form was used for controversial and propagandist ends. But long before the day of applied fiction the result of the censorship exerted by the reviewers was that booksellers looked askance at manuscripts which did not conform to the prejudice against a frank and unbiased version of life. That rarity alone, independent genius, could prevail against such wrong-headed dogmatism, and genius itself had an uphill task in making its way. Everybody knows how long Jane Austen had to wait to see her first novels in print, with the natural consequence that she kept her discouraged pen unemployed for several years of her prime. Miss Edgeworth wrote fiction that was expressly didactic, and met with immediate acceptance, although the critics were nonplussed by *Castle Rackrent*, the one among her novels that is without an extra-literary purpose.

Idealistic aims of the Gothic romancers

The revival of romance by Clara Reeve, the Lee sisters, and Mrs Radcliffe, in the latter part of the century, was due in no small measure to their revulsion from what they thought the demoralizing realism of the contemporary novel, to which they would fain provide an antidote. So these writers appear to be on the side of the reviewers and Dr Johnson. But their case is somewhat different. In espousing the theory that fiction should

---

[1] The Dublin *Literary Review* in a notice of Fielding's *Amelia* remarked : "Romances and novels, in general, have no great right to be in Literary Journals. Yet some exception may be made in favour of those not calculated for mere amusement ; and we should be very sorry to look on any book as below our notice, that may tend to the Reformation of Manners, and the Advancement of Virtue. This seems to be one, if not the chief, point from which Mr Fielding's performance ought to be considered" (quoted by W. Graham, p. 208).

portray virtue attractively and show it always triumphing over
vice, they set themselves entirely apart from those who undertook
to represent life as it is.   It was the classic theory of heroic
romance that they adopted, as enunciated by Bishop Huet:

> The principal End of *Romance*, or at least what ought to be
> so, and is chiefly to be regarded by the Author, is the Instruction
> of the Reader; before whom he must present Virtue successful,
> and Vice in Disgrace. . . . Thus it appears, That the Entertain-
> ment of the Reader, which the Ingenious Romancer seems chiefly
> to design, is subordinate to his Principal Aim, which is the
> Instruction of the Mind, and Correction of Manners; and the
> Beauty of a *Romance* stands or falls according to its Attention to
> this Definition and End.[1]

In *The Progress of Romance*, Miss Reeve surveys the fiction *Clara*
to be found at that time on the shelves of the circulating library, *Reeve on*
and indirectly puts forward an apology for her own inoffensive *romance*
work, for her qualities are chiefly of a negative order.[2]   She was
rather timid.   Her own opinions have to be gathered from a
dialogue between interlocutors who do not differ much, and the
important contrast she would draw between the fiction that she
deplores and the new and improved kind of romance which she
desires is set forth in a quotation.   This is from *A Comparative
View of the State and Faculties of Man, with those of the Animal
World*, by Professor John Gregory, and it was a good tactical
point to cite as witness on her side a philosophic writer so widely
esteemed.   He wrote, and the date is 1766:

> Notwithstanding the absurdities of the old Romance, it seems
> calculated to produce more favourable effects on the morals
> of mankind than our modern Novels.   If the former did not
> represent men as they really are, it represented them better.
> Its heroes were patterns of courage, truth, generosity, humanity,
> and the most exalted virtues,—its heroines were distinguished for
> modesty, delicacy, and the utmost dignity of manners.   The latter
> represent mankind too much what they really are, and paint such
> scenes of pleasure and vice as are unworthy to see the light, and

[1] *The History of Romances . . . by Huetius; made English by Mr Stephen
Lewis*, London, 1715, pp. 4-5.

[2] *The Progress of Romance, through Times, Countries, and Manners; with
Remarks on the good and bad effects of it, on them respectively, in a Course of
evening Conversations* (1785).

thus in a manner hackney youth in the ways of wickedness before
they are well entered into the world; they expose the fair sex
in the most wanton and shameless manner to the eyes of the
whole world, by stripping them of that modest reserve, which
is the foundation of grace and dignity, the veil with which nature
intended to protect them from too familiar an eye, in order to
be at once the greatest incitement to love, and the greatest
security to virtue.[1]

The little group headed by Clara Reeve wrote romances
which aimed to avoid the absurdities of the older kind but fell
into absurdities of their own. Had they no right to put the moral
purpose foremost and make literature subservient, seeing that they
were so candid about it and protested against the reproduction
of life in all its ugliness? At any rate, the critics had no
right to browbeat other writers for not undertaking to instruct
and edify, so long as they did not offend by coarseness or
licentiousness. But a history of eighteenth-century reviewing
would be largely a list of moralistic sentences and of acquittals
on the score, not that an interesting story or a veracious picture
of life had been achieved, but that there was no stain on the
character of the novelist. Whilst they complained of ignorance
of the world and preposterous ideas on the part of many women
novelists, the critics themselves showed a bigoted misunderstanding
of the true relation between literature and life.

*Was
Fielding's
philosophy
of fiction
not
sufficient?* But was there indeed no adequate theory of the novel widely
promulgated if not generally agreed upon? Surely, Fielding had
propounded such a theory and had illustrated it with the most
brilliant examples. Fielding, it is true, had set forth a philosophy
of fiction, which was invaluable as far as it went; but he had
not been very explicit, except in the way he applied his principles,
on the methods by which the lifelike picture of the actual world
was to be achieved. He was not the Aristotle or Coleridge of
the art of prose fiction, and did not explain in any of his discourses
how the novelist is to secure that willing suspension of disbelief
which is called poetic faith. His account of the art had not the
thoroughness of his practice. Like other craftsmen, he knew
what he was about, and understood better than any the relative
place and function and the limitations of his art; but it did

[1] Quoted in *The Progress of Romance*, ii., pp. 86-87.

not perhaps occur to him to explain how he actually worked. Like Hogarth, he succeeded in making his figures appear not only to breathe but also to think.[1] But, like Hogarth, he could not or at any rate did not discuss the secrets of draughtsmanship or describe the brushwork by which he gave body and the breath of life to his creations.

Still, *Joseph Andrews* and *Tom Jones* were before them, and the critics could not have employed themselves more profitably than in putting these works under the magnifying-glass and exhibiting the technical means by which Fielding obtained his effects; how he made his personages portray themselves and always speak in character, how his fiction was thus self-authenticated and all pretences were rendered superfluous; how, again, he so managed his scenes and links of narrative that the story seemed to tell itself, and yet all the while his was a controlled realism, conveying a clear philosophy of life at the same time as it seemed to present a polished mirror to reality. They might have applied a similar scrutiny to Fielding's rivals; examined the processes of Richardson's self-analytical portraiture, Smollett's vigorous reporting, Sterne's impressionism. Hardly any of the novelists writing in this period seemed to have a clear insight into these details of technique, except Goldsmith and Fanny Burney, who recognized their rightness with the intuition of genius.

The existence of a ready market for literary wares, even of *Change of* indifferent quality, and the ignorance or disregard of respectable *public* standards, account to a large extent for the low estate of the *temper and* novel. It was not, of course, a new thing for authors to be more *outlook;* or less at the mercy of readers; the writer for hire had from the *on the* time of Greene and Nashe to consider whether his books would *novelist* sell. But now that the old custom of patronage had gone and the writer's standing in the book-mart was fixed by the breadth of his appeal, originality was not too much encouraged and approval by the great majority was all that mattered. Defoe had written his fictitious memoirs, histories, and astonishing records of travel to catch a certain class of readers whose appetite he knew exactly. Richardson had commenced author at the suggestion of publishers who wanted a saleable kind of book;

----

[1] *Joseph Andrews*, preface.

Pamela and his two longer novels were the result. Even the man of genius is conditioned by circumstances, by the tone and temper of society and the prevailing mental and moral attitudes, by what has been aptly called the climate of his day. Defoe and Richardson, Fielding, Smollett, and Sterne were not made by their epoch, on the contrary they helped to make it; they had convictions too strong, habits of mind too well fixed, to be dominated by the vagaries and prejudices of their contemporaries. It is the lesser writers, the underlings, who are the creatures of their time and environment, who are at the beck and call of opinion, and wait upon it to take their cue; and, this being a period of the minor talents and circumstances having made the production of reading matter a trade, the average novelist was caught in a machine and turned out goods to a registered pattern.

Beginnings of senti-mentalism Formerly there had been circles of women and men, women in particular, with time on their hands and a rage for amusement, aristocratic in tastes and irresponsibility, who gave a ready hearing to the wit who had anything brilliant to say or who drew a pungent or flattering image of themselves and their world. But now there had not only been a vast extension of the reading public, the reading public was of a vastly different kind; the middle classes now formed the main portion, and the middle classes had preferences and prejudices that must not be offended. No frivolous pleasure-seekers they, or admirers of wit whatsoever its target; but earnest, solemn, puritanical; moral themselves, ofttimes ostentatiously so, and also keenly interested in practical questions of conduct, and anxious that their standards should be strictly observed by all over whom they enjoyed any influence. The cold-hearted intellectuality, the flippancy and cynicism of a little time ago seemed to be now a thing of the past. To judge by the dominant moods, the great reading public was warm-hearted, emotional, strikingly impulsive; much more inclined to feel than to think. The herd instinct was in the ascendant. Common language witnesses how this always goes with sentimentalism. He who prides himself less on being an individual than on belonging to a large and influential class is more likely to say that he feels something to be right or true than that he thinks so. He is a firm believer in human nature.[1] To such an audience the novelist could not dictate in matters of taste and offer for its entertainment whatever happened to please himself; he had to consult its inclinations and hold aloof from its aversions.

Before the end of the seventeenth century, playwrights had *Domestic* had to acknowledge the existence of the new public that was *tragedy* at length coming to self-consciousness, and to set aside the convention that tragedy was concerned only with the disasters of kings and queens and that the only use for the people in comedy was to provide laughter. The human dignity of suffering and sorrow was found to make a more powerful appeal when the victims were drawn from the same class as composed the majority of the spectators. Speaking of the Tragic Muse, Lillo in the prologue to *George Barnwell* (1731) alludes to these beginnings:

> Upon our stage, indeed, with wished success,
> You've sometimes seen her in a humbler dress—
> Great only in distress. When she complains
> In Southerne's, Rowe's, or Otway's moving strains,
> The brilliant drops that fall from each bright eye
> The absent pomp with brighter gems supply.

Comedy, also, now asked for interest and respectful sympathy for people like those who crowded the auditorium. Congreve and Vanbrugh in much better plays were still making game of the shopkeeper and everything belonging to him; the principal function of the cit on their stage was to be cuckolded. The sentimental comedy now coming into fashion expresses a warm regard for simple family life and domestic virtue. Cibber, in *Love's Last Shift* (1696), *The Careless Husband* (1704), and *The Lady's Last Stake* (1707), did not shrink from adapting himself to what he had once stigmatized as "the vulgar taste," and wrung both admiration and tears for persons who would have been beneath notice in Restoration drama.

The *Tatler* and *Spectator* had been addressed to the cultured *Senti-* classes, who were not, however, identifiable with the exclusive *mental* sets of the previous generations. But Steele's plays, *The Lying* *comedy* *Lover* (1703), *The Tender Husband* (1705), and *The Conscious*

---

[1] " Confidence in the goodness of average human nature is the mainspring of sentimentalism " (Ernest Bernbaum, *The Drama of Sensibility*, p. 2).

Lovers (1722), to which *The Drummer* (1715) of Addison might
be added, follow Cibber's lead and belong to a strain of drama
which was now growing popular, that exhibited the joys and
sorrows of the common world, the world of homely people,
treated the subject of love and marriage with due respect, and
discovered not only pathos but also edification in the tragedies of
private life. One of the plays of Richardson's friend Aaron Hill,
The Fatal Extravagance (1721), was a good example of domestic
tragedy, and the model for Edward Moore's *Gamester* (1753),
which was popular even in the next century. But the most notable
of these sentimental tragedies of middle-class life was *The London
Merchant, or the History of George Barnwell* (1731), by George
Lillo, who followed up his resounding success with another, *The
Fatal Curiosity* (1736). Crude melodramas as these are, and in
prose that rises above the commonplace only into tumid rhetoric,
they have a certain power, and their emotionalism met with a
hearty response. Lillo knew his public [1]; and when he compared
his homely stage with the loftiness of heroic tragedy, he was
sure enough that his City merchant and raw apprentice would
touch their heart-strings more movingly than the Tamerlanes
and Bajazets of his predecessors.[2] He stresses " the usefulness of
tragedy," useful because it enforces a moral; even *Hamlet* comes
in for approval on account of the lessons it teaches. The method
that he commends is " the exciting of the passions, in order to the
correcting such of them as are criminal, either in their nature,
or through their excess." Thus " Plays founded on moral tales
in private life may be of admirable use, by carrying conviction to
the mind with such irresistible force as to engage all the faculties
and powers of the soul in the cause of virtue."[3] Exactly what
Richardson undertook to do in *Pamela*, published nine years later.

For what is labelled " Sentimentalism," that unbalanced state
of mind which revels in emotion, especially grief and compassion,

---

[1] The paradox is that Shakespearian tragedy was so popular at the same
time. Could it be the same people who enjoyed the brutal directness of bourgeois
tragedy and appreciated the poetry and lofty ideality of genuine tragedy ?
[2] Lillo's dedication to Sir John Eyles, M.P., Alderman of the City of London,
and Sub-Governor of the South-Sea Company. The Abbé Prévost served as
tutor to his only son, Francis Eyles, during his first visit to England (1728-1730) ;
see Dr Mysie Robertson's introduction to the *Adventures of a Man of Quality*
(1930).
[3] *Ibid.*

and decides its moral problems according to the reactions of *Senti-* feeling, was not merely a literary but a far-reaching social phe- *mentalism* nomenon. These plays and novels with the immediate applause *a general* they won were symptoms of a general social condition, a prevailing *state of* mentality, which came over England and other countries like an *mind* epidemic, reaching its head later in the extravagances of the novel of sensibility and the *comédie larmoyante*. *George Barnwell* led on to the sentimental melodramas of Hugh Kelly, Whitehead, Cumberland, Mrs Griffith, Mrs Inchbald, and others, most of whom wrote novels of a similar complexion. It was applauded by almost everybody in France, where it was followed by a number of *drames bourgeois* gratifying the same tastes. Gay's *Beggar's Opera* (1728) ridiculed these tendencies, but did little to check them, in spite of its huge popularity. Goldsmith's and Sheridan's comedies were later counter-strokes, yet the thing survived. It had secured much too deep a hold, not merely on literature but on life.

Poetry went through the same phases as drama and fiction. *Poetry of* Pope himself had turned aside from his proper domain, satire, to *sensibility* *The Essay on Man*, his half-sincere attempt to set forth " the nature and state of man with respect to the Universe " as a harmony like the optimistic Shaftesbury's—"Whatever is, is right."

> So two consistent motions act the soul,
> And one regards itself, and one the whole,
> Thus God and nature link'd the general frame
> And bade self-love and social be the same.

After Pope, it tended more and more to become the poetry of sensibility. Akenside, in *The Pleasures of Imagination*, formally and grandiloquently celebrates " this majestic frame of things " contrived by the " Sovereign Cause " to charm us with its beauty and teach us " to behold and love what He beholds and loves," and " to be great like Him, beneficent and active," enunciating the pleasant doctrine of the Shaftesbury school of the æsthetic and moral influence of nature :

> But let not man's unequal views
> Presume o'er Nature and her laws;
> 'Tis his with grateful joy to use
> The indulgence of the sovran Cause;

Secure that health and beauty springs
Through this majestic frame of things,
!Beyond what he can reach to know,
And that Heaven's all-subduing will,
With good, the progeny of ill,
Attempereth every state below.[1]

Thomson, Dyer, and other poets of nature gave utterance to a kind of poetical impressionism; Thomson in his affection for homely life, his pathos, and his moralizing, coming very near to Steele and sometimes suggesting Richardson. But it was the optimistic deism of Shaftesbury and his followers that chiefly inspired Thomson too. Then came that group who nourished their sensibility with reveries on death and eternity: Young with his *Night Thoughts* (1742-1745), Blair with *The Grave* (1743), Hervey with the elegiac prose of his *Meditations among the Tombs* (1745-1747), Thomas Warton with his *Pleasures of Melancholy* (1747).[2] This is a strain which had powerful echoes in fiction; even the author of *Ferdinand Count Fathom* did not fail to respond to the funeral note, nor, for that matter, did the author of *Vathek*. The sentimental humour that came out in *The Schoolmistress* (1742) of Shenstone, so much more than in his elegies, is not in essence far removed from that of Goldsmith's *Traveller* (1764) and *The Deserted Village* (1770). And already Gray, whose musings on man and nature were the most tuneful and the most classical expression of the finer sentimentalism of his time, and Collins, with their enthusiastic exploration of the legendary past, were giving a direction to the next phase of sensibility, that which sought what the present could not give in vague revocations of bygone times. The rudimentary historical novel and the so-called Gothic romance owe as much to the inspiration of Gray and Collins as to the revival of chivalric sentiment by Bishop Hurd, in his *Letters on Chivalry and Romance* (1762), the stir and picturesqueness of Percy's *Reliques* (1765), the glamour of the Ossianic poems (1760-1762), or the vivid if delusive imitations of antique ballad and epic, unhappily given to the world as genuine, by Chatterton (1752-1770).

Habits of mind and feeling so deep-seated and so widely and

---

[1] *On the Winter Solstice*, 1740. [2] Written in 1745.

persistently entertained must have had some countenance from *Senti-* the leading thinkers of the age. Philosophy, in fact, had been *mentalism* for some time deeply engrossed by the problem of the moral *and the philosophers* sentiments, which novelists and playwrights were exhibiting as mainsprings of conduct and the source of personal tranquillity and happiness. From Shaftesbury to Hume, philosophers debated whether these did not constitute the very basis of ethics, as well as supply the motive forces which in the majority of men determine their acts. Probably the most widely read among them was Shaftesbury, whose lively style and genial optimism were more to the taste of the day than " the selfish system of morals "[1] of Hobbes and Locke in their less elegant attire. His was exactly the right doctrine to flatter emotional temperaments and enhance the value commonly put on keen sensibilities. In the "Inquiry concerning Virtue,"[2] it appears that man, a portion of the universal harmony, is himself a harmony. A social animal, he is inclined by his very constitution to love his neighbour, and accordingly to ensue virtue and detest vice. His instincts are altruistic; benevolence is as spontaneous as self-love, and impels him to subordinate his own interests to those of others. "To have the Natural and Good Affections, is to have the chief Means and Power of Self-Enjoyment: So *on the other side*, to want them, is certain Misery, and Ill."[3] Good and evil are distinguished intuitively and infallibly by a moral sense, counterpart of the supposed æsthetic sense which distinguishes between the beautiful and the ugly. Not to put the natural before the unnatural affections is to be lacking in good taste. The infinite wisdom and benevolence of the heart are sources of beauty and beatitude in all creatures. No philosophy could be more acceptable to the novelist who depicted characters acting upon the impulses of a generous nature, failing sometimes through mistakes of judgment or excess of feeling, but, being sound at heart, always correcting their errors and acquitting themselves in the long run to the general approval.[4]

Adopting Shaftesbury's doctrine in its main points, Hutcheson

[1] Hume.
[2] *Characteristics*, Treatise IV., "An Inquiry concerning Virtue, or Merit."
[3] *Ibid.*, Book II., pt. 2.
[4] Not only in the story of *Tom Jones*, but also in the initial chapters, Fielding displayed a philosophy of life largely acquired from his reading of the *Characteristics*, a book catalogued in the sale list of his library, now in the

Hutcheson gave it a more clarified and co-ordinated form, especially by
and more closely identifying the moral and æsthetic sense, in his
Butler treatise significantly entitled *Inquiry into the Original of our Ideas
of Beauty and Virtue* (1725). He and Bishop Butler were provoked
by Mandeville's monstrously exaggerated yet specious version of
the egoistic philosophy of Hobbes and Locke, in his *Fable of the
Bees* (1725),[1] where all our actions are imputed to the self-
regarding affections, however much we may disguise our motives
even to ourselves. Butler constructed a natural theology on
altogether different lines, but in ethics he agrees on the whole
with Shaftesbury. The moral sense or conscience is to him an
inexplicable faculty implanted by God. It is by its intuitions that
we distinguish good from evil, not because virtue is identical with
benevolence, but because we have been so constituted as to recognize at once that which is good for us as human creatures. The
benevolent affections are not infallible themselves; reason must
be called in to direct them. Hence, he says, " prudence is a species
of virtue, and folly of vice," folly being " a thoughtless want of
that regard and attention to our own happiness, which we had
capacity for." This, it has already been pointed out, is in accord
with Fielding's views on the necessity of " prudence and circumspection " as " a guard to virtue," [2] just as Hutcheson's careful
distinction between calm good-will and passionate love is in accord
with the general drift of Richardson's teaching. When Butler
speaks of men of deep research and curious inquiry whose dis-
coveries may serve the cause of virtue and religion, he might be
quoted as approving the work of the didactic novelist:

> If they tend to render life less unhappy, and promote its
> satisfactions;—then they are most usefully employed: but bringing
> things to light, alone and of itself, is of no manner of use, any

British Museum. His morality according to Sir John Hawkins was " that of
Lord Shaftesbury vulgarized " (see W. M. Cross, *History of Fielding*, iii.,
p. 163). Such a criticism would more fittingly have been applied to the
Smollett heroes. For the philosophical influence of the Stoics and of John
Locke, particularly in *Jonathan Wild* and *Amelia*, see *Die Philosophie
Fieldings* (Leipzig, 1932), by Dr Maria Joesten.

[1] First published as *The Grumbling Hive, or Knaves turned Honest* (1714).

[2] See Volume IV., p. 131. Fielding was not one of those who adopted
Shaftesbury's views only to caricature them by extravagance. He ridicules
Square and his mechanical theory that virtue produced happiness, vice misery,
as justly as Johnson caricatures the philosopher who maintained that deviation
from nature is deviation from happiness.

otherwise than as an entertainment or diversion . . . the only knowledge, which is of any avail to us, is that which teaches us our duty, or assists us in the discharge of it. . . . If then there be a sphere of knowledge, of contemplation and employment, level to our capacities, and of the utmost importance to us; we ought surely to apply ourselves with all diligence to this our proper business, and esteem everything else nothing, nothing as to us, in comparison of it. . . . Our province is virtue and religion, life and manners, the science of improving the temper, and making the heart better. This is the field assigned us to cultivate: how much it has lain neglected is indeed astonishing.[1]

The sceptical Hume was orthodox on the subject of ethics; *Hume* his views tallied with the rest. Belief is "something *felt* by the mind," it is not the result of a rational process.[2] " It is not solely in poetry and music we must follow our taste and sentiment, but likewise in philosophy. . . . When I give the preference to one set of arguments above another, I do nothing but decide from my feeling concerning the superiority of their influence." [3] In the *Inquiry concerning Human Understanding* he puts benevolence before justice, and affirms the disinterestedness of the affections or passions. " Now, where is the difficulty in conceiving, that this may likewise be the case with benevolence and friendship, and that, from the original frame of our temper, we may feel a desire of another's happiness or good, which, by means of that affection, becomes our own good, and is afterwards pursued, from the combined motives of benevolence and self-enjoyment? " [4] Elsewhere he says : "We must renounce the theory which accounts for every moral sentiment by the principle of self-love. We must adopt a more public affection." " If any man, from a cold insensibility, or narrow selfishness of temper, is unaffected with the images of human happiness or misery, he must be equally indifferent to the images of vice and virtue : As, on the other hand, it is always found, that a warm concern for the interests of our species is attended with a delicate feeling of all moral distinctions, a strong resentment of injury done to men, a lively approbation of their

---

[1] *Sermon* XV., " Upon the Ignorance of Man."
[2] *A Treatise of Human Nature*, Book I., pt. 3, sec. 7.
[3] *Ibid.*, sec. 8.
[4] *An Inquiry concerning the Principles of Morals*, App. II.

welfare."[1] Finally, as a good Deist, he declares of reason and taste : " The standard of the one, being founded on the nature of things, is eternal and inflexible, even by the will of the Supreme Being : The standard of the other, arising from the internal frame and constitution of animals, is ultimately derived from that Supreme Will, which bestowed on each being its peculiar nature, and arranged the several classes and orders of existence."[2]

Even Hartley's associationism was in loose general agreement or was at least reconcilable with the theory of altruistic sentiments and of the enjoyment afforded by feelings and acts of benevolence. We love those things and persons, those actions and those attitudes of mind which have already produced gratification; pleasurable associations end in our liking them for themselves. It is a flimsy foundation; but it served him and his disciples as an explanation of the moral sense recognized by the philosophers. A firmer psychological basis for the sentimental philosophy was provided *Adam* by Adam Smith in his *Theory of Moral Sentiments* (1759). The *Smith* source of all practical virtue is sympathy, and sympathy is the main tendency of human nature. By cultivating and perfecting our humanity we repress our selfish affections and learn to love our neighbour as ourself. From our feelings towards others we form our sense of justice and our moral faculty or conscience. Our moral sense is fundamentally a sense of our social solidarity. Man's sympathies are too deep-rooted and too acute for him to act solely for his private benefit; if he wronged his nature by so doing, he would be too conscious of the despicable figure he made in the eyes of his fellows, just as he himself would be critically aware of the shortcomings of others, not to feel intolerable shame and remorse. He cannot hoodwink his conscience, " the man within the breast," the impartial spectator, the inexorable judge, who contemplates all that we do, not merely through our own awareness, but through the mirror of other people's watch upon our behaviour. This doctrine is obviously not an ethic, but a psychology of the ethical feelings. And Adam Smith studies not so much conduct as motive, the feelings that determine action. He purged the sentimental philosophy of the imputation of being

[1] *An Inquiry concerning the Principles of Morals*, sec. 5.
[2] *Ibid.*, App. I. : " Concerning Moral Sentiment."

merely utilitarian, as it appeared to be in Hutcheson and Hume. Acting, not from pure self-love but also from sympathy with his fellows, man aims at that which he thinks will be for the general good. Utility may be a test of the value of an act measured by its results: but the moral character lies in the motive, and those acts are approved which have a philanthropic intent.

The novelists may or may not have read the philosophers, but *Novelists* at all events the sentimental philosophy of life that was accepted *and* in the world for which they wrote received its sanction from the *philosophers* thinkers held in authority by those who did read them. Some, like Fielding, were manifestly imbued with the doctrines of certain schools; Mackenzie, for instance, is the spokesman in fiction of Adam Smith. He followed Sterne in his manner of writing; but where Sterne plays the buffoon Mackenzie is serious and sincere, and *The Man of Feeling* is the *Theory of Moral Sentiments* in action.[1] Burke, later on, in his treatise on *The Sublime and Beautiful*,[2] enunciated a theory of the emotions that justified the semi-poetic treatment of natural scenery and of states of feeling in the Gothic romances. But the influence of formal philosophy on writers of fiction later in the century may stand over for the present. Many of those in which it is most evident had pretensions to be philosophers on their own account, and their relations to thinkers who were not novelists will in some cases have to be examined. For the moment, it is enough to recognize that those novels which tended to crowd out everything else in the circulating libraries were written for people who were convinced believers in the goodness of their original instincts and whose intellect was perhaps summed up in their sensibilities. The gist of the situation was that, throughout the middle tract of the century, popular taste, what passed as enlightened opinion, and the voice of philosophy, coincided with

[1] Dr H. W. Thompson notes Leigh Hunt's remark, " It is said that Mackenzie wished to illustrate the theories of Hutcheson and Shaftesbury," and rightly observes, " If Hunt had added Adam Smith to that list, he would have told the essential truth " (*A Scottish Man of Feeling*, 1931, pp. 19-20).

[2] *E.g.* " OF THE SUBLIME :—Whatever is fitted in any sort to excite the ideas of pain and danger, that is to say, whatever is in any sort terrible, or is conversant about terrible objects or operates in a manner analogous to terror, is a source of the *sublime*; that is, it is productive of the strongest emotion which the mind is capable of feeling " (Part I., sec. 7).

the fondest inclinations of the great mass of novelists. Dr Johnson's austere Puritanism and hatred of shams and affectations might eloquently rebuke these morbid and effeminate tendencies. But even his petted Fanny Burney did not quite escape the infection, and thinkers as sincere if not as restrained as Johnson, such as Henry Brooke, and as sane and anti-romantic as Goldsmith, were carried with the tide. Fielding himself, after *Tom Jones*, had lost his confidence in the sufficiency of reason to control the passions, though his belief in the goodness of common sense never wavered. In *Amelia*, we feel that life itself has got him down and will not let him maintain the superior attitude that he loved; his irony seems to have been struck dumb. So again in the *Journey to Lisbon*. But let there be no mistake. Fielding's sentiments are the promptings of true feeling; affectation was always his butt and abhorrence, and *Amelia* is as different from the typical novel of sensibility as tragedy is from the *comédie larmoyante*. Nothing, indeed, brings out better the chasm between honest sentiment and that specious thing, sentimentalism.[1]

1 *Cp.* Volume IV., especially pp. 171-177.

CHAPTER II

SOME MINOR CONTEMPORARIES

OLD fashions and new characterize minor fiction for some time *Sarah* now, and most of the writers do not fall obviously into anything *Fielding* so definite and consistent as schools. The Manley and Haywood *and* strain had not yet died out; an easy way of compiling a novel *Lennox* was to fabricate a spicy version of some scandal in high life; and even such able lampooners as Smollett and Charles Johnstone, as has been noted,[1] kept up the well-worn satirical or rather the defamatory device of secret histories and Court intrigues, infusing, however, a new pungency and precision. Mrs Haywood went on writing till her death in 1756, the last of several posthumous works being *The History of Leonora Meadowson* (1778), a diluted and adulterated *Betsy Thoughtless*. Her improvement in directness and general workmanship has been noted [2]; she had moved with the times, the times of Richardson; and even her last effort in the genre of the secret memoirs, *The Invisible Spy* (1754), jumble of oddments as it is, shows a change from the wantonly erotic to the sentimental. The fitful reactions of middling talents to literary fashions and climatic changes are fairly typified in the cases of two learned ladies of whom there has already been some mention, Sarah Fielding, sister of the great Henry, and Samuel Johnson's " admired woman of letters," Charlotte Lennox, remembered to-day chiefly as author of *The Female Quixote*. Sarah *Sarah* did better in one of her later novels than in *David Simple*. But *Fielding's* taken together her works form an odd collection, and convict her *other* of as much uncertainty in choosing a subject as in working out *works* a coherent story when she had made her choice. It must not be forgotten that she was one of Richardson's bodyguard of female intellectuals. She translated two books of Xenophon, the *Memorabilia* and the *Apologia*, and two other works make a show of classical erudition. In *The Cry* (1754) she worked in

[1] See Volume IV., pp. 227-229. [2] See Volume III., pp. 118-121.

partnership with Jane Collier, daughter of the philosophic writer, Arthur Collier, and like herself a young woman always in monetary difficulties. This " new dramatic fable " is much in the style of classical narrative and the moralizing chorus. That early attempt to make biography as readable as fiction, *The Lives of Cleopatra and Octavia* (1757), shows similar pretensions. The two stately heroines meet and tell their stories in the realms below ; in short, it is a performance in the manner of her brother's admirable *Journey from This World to the Next*, overweighted by her habitual didacticism.

" *The* Her best novel was *The History of the Countess of Dellwyn*
Countess of (1759), which comes a little nearer than her first to her brother's
Dellwyn" unerring perception of motive, and is not without some tincture of his irony. It is the story of a young woman tempted into marriage with a rich old lord, and demoralized by her consciousness of a misalliance and the unfamiliar glitter and dissipation of high life. More out of vanity than any more powerful temptation, she yields to a libertine, her infidelity is detected, and she is divorced ; and, failing later in an all but successful attempt to capture a new husband, she ends in misery and repining. Sarah Fielding had a certain gift for showing impulsive natures labouring and breaking down under the stress of moral pressure, disillusionment, flattery, the sensual lure. But she wanders off into generalities, and the book is as ill-knit as *David Simple*. Her other novel, *The History of Ophelia* (1760), about a sort of Pamela who is carried off by a young lord, runs away when she finds that his purposes are dishonourable, and is reconciled when he repents, would hardly have elicited Dr Johnson's fulsome compliment to her powers of introspection.[1] Admiring friend of one great novelist and sister of the man who was his rival and in many ways his opposite, Sarah Fielding did not escape influences from both sides, and she was not strong enough to maintain equilibrium and self-consistency.[2]

[1] See Volume IV. 118.
[2] " Pray did she not also write a book, called, *The Governess, or little Female Academy*, for the use of schools ? " asks Sophronia, in Clara Reeve's *Progress of Romance* (i. 142). This curious predecessor of the modern school story appeared in 1785. It depicts in a rather flat and lifeless way the eight pupils of Miss Teachum, their ill behaviour, and the process of correction and moral salvation. Mrs Sherwood reissued it (1820) after altering it drastically to conform to her own pietistic ideas of edification.

Charlotte Lennox was born on the other side of the Atlantic, *Mrs* her father, Colonel James Ramsay, being lieutenant-governor of *Lennox's* New York. She spent much of her girlhood at Albany, Shenectady, *"Harriot* and other frontier posts, and was sent to England at the age of *Stuart"* fifteen. Then she contracted an unfortunate marriage, and for most of her life made an uncertain income by miscellaneous writing, including five novels, some plays, memoirs, translations, and the editorship of a feminine magazine. In both her first and her last novel she turned her youthful memories of Colonial days to account, chiefly for sensation sake in the first, *The Life of Harriot Stuart* (1751),[1] which starts in America, crosses the ocean to England, and has scenes in Paris and at a French château. This haphazard sequence of flight from a parent who would marry her to a detested suitor, of kidnapping red men and pirates, escapes from ravishment and other perils, desperate estrangement and ultimate reunion of two devoted lovers, is much more sensational than any of Richardson's novels; but these theatrical effects are a poor substitute for the dramatic tension at culminating moments in such stories as *Pamela* and *Clarissa*. Mrs Lennox had no doubt been carried away by the meretricious charms of a more romantic variety of sentimental fiction, that of the Abbé Prévost, whose *Cleveland* had appeared in 1732 and was translated into English shortly after—an influence that was soon to outgo and supplant that of Richardson.[2]

Still, Dr Johnson liked *Harriot Stuart* so well that he made the Ivy Lane Club entertain the author and her husband at an all-night sitting, and at supper crowned her with laurel; and yet it is the poorest of her novels. The only one of the other four, however, that can be said to have escaped deep oblivion is *The Female Quixote, or the Adventures of Arabella* (1752), one of the many attacks under the banner of anti-romanticism upon the authors or the readers of high-flown heroics.[3] The method

---

[1] Published December 1750.

[2] Lady Mary Wortley Montagu was merely irritated by Harriot, "who, being intended for an example of wit and virtue, is a jilt and a fool in every page" (*Letters*, ed. Lord Wharncliffe, 1893, ii. 221).

[3] For others, Fielding's *Tom Thumb*, Carey's *Chrononhotonthologos*, etc., see Volume IV. 14, note; for earlier skits, Sorel's *Berger extravagant*, etc., see Volume III. 38-40; later ones—*e.g.* Wieland's *Reason Triumphant over Fancy* (1773), Beckford's *Modern Novel Writing* (1796), and Jane Austen's

is burlesque, or rather extravaganza. Arabella, daughter of a haughty marquess, is a beautiful and not unintelligent girl, brought up in a lonely castle, who crazes her brain with reading bad translations of the romances of La Calprenède and Mlle de Scudéry, and firmly believes that the world is really framed as they depict it, and that fair ladies are still liable to be carried off by lawless knights and to be rescued by champions of super-human prowess and devotion. She expects all her friends of the male sex to observe the elaborate punctilio of the Court of Mithradates, and takes it as an outrage when her cousin Glanville, the suitor approved by her father, ventures to hint his affection in a manner unsanctioned by the author of *Cleopatra*.

These words, which he accompanied with a gentle pressure of her hand, threw the astonished Arabella into such an excess of anger and shame, that, for a few moments, she was unable to utter a word. What a horrid violation this, of all the laws of gallantry and respect, which decree a lover to suffer whole years in silence before he declares his flame to the divine object that causes it; and then with awful tremblings and submissive prostrations at the feet of the offended fair ![1]

Naturally, she meets with adventures a-plenty, not all such as she longs for, and is thrown into ecstasies of alarm at things and people more harmless than Don Quixote's windmills. Glanville's suit makes scant progress. Then a new aspirant arrives on the scene, a gentleman who sees what is wrong with Arabella and perceives that the way to win the damsel is to humour her to the top of her bent. He accoutres himself in a suit of plate armour, recounts his feats in delivering oppressed ladies, and hires a ballet girl to dress up as a princess in adversity and bewail the faithless-ness of Ariamenes, whom she pretends to recognize in the person of Glanville. But jealousy reveals to Arabella that she is after all in love with Glanville, and at the end of two volumes she is cured of her folly and he receives the reward of his patience, for the capitulation of such a proud fortress was worth it.

Northanger Abbey (1818, written 1798) will be duly noticed. Marivaux himself seems to have realized that his *Pharsamon, ou les Folies romanesques ou le Don Quichotte moderne* (1712, pub. 1737), parodying the sentimentality and lofty language of Scudéry romance, was a missfire. (The note on this in Volume III. 39, is incorrect.)   [1] Book I., chap. ix.

Burlesque can easily be overdone; the authors of *Joseph Andrews* and of *Northanger Abbey* knew when to stop. *The Female Quixote* is a pleasantry done to death, though partly redeemed by the character of Arabella, whose imperiousness somehow becomes her. The dedication to Lord Middlesex was written by Dr Johnson, and there is a legend that he contributed the last chapter but one, which is described as " in the author's opinion, the best chapter in this history."[1] Both the language and the sentiments here are certainly Johnsonian, but the same could be said of many other passages; and, if the authoress could not very well pay herself such a compliment, what are we to say of Johnson alluding to himself as " the greatest genius in the present age " ?[2]

One of the best things in her next novel, *Henrietta* (1758), is " *Henri-* the arresting first scene. A stage-coach is on the point of start- *etta* " ing, full of passengers, when a young woman squeezes herself in, annoying some, and eliciting the gallantry of a young spark who makes room for her by finding himself a place outside. These people are capitally hit off: the surly coachman, the tall lean woman who has never been in a stage-coach before and is already sick of it, the fat gentlewoman who sneers at such snobbishness: " I would have you to know, Madam, your betters ride in stage-coaches. Here's a coil indeed with such would-be gentry ! "

Fielding had done this sort of thing, and so had Mrs Haywood; the novelty was in choosing such an opening, and bringing in the heroine with none of the customary formalities. We have to find out who she is and what she is about from the subsequent dialogue. When Henrietta discloses to the sallow young lady sitting next her that she is running away from home and has no settled destination, and the young lady affectedly exclaims, " Oh heavens ! my dear creature, what do you tell me ! were you upon the point of being forced to a detested match? " and swears to her an inviolable attachment, we know that Mrs Lennox is indulging again in burlesque. The sallow lady must have a more dignified name than Henrietta for her bosom friend, for they have forged a romantic friendship literally at first sight, and dubs her Clelia and

[1] The Rev. John Mitford contended that this is from Johnson's pen (*Gentleman's Magazine*, 1844, i. 41).
[2] *Female Quixote*, Book IX., chap. xi.

herself Celinda, although Celinda is to be of no further service
either to Clelia or to the plot.

The   For this is not a Richardsonian novel; it is rather in the spirit
influence of of Fielding, to whom Henrietta herself pays a charming courtesy.
Marivaux When Mrs Eccles, her first landlady in London, offers her " a
very pretty collection " of novels and plays, the vulgar creature
is taken aback because Henrietta declines everything but *Joseph
Andrews*, which she has read three times already. " And yet, I
assure you, I shall begin it again with as much eagerness and
delight as I did at first." Useless to press upon her Mrs Haywood's
novels—" Oh ! they are the finest love-sick, passionate stories;
I assure you, you'll like them vastly; pray take a volume of
Haywood upon my recommendation." The model, however, was
not Fielding, but Marivaux, whose critical detachment in handling
sentimentality is, after all, more akin to the ironic Fielding than
to the doggedly earnest Richardson. The situation is the counterpart of that in *Marianne* : a young woman thrown upon her own
resources in London, at the mercy of an intriguing milliner-
landlady, and exposed to the attentions of enterprising fellow-
lodgers and wealthy woman-hunters. She preserves her honesty,
and eventually succeeds in marrying a marquess. But if Mrs
Lennox aimed at such a difficult pattern she fell very far short of
rivalling the Frenchman : it is a superficial copy. Nothing here
of the superfine moral casuistry, the analysis of delicate shades of
sensibility, the witty clairvoyance, that constitute Marivaudage :
the English damsel, sensible in the common meaning of the word,
simple and downright, is no such masterpiece of subtle insight as
is the corresponding figure in the Parisian story. The rest of
the characters are sketchily done; some are caricatures, and are
meant no doubt as gibes at romanticism, for example, the woman
of forty who fancies herself still fresh and blooming, and thinks
her husband's fits of depression are due to the torments of jealousy
when he is simply bored.

" Sophia "   The next novel of Mrs Lennox, *Sophia* (1762), is a straight-
and " Eu- forward piece of work, but even thinner and fainter in the
phemia " character-drawing. It is seldom in either of these tales that the
chatter goes as limpidly as in the stage-coach scene; most of
the conversation is tame and literary. When in old age she wrote

Euphemia (1790),[1] other interests had come into fiction, and, though in the person of her two chief characters she revisits the country of her youth, it is a very different picture that she paints from the one in *Harriot Stuart*. Though some incidents are rather excessive, the main story is a sober example of the trials of life. The husband Euphemia has taken in obedience to her dying mother is an ill-tempered brute, and she has to bear with him and other misfortunes, that of exile to the wilds of America not being the worst, for her son is carried off by the Indians. All is righted at the end, except that Euphemia has to resign herself never to enjoy married bliss. Such earnest domestic fiction was entirely to the taste of this later day, and so were the pains she took in what did duty for local colour, the journey up the Hudson river with the Dutch skipper, the experiences with the redskins and the fur-traders, the exotic splendour of the scenery. The Indians are not now mere bogies; she makes them, not merely picturesque, but generous, loyal, brave, eloquent, high-minded; in short, exemplars of the idea of nature's noblemen now current. Mrs Lennox has not learned to be a better novelist, but her outlook is that of the late instead of the early eighteenth century.[2]

At the time when Mrs Lennox was writing her first novel, even a Crusoe story by a man who was in other respects as matter-of-fact as Defoe could not avoid sentimentalism. So far, the only noteworthy example of the imaginary voyage since Defoe and Swift had been the *Adventures of Gaudentio de Lucca* (1737), by Simon Berington, which as a wonder story is indebted to both these predecessors and as a Utopia to Swift. But the

Paltock's even a "Peter Wilkins"

---

[1] This has no connexion with Baculard d'Arnaud's play *Euphémie ou le triomphe de la religion* (1768), although the contrary has been absurdly suggested. Baculard exploited "the taste for the Horrid" (Praz, 46, n. 3) and directly or indirectly contributed to the later terrorists such as "Monk Lewis."

[2] A feebler novelist, Sarah Scott, *née* Robinson, sister and as like " as a pea " to Mrs Elizabeth Montagu the bluestocking, was a similar echo to the changes of the times. Her *History of Cornelia* (1750) is ultra-sentimental, though the plot might have been suggested by *Pamela*, and her *Agreeable Ugliness, or the Triumph of the Graces, exemplified in the real life and fortunes of a young lady of some distinction* (1754) is still more mawkish. The influence of Prévost or his imitators seems to be traceable here, the tone being more sensational and per-fervid even than that of *Harriot Stuart*. *The Man of Real Sensibility, or the History of Sir George Ellison* (1765), emulates *Sir Charles Grandison*. As to *The Test of Filial Duty* (1772), a dull epistolary novel, and two sets of frankly edifying tales, these have nothing to recommend them but their unimpeachable lessons, in the mode of the domestic-didactic fiction of that day.

contrast propounded between the advanced civilization discovered in the middle of Africa is meant as a social lesson, and is not more satirical than the pattern state imagined by Sir Thomas More. *The Life and Adventures of Peter Wilkins* (1751), published over the initials R.P.,[1] was the work of Robert Paltock, a man of Cornish blood and an attorney in Clement's Inn; it belongs less to Utopia than to the literature of the marvellous.[2] At the time, it was hailed as " the illegitimate offspring " of *Gulliver's Travels* and *Robinson Crusoe*, a depreciatory remark which is not too slanderous. After sundry escapades at home and full measure of perils abroad, Wilkins is cast away upon a vast rock in mid-ocean, where he prospers for a time in regular Crusoe style, and then goes exploring. His boat is carried by a river of sea-water through a cavern to the beautiful land of Graundevolet, and there he makes the acquaintance of the Flying Indians, a simple and blameless people who have managed to equip themselves with wings. Wilkins captures one of them, and being of an amorous disposition he is delighted to find that under the flying apparatus clothing his prize is a beautiful woman. There follows the voluptuous idyll of their union, which enthralled Leigh Hunt. But the author of *The Story of Rimini* was only a trifle more enthusiastic than Southey and Coleridge, or even Sir Walter Scott. Paltock's homely yet sensitive and graphic style might charm any lover of good English. Perhaps the reviewer in the *Monthly Review* was not far off the mark when he described the author as " an able mechanic." The glossary of terms and place-names in the land of the Glumms and Gawries is further evidence of the way Paltock's imagination worked.[3]

[1] Actually "R.S." on the title, obviously a misprint, for the dedication is duly signed "R.P."

[2] The agreement for the sale of the work was unearthed accidentally in 1835, putting the ascription beyond a doubt. But Paltock's authorship was known long before that. See a letter by E. Phillips Poole (*Times Lit. Supp.*, 4th October 1928) giving a reference to P-lt-ck dated 1759.

[3] There is no evidence whatever beyond the coincidence of the initials on the title that Paltock wrote two contemporary stories, *Memoirs of the Life of Parnese, a Spanish Lady* (1750), and *Virtue Triumphant and Pride Abased*; in the *humorous History of Dickey Gotham and Doll Clod* (1753). The former is a romance à la Prévost, the latter a coarse love tale of the chap-book order. There was, however, an imitation of *Peter Wilkins* before the year was out, in *A Narrative of the Life and Astonishing Adventures of J. D.* [*i.e.* John Daniel], a smith at Royston in Hertfordshire (1751), which came out in December, exactly twelve months later. It is a servile copy, only departing from its original by

A novel that first appeared in the same year as *Clarissa*, and *John* which must have attained an enormously larger circulation before *Cleland* its sale was stopped through proceedings against it in the Privy Council, was John Cleland's *Fanny Hill, or the Memoirs of a Woman of Pleasure*, a realistic and entirely unreserved account of the seduction and the subsequent career of a courtesan, in her own letters. The book was first issued in two volumes by Fenton (1748-1749), and then bought and republished in a single volume (1750) by Ralph Griffiths, owner of the *Monthly Review*, who is said by Lowndes[1] to have cleared £10,000 by its sale, after inserting a commendatory notice in his own review. It is rank and unmitigated pornography, made worse in one edition by the substitution of more salacious terms by a bookseller named Drybutter, who was stood in the pillory for the offence. Cleland's only excuse was that he wrote to save himself from starving. He was a former official of the East India Company who had had to resign on account of some local squabble, and he is said to have been a Westminster boy and son of the Colonel Cleland who figured as Will Honeycomb in the *Spectator*. At all events, the excuse availed with the Council, and seems to have been the reason for Cleland's being given a pension of £100 a year.

Fanny Hill is an able piece of work in a facile and purely "*Memoirs* superficial genre, and superior to the *Memoirs of a Coxcomb* which *of a* followed it (1751). This is a less daring, or, to put it otherwise, *Coxcomb*" a more expurgated treatment of the same theme, the life of gallantry, with a similar transparent feint of drawing a moral. The coxcomb describes his first disappointing love affair, and the subsequent amours for which this is his excuse, with various sorts and conditions and ages—serving wenches, courtesans, demireps, and superannuated ladies of fashion who balk him of

---

introducing a flight to the moon, after Bishop Godwin (see Volume II. 209) and Bishop Wilkins (see Volume III. 134), not to mention others.   Stories of the marvellous that more than border on the ridiculous were *The Travels and Adventures of William Bingfield* (1753), introducing the reader to " that most furious and amazing animal the Dog-bird," and *The Life and Surprising Adventures of Crusoe Richard Davis* (1756), which boasts a floating island with feathered inhabitants, one of whom Davis marries, after she has been plucked. *A Voyage to the World in the Centre of the Earth* (1755), based upon Holberg, and *A Trip to the Moon* (1764) are satires.

[1] *Bibliographers' Manual*, 1858, I., *sub voce* " Cleland " : such shady transactions are still not unknown.

his promised guerdon. It is a novel in the loose-knit Manley-Haywood style, obviously written after the advent of Richardson and Fielding.[1] Perhaps unintentionally, there is pathos in the history of Miss Wilmore, the young lady of independent means who defies scandal and takes lover after lover, but lives to repent it when she falls really in love with the coxcomb. But apparently even this is meant, like the rest of the sorry business, to show what rakes women are, and how they earn only contempt from the knowing of the other sex. For Cleland adopts without qualification the profligate's estimate of women, and most of his sallies are at their expense. The fact is, any novelist of average ability at this date, who abandoned his mind and morals to it, might have written either *Fanny* or the *Coxcomb*. Cleland's other work is of no importance.

Shebbeare   Almost as disreputable a trespasser into fiction and certainly more disliked personally was Macaulay's "wretched scribbler named Shebbeare,"[2] who wrote *The Marriage Act* and *Lydia*, and was afterwards sentenced to the pillory—a sentence very perfunctorily carried out—for his truculent *Letters to the People of England* (1755-1762),[3] assailing the Newcastle administration. Dr John Shebbeare, as he claimed to be called, had been trained as a surgeon, but his vocation was politics, in which field he enjoyed a reputation for violence and scurrility answering to the boorishness that distinguished him in society. Fanny Burney calls him " the most morose, rude, gross, ill-mannered man " she was ever in company with, and inserts a full-length dialogue with Shebbeare to show how he " absolutely ruined " an evening at Queen Square.[4] Whig libellers paired him off as the She-Bear with the He-Bear Johnson, both being regarded as Government hirelings and a blot on the Civil List, for Shebbeare, in spite of the apparent frankness of his views and fearlessness in asserting them, seems to have ratted, and made a suspiciously quick transit from pillory to pension.

1 The long account of a night in a brothel is evidently meant to compete with the famous episode in *Clarissa*.

2 *Essays* : " The Earl of Chatham."

3 Shebbeare also published *Letters on the English Nation* (1755), a pretended translation from Battista Angeloni, " a Jesuit, who resided many years in London," one of the many collections of letters by an imaginary foreign visitor sketching life and manners in London or Paris.

4 *Early Diary*, 20th February 1774. See also Daddy Crisp on " that beast Shebbeare " (*Ibid.*, April 1774).

Shebbeare's novel, or tract in the guise of fiction, first entitled *The Marriage Act* (1754),[1] was a blundering attempt to show up the effects of Lord Hardwicke's unpopular Marriage Act of the previous year, which put a stop to weddings between minors without the consent of their guardians and to other matrimonial irregularities of long standing. The writer was arrested for an attack upon the legislature, and in the second edition prudently changed the title to *Matrimony*. He exhibits various young people coerced by their parents into disastrous unions, or showing resistance and finding happiness with the partners chosen by themselves. The style is an amalgam of Fielding and Smollett; the sentiment, as the ill-connected stories proceed, becomes more and more an affectation of Richardson's sensibility.

Lydia, or Filial Piety (1755), is as ramshackle in structure and "*Lydia*" mixed of the same ingredients. An Indian chief Cannassetego, who is a nearer relation of Mrs Behn's Oroonoko than of the noble savage of Rousseau and his tribe, comes to England to lay the wrongs of his people before the king. He and Lydia sail on the same warship, and the captain, Scots surgeon, a Welsh exciseman, and other oddities, are drawn with a comic virulence evidently studied out of *Roderick Random*. The Jacobite author hates Quakers and Presbyterians, and some of his caricatures are galvanized into something like life by dint of sheer acrimony. In the love affairs of Lydia and some others, Shebbeare again follows Richardson, and at times shows real feeling. His airs of righteous indignation were not all put on, if his manner did tend to alienate sympathy. It has already been remarked that he was slipped into *Launcelot Greaves* as the wily Ferret; but Smollett was not always in the same mind about Shebbeare.[2]

A more unsavoury person who also wrote novels of a sort was Dr John the quack doctor and pseudo-polymath who styled himself Sir John Hill.[3] Two of these are scandalous chronicles like many

---

[1] *The Marriage Act, a political novel, in which the ruin of female honour, the contempt of the clergy, the destruction of private and public liberty, with other fatal consequences, are considered in a series of interesting adventures.*

[2] See Volume IV. 223, *cp.* 215, note.

[3] I have now no doubt that the temporary owner of the guinea in *Chrysal* (Book I., chap. xix.-xx.) who undertook as they came "panegyric, libel, physic, divinity, cookery, criticism, politics, ballads, botany, etc., etc., etc.," was Dr Hill, and the "doctor and author" of a later chapter must have been

others of this period in English and in French which are doubtless made up rather of fiction than of fact, but aim to gratify prurient tastes by the suggestion of facts transparently disguised. *The Adventures of Mr Loveill, interspersed with many real Amours of the Modern Polite World* (1750), might have been the pattern for Cleland's *Memoirs of a Coxcomb*, published next year; it gave Lady Mary Wortley Montagu some entertainment, though she evidently took it for a key-novel and says, "There is but one character in it that I can find out."[1] *The History of a Woman of Quality, or the Adventures of Lady Frail* (1751), was written, probably for a consideration, to make out a case for the husband of Lady Vane, who had been her own heroine in the "Memoirs of a lady of quality" inserted that same year in *Peregrine Pickle*.[2] Invention outruns both truth and probability in this vulgar and slipshod farrago.

" *Adven-* Shaped, at any rate, to look more like a novel was his *tures of a* third work of fiction, *The Adventures of Mr George Edwards, Creole* " *a Creole* (1751); but this is only a cheap-jack, catchpenny production aping *Tom Jones*, and sailing so near the wind that it narrowly skirts pornography. Edwards is the son of a rich West Indian, sent to London by his father to be under the eye of an alleged kinsman, related, however, only through the runaway or rather the stay-at-home wife of Edwards senior, who was erstwhile sent to the plantations as a convict. Although the supposed uncle undertakes to be the raw youth's guardian and counsellor, he means if he can to pick his bones. The goodness of nature and easy morals of Fielding's hero are crudely exaggerated in this young fellow, who not merely never resists temptation but eagerly pursues it; hence lickerish scenes in which the female figures are demireps or professional courtesans. Edwards is fleeced by pimps and card-sharpers, but loses his money handsomely and usually turns the tables on those who try to gull him. None too soon, the story is rounded off by his old flame Juli's uncle, who had come over from the West Indies and has been

someone else, perhaps Smollett. The identification is clinched by the allusion to his " discovery of the sleep of plants," on which he had written. I owe this correction of a statement in my introduction to *Chrysal* (1907) to Mr E. Phillips Poole, who knows this period of literary history well.

[1] *Letters*, ii. 220.   [2] See Volume IV. 214-215.

secretly watching over the prodigal, and now rewards him with Juli herself. She was not dead, as he had long been led to believe. A would-be lively and dashing style, exuberant to the point of verbosity, made this conventional stuff go down, even with the reviewers.

There is not much to choose between such rudimentary fiction *Versions* and the base imitations which were made up of or heavily spiced *of society* with flagrant versions of society scandals. Titles, and more *scandals* especially sub-titles, were often promises of revelations which the authors failed to make good. Lady Mary Wortley Montagu had reason to be annoyed at not finding the " many real amours of the modern polite world " which were stated to be interspersed in *Mr Loveill.* Lady Vane's matrimonial history had masqueraded as a novel and had been foisted into another to serve in the one as defence and in the other as counter-attack. But most of the scandal-mongering novelists made no claim to any righteous purpose, such as exposure or vindication; nor did they pretend that they were studying an authentic bit of the drama of life from the point of view of an expert in human characterization; they were merely trading on the prurient curiosity of the world, and making easy if not fraudulent profits. Mrs Manley, who wrote so many secret and even " genuine histories " [1] which were anything but genuine, was probably responsible for a typical specimen of a story closely adhering to facts that were generally known, entitled *Dalinda, or the Double Marriage. Being the Genuine History of a very Recent, and Interesting Adventure* (1749). This, although the actors are given romantic Italianate names, is a fairly literal account of the infamous business of Mr Cresswell and Miss Scrope, and of the legal proceedings by which the lady brought the profligate to book, without however securing her own freedom to marry the man she loved.[2]

[1] E.g., *The Fortunate Foundlings : Being the Genuine History of Colonel M . . . rs, and his Sister, Madam du P . . . y, the Issue of the Hon. Ch . . . es M . . . rs, Son of the late Duke of R . . . L . . . D. Containing Many wonderful Accidents that befel them in their Travels, and interspersed with the Characters and Adventures of Several Persons of Condition, in the most polite Courts of Europe* (1744). It is the story of a young woman in much the same situation as Marivaux' Marianne, and of her twin brother, whose adventures are reminiscent of Courtilz de Sandras or the Abbé Prévost.

[2] On the question of authorship, see G. F. Whicher, *The Life and Romances of Mrs Eliza Haywood*, 94.

The second half of the century saw affairs enough in high life, from the royal family downwards, to keep the bookseller's hack busy; some were commonplace intrigues, some irredeemably ugly, others not ungilded by romantic pathos. Many stories to which everybody held the key appeared about 1770, which was the exact date of one having a strong personal appeal, the *Theodora* of Lady Dorothea Du Bois, a daughter of that iniquitous personage the sixth Earl of Anglesey. She had proclaimed her wrongs already in *Poems by a Lady of Quality* (1764). The Earl had repudiated her mother, and entered into another alliance, which was afterwards legitimized. This was the burden of her complaint. But disputes as to wives or concubines and the legitimacy of offspring were no novelty in the Anglesey family. The earl had also managed to get his nephew, claimant and probably rightful heir to the title and estates, shipped as a slave to America, as Smollett recounts at great length in *Peregrine Pickle*, through the mouth of Mr M., that is, Mackercher.[1] It sounds as improbable as the wildest inventions of Mrs Haywood or the disciples of Prévost. But plenty of subjects were to be found without going far from home. The elopement of that famous beauty Lady Sarah Bunbury, who in her teens as Lady Sarah Lennox had captivated George III., furnished material for at least two novels, *The Lovers; or the Memoirs of Lady Sarah B . . . and the Countess P. . .* (1769), by the Frenchman H. P. Treyssac de Vergy, an unblushing purveyor of high-flavoured scandals, and *The Unhappy Wife* (1770), a feeble epistolary novel by "a Lady." A still more notorious case, that of the Duke of Cumberland and Countess Grosvenor, is the theme of *Harriet; or, the Innocent Adulteress* (1771), the anonymous author of which endeavours to exculpate her heroine. The Duke had had to pay £10,000 damages. It was he who afterwards made a misalliance with Mrs Horton, sister of Colonel Luttrell, Wilkes's adversary, the subject of bitter invective in the *Letters of Junius*. Entirely opposite was the intention of such pamphlet-novels as *The History of Miss Dorinda Catsby and Miss Emily Faulkner* (1772), giving a vituperative account of the sexual irregularities of the second Earl of Halifax, or *The Life, Amours, Intrigues, and Adventures of Jemmy Twitcher*

[1] Chapter xcviii.

(1770), and *The Life and Amours of Sir R. P.* (1770), which perform the same spiteful office for the Earl of Sandwich and Sir Richard Perrott respectively.[1]

These productions kept more or less to the form and manner *The* of a novel, but a device that puts them in a different category was *inanimate* employed in a number of works, chiefly satirical, two of which, *witness* Smollett's *Adventures of an Atom* and Charles Johnstone's *Chrysal, or the Adventures of a Guinea*, have already been mentioned.[2] In these, some article that was passed from hand to hand was given attributes akin to those postulated by the occult science of psychometry, and the things it witnessed were described rather in the accidental manner of a picaresque story. Sometimes the observer was an animal, as in *The Life and Adventures of a Cat* (1781) or *Memoirs of a Flea* (1785). The machinery is thus of the same kind as the peregrinations of the halfpenny and the shilling in Richard Bathurst's and Addison's stories in the *Adventurer* and the *Tatler*; but the temper and purpose are very different, at any rate in the Scoto-Irishman Charles Johnstone's elaborate satire. His witness and narrator is meant to be regarded as a supernatural being, the Spirit of Gold, and to be possessed of faculties that penetrate the hidden motives, thoughts, and the past lives of those with whom he consorts; in a word, this is a demon like Asmodeus, who in *Le Diable boiteux* of Lesage (1707) shows his master all the wicked things secretly going on in Madrid.[3] Chrysal relates to his adept the inner history of public and private transactions, in England and abroad, during the period of the

---

[1] Miss Husbands mentions a couple of novels that typify two special strains of revelations in the guise of fiction, *The Life and Extraordinary Adventures of Timothy Ginadrake* (3 vols., 1770-1772), a coarsely humorous account of a musician at Bath and of the squabbles over the appointment of various Masters of the Ceremonies, and *The Adventures of a Jesuit, interspersed with several remarkable Characters and Scenes in real Life* (1770), a picaresque effusion pretending to show up the licentious morals prevalent in that Order. Plenty of later novels thrive on pretended disclosures, but at no date was there such a crop as at this particular time. Fanny Burney mentions more than once *The Correspondents* (1775), accepted by many as composed of the love-letters that were actually exchanged by Lord Lyttelton and Mrs Peach; they took in even Horace Walpole; they were repudiated, however, by Lyttelton's executors. The book " proves to be a very impudent forgery," observes Fanny (*Diary and Letters*, ii. 74).

[2] See Volume IV. 227-229.

[3] Le Sage borrowed the idea of his spirit from *El Diablo cojuelo* (1641) of Guevara.

Seven Years War and the Wilkes imbroglio, and paints virulent but life-like portraits of the chief agents and their understrappers. But, as Scott pointed out, Johnstone's was not the Horatian temper of Le Sage, the good humour and tolerance of comedy, but was nearer akin to Juvenal.[1] In truth, he was still more atrabilious, and admitted that misanthropy was the inspiration of his satire : " For, blazon it out as pompously as you will, nothing but ill-nature can make a man take delight in exposing the defects of others ; and the more forcibly he does it, the more powerful must that principle be with him." [2]

Similar stories of the same period   Among Johnstone's other works were *The Reverie, or a Flight to the Paradise of Fools* (1762), the satire of which is aimed at more obscure targets ; *The Pilgrim, or a picture of life* (1775), a satire on life and manners as observed by a Chinese philosopher in London ; and *A History of John Juniper, Esq., alias Jack Juniper* (1781), in which " a certain republican character now living " is portrayed with the sardonic irony of Fielding's *Jonathan Wild*.[3] *Chrysal* was the best of his works, and also the best of all these diaries or note-books of non-human detectives. Like much else considered in the foregoing pages, they were a misuse and often a prostitution of the craft of the novelist, an easy means of emptying a store of anecdote, miscellaneous observations, surreptitious libels, and what-not, and their literary interest is insignificant. It will suffice to enumerate most of the others. Mrs Haywood in this case too was one of the earliest to snatch at such a device for evading the difficulties of well-knit narration. Her *Invisible Spy* (1755) was not very different in contents from her so-called memoirs ; she simply introduces a spectator with a note-book and a belt of invisibility. Equally superficial imitations of Le Sage are *The Sedan* (1757), *Chiron, or the Mental Optician* (1758), *The Adventures of a Black Coat* (1760), and *The Adventures of a Bank-Note* (1770-1771), by Thomas Bridges. Bits of farcical liveliness relieve the monotony of the two last ; Bridges

---

[1] *Lives of Eminent Novelists and Dramatists*—"Charles Johnstone."

[2] He actually puts these sentiments into the mouth of the character representing Wilkes (*Chrysal*, xlix., " Reflections on the origin and use of satire ").

[3] Dr Tompkins is prepared to accept the British Museum ascription to Johnstone of the picaresque *Adventures of Anthony Varnish* (1786), which seems to have suggested an important episode to Bage, in *James Wallace* (1788).

tried to write like Fielding. *The Adventures of a Hackney Coach*
(1781) is topical in a way that *Chrysal* was not; that is, it
brings in homelier personages, not less known in their day, and
is as kindly as that was savage. *The Adventures of a Rupee*
(1782), " wherein are interspersed various Anecdotes Asiatic and
European," *The Adventures of a Watch* (1788), *The Adventures
of a Pin, supposed to be related by himself, herself, or itself* (1796),
belong to the genre, and so too at no great remove does *The Devil
upon Two Sticks in England* (1790), a continuation of Le Sage by
that Jack of all trades, William Combe, author of the *Tours of
Dr Syntax*.[1]

*The History of Pompey the Little ; or, the life and adventures of " Pompey
a Lap-Dog* (1751), is connected with this group only by similarity *the Little"*
of title. The author, pretty certainly, was the Rev. Francis
Coventry, a confessed disciple of Fielding, whom he places
" foremost in this species of composition," though he must have
enjoyed Smollett almost as much.[2] The dog is not a mere thing,
passing from owner to owner, but a character, who has temperamental experiences with the other characters, ranging from people
of fashion, such as Lady Tempest, another Bellaston, to the lower
sort of men-servants, fishwives, highwaymen, and the blind beggar
in whose company he finds his way to Bath. Fielding is indicated
when the author holds forth on the insolence of servants, who love
to vilify the reputations of their employers. But Coventry is more
unkind than Fielding, and the sketch of the methodistical Lady
Betty's mother and of Whitefield as an unctuous and sensational
religious demagogue is in the Smollett fashion.[3] On the other
hand, there are echoes of Fielding in the sentiments on society,
fops, snobs, debauchees, drums, intrigues, and the like; and the
scenes in the watch-house and the drama of the highwayman, the

[1] Miss Husbands has unearthed several of these, together with *The Adventures
of a Corkscrew, in which, under the pleasing method of a Romance, the vices, follies
and manners of the present Age are exhibited and satirically delineated. Interspersed
with striking Anecdotes, Characters and Actions of Persons in Real Life ; all drawn
to promote virtue, expose Vice, and laugh Folly out of Countenance* (1775). Watt's
Bibliotheca Britannica also catalogues the *Adventures of a Seven-Shilling Piece*
(1871).
[2] *The Adventures of an Atom* was not yet published.
[3] There is a curious resemblance in the names of Lord and Lady Marmazet
and the Mr Marmozet, in *Roderick Random,* Smollett's malevolent caricature
of an actor (Garrick) in Melopoyn's story.

blind beggar's son, passing himself off at Bath as a person of quality and all but marrying Miss Newcome, with the candid and caustic repartee, recalls *Jonathan Wild*, though the cynical tone is very different from Fielding's profound irony.[1]

[1] Lady Mary Wortley Montagu could not go to bed till she had finished *Pompey the Little*, although her eyes were weary with reading *The History of Charlotte Summers, the Fortunate Parish Girl* (1750). " It was a real and exact representation of life, as it is now acted in London, as it was in my time, and as it will be (I do not doubt) a hundred years hence." She found many of her acquaintance, and even recognized herself in the character of Mrs Qualmsick (*Letters*, ii. 218).

CHAPTER III

THE ORIENTAL STORY FROM *RASSELAS* TO *VATHEK*

AT the beginning of the eighteenth century appeared the first *The cult* translation of the *Arabian Nights* into a Western language, in the *of Oriental* French of Antoine Galland, which was turned into English forth- *story* with, to be rapidly followed by renderings or pretended renderings of other Oriental tales and by a large number of works in imitation of the style. Thus was inaugurated a renaissance of interest in the genius of the Orient, and more particularly in Persian and Arabian fiction and myth, the wild and wayward fancy of which, the sarcastic humour, and cool, matter-of-fact, fatalistic philosophy, differed curiously from what the Western mind was used to, and were therefore all the more seducing to readers avid of novelty and by no means averse to the outlandish. The event was a repetition in a sophisticated age of what had happened long ago when the East was introduced to the West in the Middle Ages. But the circumstances had changed. In that remote time, folk-tales and legends made their way by primitive modes of trans-mission into Western Europe and were received into the general stock, or were collected and translated into Latin in learned com-pendiums for use as illustrations in teaching or preaching.[1] The West had been able to assimilate the East because to simple minds the marvels and magic and grotesquerie of the one seemed not very different from the extravagances that were native to the other. The new stories took their place side by side with the old, and provided just as good material for the *fabliaux* and metrical romances, Eastern elements mingling and blending with those of Celtic or Teutonic origin without any manifest incongruity.

But in this later age such assimilation was impossible; East and West were never less likely to meet and embrace than at the

---

[1] See Volume I., Index : " Oriental folk-tales," etc.

An exotic genre, apt for satire or edification beginning of the eighteenth century. Any approximation must needs be of a superficial kind, in externals only, in setting and machinery, not in spirit and ideas. In fact, the most potent charm of Oriental story for the cultivated Western mind at this time of day was its strangeness and uncouthness, more even than its splendour and beauty. The masterpieces of the orientalizing cult were those which set these two incompatible worlds in subtle opposition, whether for satiric or for philosophical purposes. Western attempts at thorough imitation were uninteresting, unless they outdid the original for the sake of burlesque. The finest of the works in this alien style were, no doubt, very inaccurate representations of Oriental life and character; but that would have been a pointless criticism. They were not meant to rival the genuine article on its own merits; they were not written for Eastern readers but for Westerners, and verisimilitude in the Oriental details had only an instrumental value. Writers availed themselves of a medium brilliantly adapted by its arresting and malleable features, fascinating by the charm of beauty and strangeness, and made this serve purposes of their own. It was a pure accident that the cult of Orientalism coincided with their wish to expound a social philosophy or to satirize things as they were. Voltaire adopted Western picaresque for *Candide*, but threw *Zadig* into an Eastern mould. Johnson, on the other hand, chose a vague Oriental background for *Rasselas*, which enunciates a similar philosophy to that of *Candide*. Montesquieu and Goldsmith employed the method of contrast between Eastern and Western manners and ideas, but might conceivably have been just as incisive had they sought their contrast in the backwoods of America, as so many other writers actually did. Even *Vathek* is in essence a tale of terror like many other Western romances of stupendous marvels and violent sensations, in short, a Gothic story. It was a question of putting native wine into bottles of foreign make, and it was the quality of the vintage not of the imitation bottles that mattered.

An ephemeral vogue Thus the vogue of the pseudo-Oriental tale was bound to be transient and to leave no indelible mark upon the history of fiction. The aptitude of these daring fantasies and trenchant fables for philosophic satire made the form singularly acceptable to those

French writers who were promulgating views that, if generally accepted, must either mend or end the established order. But in England there was no such dissatisfaction with the established order. Tales and allegories in the Oriental style were used to ridicule social anomalies or as pithy illustrations of moral truths. But when, a little later, novelists with revolutionary leanings wanted to criticize or satirize, to speculate or discuss, they preferred to be realistic and direct. For a while everybody read Oriental tales, and most writers whether in prose or verse dabbled in the exotic style. Then the craze died down. It was never a genuine interest in Oriental life-and thought. That came later with the more accurate knowledge of Eastern countries of which the foundations were laid by Sir William Ouseley and Sir William Jones, and when, still later, the Oriental classics were made accessible in scholarly and unadulterated editions. But if short-lived, the cult yielded several notable works. *Rasselas* and *The Citizen of the World* can hold their own even in comparison with the masterpieces of Montesquieu and Voltaire, and would confer prestige even on an ephemeral fashion, and there were minor productions that do it no discredit. There may be some little truth in the suggestion that the Oriental example helped to teach Western novelists the value of ingenious plotting, the emotional effect of suspense, the charm of a paradoxical conclusion.[1] But they would probably have got on without this legacy, if such a legacy be not repudiated. The remarkable improvement in this respect observable in the best eighteenth-century fiction was mainly due to the example of the contemporary play; Fielding was neither the first nor the last of the novelists who had practical experience of stage-craft.

Galland's translation appeared in English (1704-1717) with the title *Arabian Nights' Entertainments : consisting of One Thousand and One Stories told by the Sultaness of the Indies to divert the Sultan from the execution of a bloody vow.* Compared with the fullness, accuracy, and vigour of Payne's and Burton's modern renderings, or even with the more intelligent though dull and still incomplete translation by Lane, it is a garbled, emasculated,

Galland's "Arabian Nights" and its imitators

[1] *The Oriental Tale in England in the eighteenth century,* by M. P. Conant (1908), 242. Miss Conant's is by far the fullest and best account in English of this literary cult.

and uninspired version; yet it served to introduce the West to this great body of Arabian story and to whet the appetite for more.[1] Even before the concluding volumes were issued, there came hot from the press the first of many translations of other Oriental story-books, the more satirical *Turkish Tales* (1708),[2] to be quickly followed by *The Thousand and One Days, Persian Tales* (1714-1715), more fantastic and sentimental, and by Thomas Simon Gueullette's *Chinese Tales* (1725). All were Englished from versions that had come out recently in French. Gueullette was less a translator than an imitator, and a rather clumsy and shallow imitator, who had been stirred to rivalry by the brilliant extravaganzas of Count Anthony Hamilton, *Fleur d'Épine, Les Quatre Facardins*, and the rest (1704-1720),[3] the light-hearted mockery and oft-times pointless exaggerations of which outdo even burlesque. Gueullette's *Chinese Tales* were put forward as renderings from a genuine original; so too his *Mogul Tales* (1736), his *Tartarian Tales* (1759), and *Peruvian Tales* (1764),[4] all which, especially the last and worst, are composed of shreds and patches of fantastic, moralistic, or sentimental romance, collected from here, there, and everywhere, with a colouring of Orientalism that is for the most part a transparent sham. The best parodies after those of Hamilton were contained in the framework collection translated into English as *Oriental Tales* (1745), from the Comte de Caylus, son of the famous marquise.

Letters of a foreign observer   Of a higher and totally different order were the *Lettres persanes* (1721)[5] in which Montesquieu urbanely and bitingly portrayed Western manners and ways of thought as they struck a pair of Asiatics in exile at Paris, one a severe philosophic observer, the other a lively satirist. He had had an artless precursor in the once popular *Turkish Spy* (1687-1693),[6] and a nearer one in C. R. Dufresny, author of *Amusemens sérieux et comiques* (1699) giving

---

[1] E. W. Lane's translation (1839-1841), John Payne's (1882-1884), Sir Richard Burton's, based on Payne, with the additions and corrections of a first-class Orientalist (1885-1886).
[2] *Turkish Tales; consisting of several extraordinary Adventures; with the History of the Sultaness of Persia and the Viziers.*
[3] Generally known collectively as his *Contes de Féerie*; see Volume III. 39.
[4] These are the dates of the earliest-known English translations.
[5] Translated 1730.
[6] See Volume III. 143, note.

the observations of a Siamese visitor in Paris. The latter had been paraphrased in a racier and more pointed form by the facetious Tom Brown of Shifnal, in *Amusements Serious and Comical Calculated for the Meridian of London* (1700).[1] Montesquieu's satire was copied by Lord Lyttelton in *Letters from a Persian in England to his friend at Ispahan* (1735), and through Lyttelton or directly it was a model and a fount of ideas to Goldsmith, in his *Citizen of the World* (1762). But the greatest of all the pseudo-Oriental works were the philosophic tales of Voltaire. *Zadig, Babouc, Le Taureau blanc, Memnon ou la sagesse humaine,* and the *Histoire des voyages de Scarmentado* were published in English (1746-1767) almost as fast as they appeared in French; and they were read by educated people, as many allusions show, even before these expeditious translations arrived.

From the time when the English translation from Galland was *Oriental* appearing tome by tome, the periodical writers availed them- *tales in the* selves freely of material so apt for illustrating their criticisms of *periodicals* manners and fashions and their moral homilies. Addison had always been fond of allegory and edifying fable, visions, bits of myth, and fairy-tales, and now frequently culled an apposite morsel of Oriental lore or an anecdote or story to point an argument. His " Vision of Mirza " and " Story of Hilpa, Harpath, and Shalum," each fill or more than fill one of his periodical leaflets, and are minor classics.[2] These are in the *Spectator.* The *Guardian* contains his tale of Schacabac and the mock feast, reminiscent of the banquet of dry bread with which

[1] Voltaire described the *Lettres persanes* as " Ouvrage imité du *Siamois* de Dufresny, et de *l'Espion turc* ; imitation très-supérieure aux originaux, mais au-dessous de son génie " (*Commentaire sur l'Esprit des Lois* : avant-propos). Elsewhere he remarks : " Il ne manque à cet ouvrage qu'un sujet plus solide " (*Lettres familières,* in *Œuvres complètes,* 1879-1885, xxiii. 399).

[2] For a list of Addison's and Steele's contributions in the genre see Conant, 271-273, where, however, the extent of Addison's loans from this source are exaggerated. In the first item cited, " Observations by four Indian Kings," the kings are certainly Indians, but not from the Orient ; they are Iroquois. *Spectator* 94 quotes a story from the *Turkish Tales,* 195 from the *Arabian Nights* ; 237 concludes with a brief anecdote from Chardin's travels, 293 with a little Persian fable of the drop of water that became a pearl. No. 343, the autobiography of Pugg the monkey, is an Indian tale of transmigrations ; 349, an episode of a Portuguese invasion of Morocco ; ∙ 587 comes from the life of Mohammed. Thus the derivation is exceedingly various, and only a minority come from the story-books which supplied the staple of Oriental fiction.

Peter regales his brethren in the *Tale of a Tub*,[1] and concludes
with the longer story of Helim the great physician, which he
pretends had been "lately translated out of an Arabian manuscript." Steele gave a very elaborate example of the letter from
foreign parts, in the epistle of the Emperor of China to the Pope
set out in both Italian and English in the *Spectator*[2]; and
borrowed from the *Turkish Tales* the story of the Santon Barsisa,
which was to give Lewis by his own admission "the first idea"
of *The Monk*.[3]

*Didactic
trend*

Eastern tales were great favourites again with the later periodical essayists; but there is a change of tone in those related by
Dr Johnson and Dr Hawkesworth. By this time, Montesquieu
had written the *Lettres persanes*, and Voltaire was busy with his
inimitable tales: pseudo-Orientalism had gone up in esteem as
a vehicle for serious thought as well as diverting satire. Johnson
and Hawkesworth adopted a gravity of tone befitting moral or
philosophical admonitions; and, unfortunately, in straining to
mimic the voice and manner of the East employed a formal
and pompous diction which they thought typical. The moralistic
tradition was to be kept up to the end. Goldsmith maintained
it in his "Asem the Man-hater," a Johnsonian "vindication of
the wisdom of Providence in the moral government of the world,[4]
and in many of the *Chinese Letters*; Mrs Sheridan followed it
in *Nourjahad*; and even Beckford, when he was not merely
flippant and fantastic like Hamilton and Bignon, when, that is,
he yielded to his imagination, affected the tone of the Judgment
Day. Miss Edgeworth was to write a sort of belated footnote
to the genre in her excellent piece of edification "Murad the
Unlucky," in the *Popular Tales* (1804).

*Satirical
trend*

Some of the items in the periodicals were the germs of lengthier
stories afterwards published separately. Such was Johnson's tale
of Seged, lord of Ethiopia, which occupies two numbers of the
Rambler,[5] and tells how the monarch of forty nations failed in
his persevering endeavour to secure even one day of perfect
happiness. It clearly foreshadows *Rasselas*. Such too was
Hawkesworth's tale of Nouraddin and Amana, in the *Adventurer*,[6]

---

[1] See Volume III. 232-233. [2] *Spectator*, 545. [3] *Guardian*, 148.
[4] *Essay* XVI. [5] 204-205. [6] 132-133.

which he expanded into the very popular *Almoran and Hamet*. In one of his later stories, of Ortogrul of Basra, Johnson returned to the theme of having an object in life, as a way of escape from the wretchedness of mere empty leisure that " soon made him weary of himself." [1] The appearance in English of Count Hamilton's tales (1760) and then of the *Contes moraux* of Marmontel,[2] some of which were Oriental in setting and colour and many others akin in their satiric or lightly moralistic aim, was a sign that the popularity of the fashion was not exhausted and also an incentive to further imitation. Horace Walpole adopted the well-accredited form of the letter from an Oriental to his friend at home, to ridicule the absurdity of English justice as illustrated in the execution of Admiral Byng, in *A Letter from Xo-Ho, a Chinese Philosopher at London* (1757), wittily and scathingly enough, though not with more effect than Voltaire's quiet " Dans ce pays-ci il est bon de tuer de temps en temps un amiral pour encourager les autres." [3] Goldsmith, himself utilizing the popular framework in his *Citizen of the World*, bantered those amateurs who thought they could shine in it by a supposed Oriental magniloquence: " There is the true eastern taste for you; every advance made towards sense is only a deviation from sound. Eastern tales should always be sononous, lofty, musical, and unmeaning." [4]

Thus it was natural for Dr Johnson to employ the Oriental convention in *Rasselas* (1759); he had already found it acceptable and effective for philosophical fabling. Though apparently written at high speed, perhaps in the evenings of one week, as Boswell says that Johnson told Reynolds,[5] it is the longest and most sustained of his sermons on the vanity of human wishes, the gravity of tone deepened to melancholy by his late bereavement, for it was in order to meet the expenses of his mother's funeral and pay off some debts she had left behind that he was

Johnson's "Ras- selas"

---

[1] *Idler*, 99.

[2] Marmontel appeared in English piecemeal; e.g. *Select Moral Tales*, translated by a Lady (1763), a later collection selected and abridged by Mrs Pilkington (1799), *Moral Tales* (in an edition mentioned by Conant, 1764-1766?), and *Moral Tales*, translated by G. Dennis and R. Lloyd (3 vols., 1781). They appeared in French (1761-1765), and *Nouveaux contes moraux* (1790-1801).

[3] *Candide*, xxiii.

[4] Letter XXXIII.

[5] Points settled once for all in R. W. Chapman's edition of *Rasselas* (1927).

in a hurry to finish it and receive the price agreed upon. The subject was one of the commonplaces of the time, the impossibility of unmixed happiness in such a world as this. It was Voltaire's theme in *Zadig, ou la destinée,* in *Scarmentado,* in *Memnon,* in *Jenni,* where the doctrines of Mandeville are severely reprobated, and in *L'Homme aux quarante écus,* where the problem is considered in relation to the body politic. It was the theme of *Candide,* which appeared only six weeks before *Rasselas.*[1]

Contemporaneous with "Candide" It was a remarkable coincidence, though not so astonishing if we remember that both men were continually writing refutations of optimism, Voltaire as a disillusioned philosopher, Johnson as moralist. The purpose, a satire of that enervating doctrine, and the scheme, a survey of the world to test its application, were pretty nearly identical; it is the manner and tone that bring out the difference between the mocking Voltaire and the grave and reverent Johnson. Close contacts there were bound to be, in these and in others of their works, between two such realists, such defenders of common sense against any abstract or abstruse philosophy whatever. Events teach Candide to moderate his desires and accept the world as he finds it; his story is as full of incident and surprises as any picaresque romance. Very little happens to the prince of Abyssinia and his sister Nekayah, from the day when they voluntarily quit their Eden till their disenchanted return, except ample opportunities to view and discuss the different modes of life met with in the course of an extended tour. The kidnapping of the princess's maid by Arabs hardly ruffles the surface. Yet both stories lead to a like conclusion. Do the duty that lies nearest to your hand, and in doing it you will find what happiness is within human reach.

Vacuity and ennui the enemy For the direct pursuit of happiness is the pursuit of a mirage, which flies us as fast as we seem to approach. What afflicts us is ennui, boredom, vacuity, the lack of an object in life. An inexhaustible supply of pleasure does not ensure happiness.

---

[1] Johnson's remark, reported by Boswell, that had not the one book followed the other so closely " it would have been vain to deny that the scheme of that which came latest was taken from the other," is considered *Ibid.,* xvi. The possibility cannot be entirely ruled out; but " no one will doubt that Johnson, when he wrote *Rasselas,* had not seen *Candide.*"

Rasselas sees that every beast is satisfied when hunger and thirst
are appeased; but, he says, "when thirst and hunger cease, I
am not at rest. . . . I long again to be hungry, that I may
again quicken the attention." The birds sit in seeming happiness
on the branches; "I likewise can call the lutanist and the singer;
but the sounds that pleased me yesterday weary me to-day, and
will grow yet more wearisome to-morrow." Like Voltaire's
Zadig, he has found that "toujours du plaisir n'est pas du
plaisir."[1] "Give me something to desire," Rasselas cries. And
he finds himself happy when he has something to do, an object
to strive for. Even when his efforts to find a way out of the
happy valley were fruitless, the time passed cheerfully away;
"he rose with new hope" and "slept sound after his fatigue,"
he rejoiced in the variety of interests that had been revealed to
him, and was half prepared to abandon his quest and solace
himself with the delights of contemplation.[2]

But having realized their purpose and escaped into the great
world, they discover mankind everywhere a prey to disappointment and discontent, and soberly wend their way back to the
place they had left. Variety after all has not satisfied them. Life
can be made tolerable only by our having something to do. It
is a minor matter what the vocation is, so long as it engrosses
our attention. "The choice of life is become less important,"
says the princess; and the pious Johnson makes her add, "I
hope hereafter to think only on the choice of eternity." The
employment that she actually selects is to preside over a college
for women, whilst the prince would set himself to administer
the affairs of a little kingdom. "Travaillons sans raisonner,"
said Martin at the end of *Candide*. Both Voltaire and Johnson
forestall Carlyle's injunction to work. As to the nature of the
work, practically anything will serve. "Cela est bien dit,"
answered Candide to the demonstration of Pangloss that everything had happened by an intelligible process of causation; "mais
il faut cultiver notre jardin." Here is the remedy for the ennui

---

[1] *Zadig*, vi.

[2] So Ortogrul says to himself, "How different, Ortogrul, is thy condition,
who art doomed to the perpetual torments of unsatisfied desire, and who hast
no amusement in thy power that can withhold thee from thy own reflections!"
(*Idler*, 99).

of which the old crone had been eloquently complaining, and the best refuge after the diversity of ills they had suffered in the world at large.[1]

" Dinar-bas,"
sequel to
" Ras-selas "

Late in the century, an Ellis Cornelia Knight [2] had the temerity to provide a happy ending to *Rasselas*, in a story of much the same length entitled *Dinarbas*, published anonymously (1790). When the inundation which kept them talking had subsided, Rasselas and Nekayah, with Imlac, Pekuah, and the deranged astronomer, set out on the return journey to Abyssinia; but are stopped on the frontier, and conducted to a fortress, where the governor, the venerable Amalphis, and his son Dinarbas converse with them on the unexhausted theme of happiness. Some alarming incidents occur through an attack on the fortress by Egyptians and Arabs; Dinarbas and Rasselas both distinguish themselves, but the former falls apparently dead and the latter is taken prisoner. In confinement, Rasselas meditates on the resources of solitude, and learning resignation finds captivity rather a good than an evil. Dinarbas comes to life again at the moment of his stately obsequies, and declares his affection for the princess Nekayah. There are further troubles in Abyssinia, which serve to display the wisdom and prowess of Rasselas. Soon he succeeds to the throne, and the marriages of Rasselas and Zilia, daughter of Amalphis, and of Nekayah and Dinarbas are solemnized shortly after. The style is a close imitation of Johnson's; not unsuccessful, except that his strength and fearlessness are lacking, and the aphorisms are mere platitudes.

A notable difference between Dr Hawkesworth's Oriental tale, *Almoran and Hamet* (1761), and *The History of Nourjahad* (1767)

---

[1] Voltaire's deistic theory, set forth in *Zadig*, " Il n'y a point de hasard ; tout est épreuve, ou punition, ou récompense, ou prévoyance " (*Zadig*, xx.), is not much at variance with Johnson's belief in Providence. Each author has a philosopher prominent in his story, and Pangloss is superior to Imlac, not merely in being much more entertaining, but in playing a more consistent rôle. Imlac merely enlarges in Johnsonian language on the situations brought about by circumstances ; and, except that he draws some fine distinctions and sometimes puts the other point of view, he shines more as a talker than as a philosopher : he does not furnish much positive instruction. He says, when the whole question has been brought to a focus, " I am afraid to decide in either part " (*R.*, xlvii.). The decisive glimpses of truth are caught by the others from their commerce with realities.

[2] She became companion to Queen Charlotte and later to Princess Charlotte of Wales, and her posthumous autobiography is interesting for its glimpses of life at Court.

by Mrs Sheridan, best known as the author of *Sidney Bidulph*, " *Al-* both of which serve the purposes of apologues, is that in the latter *moran and* magic is discarded, whence it is an early instance of the rationalism *Hamet"* that induced Mrs Radcliffe to provide an explanation for her seemingly supernatural occurrences. She plunges us at the outset into what appear to be monstrous enchantments, but shows at the end that all the miracles were stage-planned. In Hawkesworth's tale, the king of Persia divides the kingdom between his two sons. Almoran is vain and voluptuous, Hamet, temperate and gentle. Almoran affects a mien of resignation, but plots to depose his brother and seize the whole empire. He also schemes to possess himself of the beautiful lady who loves and is beloved of the amiable Hamet. And his machinations prosper, for on his side appears an irresistible genie. But though all else is in his grasp, he cannot subdue the lovely Almeida. At this juncture, the genie puts at his service a talisman. Almoran is able to assume the form and speech of Hamet, and Hamet, all unwittingly, appears as Almoran. Almeida is almost vanquished by the supposed Hamet, but is bewildered to find her lover proposing conduct that belies all she has believed of his goodness. It is a situation offering a great opportunity for dramatic irony. But the traitor, in the shape of his rival, not only has to digest the most crushing denunciations of himself, but ultimately, after agonies of terror and suspense, is forced to recognize that every intervention of the genie has brought some calamity upon his own head. Tried by the celestial powers and proved disobedient, Almoran is changed to the likeness of a misshapen rock, whilst Hamet is elevated to the highest honours. It is a sensational story, dealing with the problem of human happiness in a cruder way than *Rasselas*, and like *Nourjahad* it enjoyed considerable popularity.

Mrs Sheridan's hero is the favourite of the Shah of Persia, but " *Nour-* has been found on trial to be the slave of avarice and licentiousness. *jahad"* A genie offers to put him in possession of inexhaustible riches and bestow the gift of immortality, with the proviso that at times his life would be interrupted by trances like unto death. Nourjahad begins a career of unbridled luxury, shutting himself up in a palace more splendid than that of his sovereign, and dressing up the women of his harem to impersonate the peerless virgins of paradise.

This is the moment when one of the intervals of sleep foretold by the genie descends upon him. He wakes, as if from a few hours' slumber, and calls for his household. But Nourjahad has been asleep forty years, and here comes one of the brilliant scenes of the tale.

The slave retired in respectful silence; and presently after, all the ladies of his seraglio entered his apartment. They were, according to the custom, covered with veils; but on appearing in their lord's presence, they threw them off. But, oh Heaven! what was Nourjahad's anger and astonishment, when instead of the beautiful Houris whom he expected to see, to behold a train of wrinkled and deformed old hags.[1]

When he learns from his faithful steward what has happened, Nourjahad fills the place of his superannuated wives with a fresh troop of virgins, and resuming his abandoned courses goes from bad to worse. At length in a fit of rage he perpetrates a crime that brings him to a sense of his iniquities. True happiness has eluded him, and he is in danger of losing his soul. Then the genie reappears in the shape of his guardian angel, and the whole secret is revealed. All has been contrived by the sultan. Nourjahad was drugged with an opiate, and by the aid of a beautiful lady and a troop of deformed women he has been duped with the apparent fulfilment of his desires, only interrupted by one of the periods of trance that had been decreed. "There was not an action of thy life," says the sultan, "but I was made acquainted with; and whilst thou didst triumph in the joys of my successful illusion, I sometimes pitied thy weakness and sometimes laughed at thy extravagance." But Nourjahad has repented of his own initiative; he has now learned to despise riches, and shown his readiness to die; wherefore he shall now be permitted to live.

Gold-smith's Oriental-ism Before Goldsmith wrote his "Asem" (1765), which belongs to the same didactic category, he had produced the finest example in English of the social satire in the form of letters sent to his friends at home by a supposed foreigner. The idea of reviewing the Western world from the point of view of a travelled and reflective Chinaman may have been derived from Voltaire, who

[1] *The History of Nourjahad* (1767), 37-38. It was dramatized by Sophia Lee and acted (1788).

in the *Dictionnaire philosophique* and elsewhere had contrasted the stable and enlightened civilization of China with European shallowness and inconstancy.[1] But it was in any case an obvious variant of Montesquieu's scheme and of that of his continuator Lyttelton, whose *Letters from a Persian in England to his Friend at Ispahan* (1735) met with a warmer welcome than their merits deserved on account of the popularity of the original *Lettres persanes* in their English form. And the Marquis d'Argens had given Goldsmith a definite lead with his *Lettres chinoises*[2] (1739), published in English as *Chinese Letters* (1741), the very title by which Goldsmith's were to be known in their first form as serial contributions to a periodical. Goldsmith took a trial flight in the *Bee* (1759) with "A Letter from a Traveller," dated from Cracow, followed by one from Stockholm in the next issue; though, characteristically, he helped himself to all his material from the accounts of a person who had actually been to those places. Obviously, he was not so much trying his wings as seeing what would go down in a popular miscellany. When John Newbery enlisted him as a contributor to the *Public Ledger*, started at the beginning of 1760, Goldsmith had his opportunity.

The *Chinese Letters* commenced in an early number and came out with fair regularity until the middle of the following year, proving so popular that Goldsmith lost no time before revising and touching up what had been produced under the stress and haste of journalistic writing and publishing the whole with a new title, *The Citizen of the World* (1762), which its cosmopolitan outlook warranted.[3]

"The Citizen of the World"

The genial and accomplished mandarin who is Goldsmith's spectator, product of a civilization as much as possible the antipodes of ours, sends to his confidential friend in Pekin sketches of

---

[1] This is stressed by H. J. Smith (*Goldsmith's "Citizen of the World,"* 1926, pp. 14-15).

[2] *Lettres chinoises, ou correspondance philosophique, historique et critique entre un Chinois voyageur à Paris et ses correspondants à la Chine, en Moscovie, en Perse et au Japon.*

[3] A. L. Sells (*Les Sources françaises de Goldsmith,* 1924, pp. 96-97) wonders whether he did not borrow the title from a work of Fougeret de Monbron, *Le Cosmopolite* (1750), which in the issues of 1752 had the sub-title *ou le citoyen du monde,* and exhibits other coincidences. The phrase was, however, not unknown in English already (see, *e.g.*, Conant, 188-189, note, and also H. J. Smith, pp. 29-30).

what he sees, with a running commentary, by turns puzzled or embarrassed, by turns shrewd and penetrating, in the now established manner. Nothing escapes his well-trained eye. Walking the streets or going into houses, he marks and quizzes strange modes of attire and of behaviour in the populace and those of higher station; he notes extravagant fashions, irrational observances, eccentricities of the day, the vices of all time. He visits churches, the playhouse, the courts of justice, witnesses an election, goes to a public dinner and to an authors' club, is initiated into social and domestic life; and his misunderstandings are more diverting even than his acutest perceptions, both having a pungency due to the remoteness from his habitual scale of values. In all this, Goldsmith for a while remembers that his commentator is from another hemisphere, and he plays as dexterously as Montesquieu with the double perspective; then he contents himself with the simpler and more literal method of Lyttelton and the Marquis d'Argens. At times he approaches the withering satire of Swift, at others he is on a level with the slap-dash Tom Brown. And then Goldsmith will forget that he has a part to sustain, the Irishman lets himself go, and he talks feelingly and yet humorously about things that must often have made him wince, literature and its professors, and the lot of the drudge who compiles books for a living. Notwithstanding these differences of tone and the transitions from philosophic analysis to irony and from pathos and indignation to the lightest persiflage, there is small reason to suppose that Goldsmith was ever aiming deliberately to parody his predecessors in the style.[1]

This form of satire and its analogues   Satire of the kind that forms the gist of the *Citizen of the World*, and the whole of Montesquieu's *Lettres persanes* and of several of Voltaire's most brilliant stories, is obviously the analogue of Gulliverian satire and parallel to that of the inanimate observer, typified by *Chrysal* or *The Adventures of an Atom*; for the ostensible object of the convention in each case is to clear away the veil of familiarity and by changing the point of view to show facts as they really are, to substitute something like absolute for relative vision. There had been many such attempts before, and there have

---

[1] Sell touches on this possibility (p. 90), and notes that Frankfort Moore once suggested a parallel between *The Citizen of the World* and *The Mikado*.

been many since. Mrs Behn, in *Oroonoko*, had opposed simplicity and innocence to sophistication and corruption; and like symmetrical contrasts were to be the basis of works so different in their range of ideas as Voltaire's *Ingénu*, Bage's *Hermsprong*, and Mrs Inchbald's *Nature and Art*. Goldsmith was an unsystematic thinker, given to stringing desultory ideas together; and the evident hurry in which many of the *Chinese Letters* were composed did not make for thorough consistency, which, again, does not seem to have been the main object of his subsequent revision. Those letters which are brief dissertations or essays in the style of the *Bee* have a family resemblance to the whole progeny of Steele and Addison. The subjects are various; so too are the points of view. In the *Bee*, Goldsmith had imitated and even plundered Marivaux, author of the Addisonian *Spectateur français*. And now to Marivaux must be added La Bruyère, author of *Les Caractères*, and Voltaire of the *Lettres philosophiques*.[1]

Goldsmith's mandarin had quitted China without the emperor's leave, and his possessions had been confiscated, his wife imprisoned, and his son obliged to flee to Persia. These misfortunes are the burden of some of the replies to his letters to China; and Goldsmith utilizes them, especially the son's adventures, to improvise a romantic plot and so round off the story. By introducing a love affair he was following an example as old as Marana's *Espion turc*. All this is flimsy and far-fetched; but the other features in which *The Citizen of the World* approaches the novel of manners are among the best things in it. The Man in Black, the gentleman who so improbably turns out to be the father of Zelis, the beautiful captive rescued from a Persian harem by the mandarin's son, who in due course unites West and East by marrying her, is a mere outline, yet an engaging and unforgettable figure, a paradoxical blend of the soft heart and the sarcastic demeanour. " He takes as much pains to hide his feelings, as any hypocrite would to conceal his indifference; but on every unguarded moment the mask drops off, and reveals him to the most superficial observer." The mandarin profited by his conversation, and held him in the warmest esteem. " His manners, it is true, are tinctured

Approximations to the novel

---

[1] See Sells *passim*, but especially pp. 110-124. Goldsmith evidently oscillated between acceptance of the doctrines of Rousseau and those of his opponents.

with some strange inconsistencies: and he may justly be termed an humorist in a nation of humorists."[1] Beau Tibbs is a more extravagant droll, more roughly sketched, and perhaps hardly developed enough to be altogether credible, with his wife, a figure of the same grotesque order. But their speech is so perfectly in character that it touches them into life.

Gold-smith's plagiarisms One of the least inventive of great writers, Goldsmith borrowed without stint from those who were worth borrowing from. If the journalist with the printer's imps at his door, at his wits' end for matter to fill a sheet, could put his hand on anything that would do or could be turned to account without much trouble, he took it without a qualm, and with little disguise when the source was not too well known. The *Lettres persanes* were well known; he accordingly used Montesquieu rather as a pattern than a source; but Lyttelton, d'Argens, and others of less prestige furnished material for lengthy passages in the *Chinese Letters*.[2] He was a good French scholar who kept himself abreast of the current literature. He knew his Montaigne, Molière, and La Bruyère from his youth up; he was such an admirer of Voltaire that he wrote his life, though the hero was to outlive the biographer. Goldsmith was the freebooter of genius, who is a law unto himself. At any rate, it is admitted on all hands that he nearly always bettered inimitably everything that he appropriated; so that it is less as literary spies than as students keenly interested in the secrets of style that we look into the accounts which have been carefully drawn up and audited of his multifarious debts. Of a different and of a less questionable nature are the details of manners and customs and the other materials for his background which he obtained from the contemporary authorities on the geography and history of China, Le Comte and Du Halde, the former of whom, we remember, had been similarly utilized by Defoe for the *Further Adventures of Robinson Crusoe*.[3]

[1] Goldsmith's father was the original of the Man in Black's father, who is sketched touchingly in Letter XXVII.; he was also the village preacher of *The Deserted Village* (*Collected Letters of Goldsmith*, ed. K. C. Balderston, 1928, pp. x. and 170).

[2] For parallels with Montesquieu, see H. J. Smith, 45-52, and Sells, 106-109; for passages from Lyttelton, Smith, 52-58; from d'Argens, Smith, 58-77, Sells, 102-103.

[3] See Volume III. 151, 170. The Père J.-B. Halde's *Description géographique, historique, chronologique . . . de la Chine* (1735) had been Englished (1736).

The Oriental craze was still at its height among readers, and *Clara* the taste for Chinese temples, furniture, and bibelots which *Reeve's* Goldsmith scoffed at in his fourteenth letter. The poets were *"Char-oba"* writing Chinese and other Oriental eclogues and pastorals, and the translating business from the French went merrily on.[1] Hardly any, however, of the later pseudo-Oriental fictions are of the slightest historical importance, except Beckford's *Vathek*; and only two others need be mentioned, the romance of some thirty pages with which Clara Reeve filled out the second volume of her *Progress of Romance* (1785), and that curious departure from his wonted sociological preoccupations, *The Fair Syrian* (1787), of Robert Bage, recounting in his favourite epistolary form the adventures of a young Englishwoman among the Turks. Clara Reeve's little story is of interest as the source of Landor's *Gebir*, and it has merit of its own. *The History of Charoba, Queen of Ægypt*, was redacted by her from a translation by J. Davies (1672) of a history of Egypt by Pierre Vattier, taken from the Arabic.[2]

Landor's protagonist Gebir seeks to marry the queen and so become lord and master of Egypt, but is hindered by enchantment in his attempt to build a city on the Nile, and at last is killed by the desperate Charoba with "a regal garment which was poisoned." Clara Reeve's story is of Charoba and the subtlety which she opposes to her formidable suitor Gebirus. It opens with her accession to the throne, blessed, we are told, by the patriarch Abraham, who was her friend; and it ends with her death, three years later. Landor's episode of the journey into Hades is based on the descent of Gebirus into a subterranean place of tombs where he finds rich treasures, a passage using some of the Oriental lore out of which Beckford evolved his grandiose Hall of Eblis. In form and diction, Miss Reeve's version is admirable; no wonder it impressed Landor.

But the most imaginative of the English attempts to rival the *Arabian Nights* was William Beckford's *Vathek* (1786), a story

---

[1] There was an Oriental play even, by the bookseller-novelist S. J. Pratt, alias "Courtney Melmoth," founded on Hawkesworth's *Almoran and Hamet*, and entitled *The Fair Circassian, a tragedy*. It was produced at Drury Lane in 1781 and went through three editions the same year.

[2] *The Egyptian History* " written originally in the Arabian tongue of Murtadi," translated from *L'Egypte* (1666), which was itself derived from Murtadha ibn Alf-Khafif.

William Beckford

designed in the frivolous spirit of Hamiltonian burlesque, which would have been no whit superior to the fantasies of Hawkesworth and Mrs Sheridan had not the author's imagination caught fire as he approached the catastrophe, so that what begins in farce concludes in Dantesque gloom and terror. On his mother's side, Beckford, only son of the Lord Mayor who braved George III., came of the Hamiltons, Earls of Abercorn, and while writing his Arabian tales he told Henley, who helped him with the Oriental details, that he thought his dead kinsman Count Hamilton would smile upon him when they were introduced to each other in paradise.[1] If he inherited his insubordinate and headstrong disposition from the Beckfords, the intrepid imagination and the mischievous humour came to him either from the Hamilton blood or from his enthusiasm for the *Contes de Féerie* and their author. He gave a loose to that humour in his *Biographical Memoirs of Extraordinary Painters* (1780), originally a jest at the expense of the housekeeper at Fonthill, in the shape of a burlesque guide to the pictures. Later, he hoaxed his half-sister Mrs Harvey, and other writers and readers of sentimental fiction, with a pretended Radcliffian effusion, *Modern Novel Writing, or the Elegant Enthusiast, a rhapsodical romance* (1796), in the wildest emotional language and most disjointed narrative style, and with another burlesque novel *Azemia* (1797).[2] Neither has any merit beyond cleverness and scorn of affectation.

His romanticism

Beckford, however, must have let the romantic influences around him sink in. He was only four years older than Mrs Radcliffe, whom he was to outlive, like the still unborn Byron, by more than a decade; that is to say, he was a youth in the age that meditated among the tombs, revived the ballads and mediæval legends, and built pseudo-Gothic castles and abbeys and proceeded to live in these monstrosities. Ossian he must have read as voraciously as he devoured Galland and Gueullette,

---

[1] Letter to the Rev. Samuel Henley, quoted by Lewis Melville, in the introduction to *The Episodes of Vathek*, 1912, p. x. Count Hamilton, however, died a bachelor, and was not Beckford's ancestor, as Melville and a recent biographer, Marcel May (*La Jeunesse de William Beckford et la genèse de son "Vathek,"* 1928), repeatedly state.

[2] The sub-title ought to have raised suspicion : " a descriptive and sentimental novel, interspersed with poetry." That of the former, " and interesting emotions of Arabella Bloomville," was equally suggestive.

to judge by that singular diary of his meditative wanderings all over Europe entitled *Dreams, Waking Thoughts, and Incidents* (1783), a book that was hastily withdrawn, perhaps because some of the half-fictitious incidents referred too clearly to an affair that had won the reverse of approval from his relatives. Its prose is as poetical as the *Childe Harold* of thirty years later, whose author Beckford professed not to admire, and like that it reads like the musings of a mental valetudinarian. Beckford was at least as great an egoist as Byron, though a less theatrical one, and too idle or too contemptuous of public appreciation to write a *Don Juan*. Instead, he wrote *Vathek*, which fuses the romanticism of his own time and place with the romanticism of the East.

In the enthusiasm with which he abandoned himself to the double spell, the man's character and the singularity of his lot in life had a decisive part. Born in the purple of enormous wealth and social exclusiveness, he was brought up like the heir of an Eastern potentate. His father's palace of Fonthill was his Bagdad; he said that the dark colonnades of its Egyptian hall gave him the idea of his Hall of Eblis. It was the solitary and artificial education and the right environment to foster extravagant dreams, and the enormous fortune, inherited at the age of thirteen, gave him the means to realize them. Hardly out of his adolescence, he was sent to Geneva to complete this remarkable preparation for life, and there continued to read and to dream, and to turn all external influences to the further nourishment of his visions. He visited Ferney, and received the aged Voltaire's benediction; the streak of sardonic humour that marked his love of the mysterious and fantastic, like the affinity of both to Count Anthony Hamilton, was a link between them. He was on an intimate and affectionate footing with Henri Mallet, author of the *Northern Antiquities* that was exciting as much attention in England as on the Continent, and with the savants Bonnet and Huber. For Beckford was also an ardent reader of the latest scientific literature, though what attracted him seems to have been less the study of phenomena than the theories and speculations to which this led on the nature of the cosmos, and on the ultimate problems of the sources of energy and the origin of life. Beckford was a young Faustus

His passion for universal knowledge

aspiring to universal knowledge, the key to all the mysteries. Whether he had read Lessing's recent utterances on the Faust legend or the *Faust* of the poet Müller, published during his sojourn in Switzerland, there is no saying; but he must have been familiar with a subject so congenial, then in the air.[1]

Sources and materials

There is no evidence for the tradition that Beckford wrote *Vathek* at a sitting, no matter of how many days and nights, but ample proof that he spent a good deal of time upon it from when in January 1782 he had begun it to the middle of 1785 when he was still anxious to improve certain passages; he was reporting progress at intervals all that time to Henley, who eventually received the manuscript with the commission to translate the French in which it had been written into English. Beckford drew upon the general repertory of Oriental tales, Galland's *Arabian Nights* especially, for details and general colour, and, it appears from the notes with which it was Henley's duty to garnish the work so as to give it a learned air, he often consulted the *Koran*, d'Herbelot's *Bibliothèque orientale*,[2] and Picart's *Cérémonies et coutumes religieuses*, together with the large and often sumptuously illustrated books of travel to be found then in any gentleman's library and actually recorded in the catalogue of Beckford's. It has been shown that he borrowed largely from a complicated story, *Adventures of Abdalla, son of Hanif*, translated from the French of J. P. Bignon (1729), which brought in other stories dealing freely with the horrid and the grotesque.[3] From the *Mogul Tales* of Gueullette he derived and transformed, among other things, the circumstance of the perpetually burning hearts, which is the dread punishment of the damned, in the Hall of Eblis.[4] The intense actuality which Beckford gave to such details, and indeed to the mere extravagances of the earlier scenes, was an innovation in pseudo-Oriental fantasy.

[1] May, 262-264. M. May thinks he can find reminiscences of Marlowe's *Faustus* in *Vathek*.

[2] B. d'Herbelot de Molainville, *Bibliothèque orientale, ou dictionnaire universel, contenant tout ce qui regarde la connaissance des peuples d'Orient* (1697), a work completed by Galland. There were editions in 1776 and 1777-1779, and one " réduite par Desesserts " in 1782. Voltaire appears to have used the Maestricht folio of 1776.

[3] Conant, 38-41.

[4] *Ibid.* 37-38.

Obviously, Beckford drew from himself in the overweening *Origins* hero: the caliph's unscrupulous and insatiable ambition is *of his* Beckford's egoism and boundless curiosity pushed to the verge *characters* of monomania. He is reported to have said that the other characters were drawn from individuals in the domestic circle at Fonthill. But there are no characters, only figures, impersonations of passions, vices, or eccentricities. Nouronihar may be the woman he is said to have loved; that fearful termagant Carathis may be the monstrous likeness of another recognizable person. But writers like Beckford create their shadow-people out of themselves. Vathek and the debonair Eblis and the tortured Solomon, brooding over the annihilation of his earthly grandeur, are simply types of human nature in its excess; the amiable Gulchenrouz typifies its epicurean moderation; hence all are as it were facets of Beckford himself.

The book is not a masterpiece. The larger part is common-place and marred by horse-play and wanton coarseness. But there is no failure in gloomy pageantry and grandiose horror after the genius warns Vathek and Nouronihar to turn back at the foot of the mountains beyond which " Eblis and his accursed dives hold their infernal empire." Hence to the moment when they find they have been ensnared by the Giaour there is a steady crescendo of tragic agony. They hear " the awful and irrevocable decree," and their hearts taking fire they immediately lost " the most precious gift of heaven—HOPE."

It is a familiar story how the Rev. Mr Henley stole a march *The* on Beckford by publishing *Vathek* in English before the author *English* was prepared to bring it out in the original French. His excuses *and* were plausible; but, unfortunately, he was not content with the *French* rôle of editor and annotator and tried to figure as the author.[1] *editions* Probably Beckford employed a hack writer to translate the English version back into French; hence the slovenly version published at Lausanne; the later one at Paris received his corrections, the English manuscript perhaps never being recovered.[2]

The Episodes of Vathek were of course intended to appear along with the main story, but were now thrown aside, and

[1] May gives a photograph of Henley's signature to a presentation copy as " from the author."

[2] May, 412-413 ; see also Melville's introduction to the *Episodes*, xx.-xxix.

"The Episodes of Vathek" remained unpublished till the manuscripts were discovered by Lewis Melville and given to the world in an English translation along with the French text (1912).[1] They form the proper complement to his " Arabian tale," and are the best of our imitations of Galland's *Arabian Nights* produced in the eighteenth century. Other victims of the infernal justice tell the stories. In " Prince Alasi and the Princess Firouzhak," it is a woman-hater who has allowed himself to be dominated by a beautiful woman disguised as a youth, at her instigation commits fiendish crimes, and abjuring Mohammed devotes himself and his accomplice to the fire-worshippers. In " Prince Barkiarokh," a peri finds it so dangerous to employ her supernatural powers in human affairs that her interference seems always to bring fatal mischief when she intends good. The unfinished " Zulkaïs and Kalilah " is parody of a macabre and grandiose kind. Although they never reach the altitude of the scene in which the main story culminates, the episodes are of very even and admirable workmanship.

[1] *The Episodes of Vathek*, by William Beckford, trans. by Sir F. T. Marzials, with introduction by Lewis Melville, 1912.

CHAPTER IV

THE AFTERGLOW OF THE AUGUSTANS

THE quarter of a century following the publication of *Rasselas* *The* was the age of the progress and triumph of sentimentalism. *spread of* Johnson's apologue was read with respect, but the doctrines *senti-* contemned did not cease to flourish and fructify in letters and *mentalism, in spite of* in life. The same year as *Rasselas* and *Candide*, appeared the *Dr* *Theory of Moral Sentiments* and also the first two volumes of *Johnson* *Tristram Shandy*; the subsequent year saw the apparition of *and* the alleged Ossianic poems. Then for two decades and more it *Goldsmith* is only a small proportion of the novels published that are not imbued with the new sentimentalism. For this is a thing radically different from the sentimentality of Richardson. That had by no means antagonized Dr Johnson. It had been a temperamental disposition, a congenital habit of mind, fostered and indulged by Richardson and recommended as a thing to cultivate. It had made him cleave earnestly to the orthodox code of ethics and to its sanctions in the orthodox religion. None would have been more shocked than the straitlaced printer could he have perused the novels, plays, poems, treatises in which the thoroughgoing sentimentalists of a new generation expounded their philosophy of life. Johnson had been almost prophetic in discerning the trend of the new ways of thinking, and perceiving so clearly the fundamental opposition between the ideas of the sentimentalists and the tenets of the old school to which he and Goldsmith were loyal, notwithstanding some truant impulses of the younger man —between mere complacent trust in human virtue and the essential goodness of the world, and the age-old philosophy which acknowledged evil, and taught that it could be vanquished, but only by self-discipline and stoical endurance. The noise of the controversy is now so faint that we wonder what could have evoked from Dr Johnson such a formidable reply. As to *The*

77

Vicar of Wakefield, She Stoops to Conquer, and the comedies of Sheridan, all that was of a polemical nature seems to have dissolved away and left them for us to enjoy simply as charming works of art. They are among the few literary treasures left us by that period. And yet the other side had the best of it for the time being by sheer weight of numbers.

Oliver
Goldsmith
The *Vicar of Wakefield* has been the best-read from that day to now, all the world over, of the books of the Fielding epoch, though its fondest admirers would scarce seriously contend that it is a finer work than *Tom Jones, Roderick Random, Clarissa,* or *Tristram Shandy.* Even on the Continent, it would be difficult to find among educated people anyone who has not read it. But like so many authors of masterpieces Goldsmith was not a regular novelist. He was, to put it bluntly, a journalist, ready for any kind of work that would keep him alive, and seldom having time to write for his own pleasure. He wrote for the day, he wrote from hand to mouth. But he was a true man of letters in the sense that he could not write less than gracefully, even if through haste he was sometimes careless and dishevelled. And in two or three poems, one or two plays, some essays, and this book which we put beside the great novels, he fell short only of the finest work in those particular kinds, and surpassed even the best in a peculiar ease and charm, which was in truth the whole of his originality.

His mis-
cellaneous
writings
Coming home from his happy-go-lucky life abroad, the account of which in his history of the philosophic vagabond George Primrose[1] is suspiciously like that recounted elsewhere of the Baron Holberg,[2] he became a bookseller's hack, and a very good hack. He wrote biography, from which it is but a step to writing fiction. His memoir of Voltaire was a tribute to his hero-worship, for Voltaire was one of his intellectual gods. He wrote a life of Beau Nash, without much research, but he knew the man, and had some letters, and the result was a good generalized portrait, which he made critical and edifying in the manner of a didactic novel. His periodical essays are not markedly original, but the most readable ever written. Even his compilations on subjects

[1] *Vicar of Wakefield,* vol. ii., chap. i.
[2] *Enquiry into state of Polite Learning,* vi.

outside his proper range are nothing to be ashamed of, save that it is a pity he was not better employed. Goldsmith was a journalist who took up the novel as he took up the essay, because it was handy and congenial, and he could put himself into it. From the Addisonian *Bee*, he went on to the *Citizen of the World*, a miscellany which he made into a story, with regular beginning, middle, and end; and then he wrote *The Vicar of Wakefield*.

Although it was not published till four years later, there is *"The* evidence that Goldsmith had finished *The Vicar of Wakefield* in *Vicar of* 1762, the year when his *Citizen of the World* appeared as a book. *Wake-* The story has been told in various terms of Johnson's hearing *field"* that his friend was threatened with gaol for a debt to his landlady, and how going as soon as he could to Goldsmith's lodgings, first sending him a guinea, he found the improvident one happy over a bottle of Madeira for which he had changed the coin; how Goldsmith then produced the manuscript, which Johnson sold at once for £60, and so the rent was discharged. Thus the novel went into the hands of the publishers; but, whatever the exact date of the incident, a long delay intervened before the book was issued, the likeliest explanation being that it was held up until the stir caused by the publication of *The Traveller* (1764) enhanced its prospects of success.[1]

Superficially, *The Vicar of Wakefield* is an idyll, the benign *Super-* comedy of simple domesticity and human charity, picturing a *ficially an* little household of blameless souls whose affection for each other *idyll* and inward peace of mind are proof against the harshest shocks of circumstance. At the head of them stands that amiable sage and simpleton, the Vicar, "quite a darling character," as Fanny Burney called him,[2] the Quixotic champion of monogamy, who as a character in fiction is a minor masterpiece in the line of Parson Adams and Uncle Toby. Then there is his wife, a not unworthy pendant to Mrs Shandy; and after the daughters, one a slip of hackneyed romance, the other a delicate study of intelligent

---

[1] Professor Doughty (Introduction to *Vicar of Wakefield*, 1928) collates the different versions of the incident, variously dated, and points out that an entry quoted from a printer's account-book in the life of John Newbery (*A Bookseller of the Last Century*, by Charles Welsh, 1885) shows that £21 had been paid for a third share in the book on 28th October 1762.

[2] *Early Diary*, i. 14, note.

girlhood, come the charming boys and the circle of friends, as pretty a group of oddly assorted idiosyncrasies as can be found anywhere in fiction. It is sweet Auburn, or an idealized Lissoy transplanted to England.[1] The gadabout and homeless Goldsmith lets his fancy roam in the almost lyrical enjoyment of his exquisite family group, finding here in imagination what he had missed in life.

The catas- Then the scene changes, the peace and content are shattered. *trophe and* But unmerited misfortunes serve only to bring out more clearly *its reversal* the sterling worth and unconquerable loyalty of parents and children. And presently they are rewarded, as at the touch of a wand, by a complete restoration to happiness. It is as marvellous as a fairy tale. The sudden reversal of the catastrophe is incredible, the plot glaringly makeshift. All this may be a very pleasing version of mundane affairs, but things do not actually turn out so. Where is the insight and sanity which Goldsmith displays in minor episodes and in the sententious wisdom falling from the lips of the Vicar and Mr Burchell, but which seems to fail him at the decisive moments of the story? Yet it is a captivating idyll, and the reader is disposed to make large allowances. Goldsmith indeed asks for such, when he covertly apologizes for the accidental nature of his plot and its artless disentanglement:

> Nor can I go on, without a reflection on those accidental meetings which, though they happen every day, seldom excite our surprise but upon some extraordinary occasion. To what a fortuitous concurrence do we not owe every pleasure and convenience of our lives!

Nor need we go on; it is a lame excuse. Had Goldsmith enlarged upon the accidents and surprises of his own life it would have been more to the point. But it is something quite different that has endeared the book to all the world and made it a minor classic, unscathed by criticism of its many blemishes. Here, we feel, he whom Johnson called, in spite of his frailties, " a very great man," [2]

---

[1] Professor Doughty (pp. xxii.-xxiv.) discusses at length whether Wakefield in Yorkshire, Goldsmith's boyish home Lissoy, or the hamlet of Springfield, near Chelmsford, where he may have spent a happy summer, was the original of his idyllic Wakefield.

[2] Boswell : Letter to Bennet Langton, 5th July 1774.

put more of himself than even elsewhere in his writings, intensely personal as these are, without exception. It matters little whether the Vicar was drawn from Goldsmith's own father, or from his Uncle Contarine, or from the brother Henry whom he adored, or whether other Goldsmiths figure in that admirable family group. The Arcadian picture of domestic bliss links this with his most idyllic poem, strict criticism of which has to be met with the same apologies.

But this is far from a complete account of *The Vicar of Wakefield*, *But the* and does not explain why it puzzled those who first reviewed it, *story had* seemed to Fanny Burney altogether inferior to a feeble didactic *a very different* novel which she had just been reading, and has been so variously *object* estimated ever since.[1] There is good reason for misunderstanding, for, to put it briefly, Goldsmith started in one direction, lost his way before he had gone far, and presently found himself going, without being able to stop, in a direction entirely opposite. The idyll was to have been a comic idyll, a bitter-sweet pastoral, the bitterness concealed in the irony. Fielding had shown the possibility of a comic epic in prose; but whether the comic and the idyllic will go together is another question, assuredly not settled by Goldsmith. It was to be a fable at the expense of sentimental optimism, complacent trust in the supremacy of good, confidence that honesty will have its reward without a cautious sense of the wickedness of the world and the guile and unscrupulousness of others. The Vicar, so full of sound maxims, out of conceit in his own sagacity, out of the overweening optimism that he is always reproving, out of blindness to the perils which he loves to point out to his wife and children, is chiefly responsible for bringing calamity upon his own head and theirs.

Goldsmith handles him tenderly enough; he might even be *The Vicar* thought to be laughing apologetically at his own soft-heartedness. *originally intended to* But the Vicar is conceived as a comic character, however much *be a type* both author and reader love him. No one so tactless. He cannot *of unwise* resist showing his pamphlet on absolute monogamy, that fatal bee *optimism*

[1] Dr Johnson was not satisfied with it. Talking to Mrs Thrale about Fanny Burney's fondness for the book, and asked if he liked it, " No, madam," he replied, " it is very faulty ; there is nothing of real life in it, and very little of nature. It is a mere fanciful performance " (*Diary and Letters of Madame d'Arblay*, i. 77).

in his bonnet, to his rich friend Mr Wilmot, who was " at that time actually courting a fourth wife "; and so his daughter's engagement is broken off on the eve of the wedding, and also on the eve of the family's financial misfortune, which makes it doubly ill-timed. He is unable to see through Squire Thornhill's snares, and lets his matchmaking wife throw the inexperienced Olivia into the arms of a seducer, against whom they had been warned by Mr Burchell. He is as purblind as his wife and daughters in misreading the letter sent by that stanch protector to denounce the squire's baseness, and plumes himself on having unmasked their old friend and sent him away with a flea in his ear. How comic the irony of his pity for that " poor forlorn creature," on an earlier page ! " What a strong instance," said I, " is that poor man of the miseries attending a youth of levity and extravagance. He by no means wants sense, which only serves to aggravate his former folly." Even after the lesson of the gross of green spectacles for which Moses parted with the colt, the Vicar lets himself be swindled out of the remaining horse through a crafty appeal to his vanity. Compared with these and other blunders, the unseasonableness of his reminder to his soldier son going to the wars that it was perhaps to die, is but a minor instance of the things that he should have left unsaid.[1]

Mr Burchell the one person to be wholly approved

The one person whose conduct and opinion we are expected always to approve is Mr Burchell. His the insight that never goes wrong, his the prudence that overlooks none of the pitfalls of life. His follies and excesses were the natural aberrations of youth ; he is still only thirty, but they have taught him to see the world as it is, whilst the Vicar, misled by a shallow optimism, has arrived at maturity, only to be full of wise saws but unable to apply them. Sir William Thornhill, alias Burchell, is Goldsmith's Mr Allworthy,

[1] Professor Doughty (p. xliii.) speaks of " a certain intellectual stupidity which Goldsmith, like Fielding before him, apparently considered a necessary concomitant to that elemental goodness which springs from the unsophisticated heart rather than from the head." This *à propos* of the Vicar's fatuousness in hanging his wife's epitaph over the mantel for her to read it daily. But is this not to miss the irony of both writers ? There is a sort of conspiracy among critics to ignore the irony which was assuredly Goldsmith's intention, though he found it difficult to sustain. Can we agree with Professor E. Bernbaum, for instance, that " the interpretation of life " here " is akin to that of the sentimental school," when this was the very interpretation that Goldsmith set out to prove misleading ? Yet Professor Doughty cites Goethe's admirable dictum, " this high, benevolent irony," which sums up the intention perfectly.

and a more living embodiment of wisdom and goodness. This is Goldsmith as he would be; the man of sense and humour, generous but keen of insight, who revolts from flattery and affectation, and after the widest and ripest experience of the world realizes in his own conduct of life the lessons of *The Traveller*. At the crucial turns of events, it is always the Primroses who are wrong, and Mr Burchell who is right.

Whether Goldsmith meant him from the outset to be the good *Goldsmith* angel as well as the faithful but disregarded counsellor remains *muddled* an open question. It is evident that he found himself in such a *the story* perplexity towards the end of the story that he had to make a bee-line out of the wood. He was too soft-hearted to let the Primroses suffer all the consequences of their imprudence, and so at length he dismisses them with his blessing. Goldsmith was the last person in the world to be a consistent ironist, he was always too lax to stick to one point of view. So in the end he manages to have it both ways. Imprudence, though it always meant well, has come to grief. And now the good genius, in the shape, Goldsmith might plead, of Prudence personified, comes to the rescue. But the reversal of fortune, if strictly interpreted, reverses the moral, for it is not repentance and amendment that is the agency of their salvation, but mere coincidence. Thus Goldsmith shuffles off his comic pose, and out of pure tenderness for the children of his brain gives everybody a prize. Even the villainous seducer, a meaner scamp than Jonathan Wild himself, is left in a fair way of redeeming his character and being united to the fair Olivia after all.

It has often been remarked that the Vicar deteriorates towards *Consequent* the end as a piece of consistent character-drawing. The reason is *inconsist-* obvious: the gentle irony, the sly touches of caricature that *encies* chastened while loving him, have been dropped; the indirectness that saved the character from the usual fate of the autobiographer in fiction has been changed for directness. His faults now are not due to conceit in his infallibility, and are not shown up by quiet ridicule; they are not even consistent with his old self. Can we believe that he would have been so overjoyed at finding his beloved daughter really and truly married to the infamous Mr Thornhill? Surely, here is some lapse from the dignity which he used to maintain even when humbled to the dust. As to his sermons to his fellow-prisoners and his scheme for bettering their lot and giving them something to live for, all this is not out of keeping with his ingrained quixotism. But in his discourses we are simply listening to Goldsmith the essayist, borrowing ideas from Marivaux and Rousseau.[1] It is amusing how often the sentiments expressed here, and evidently with Goldsmith's approval, are in accord with the doctrines of Rousseau, which elsewhere he criticizes severely. But if his entrancing picture of rustic innocence owes anything whatever to that source, he made it the starting-point for an argument definitely anti-Rousseau on what is the basis of human happiness.[2]

"The Vicar of Wakefield" a didactic work, but otherwise akin to Fielding's

The Vicar of Wakefield is a didactic work, but except in these set discourses the didacticism is indirect, in consonance with the general indirectness. How thoroughly didactic a glance at the table of contents forcibly brings home. "What we place most hopes upon, generally proves most fatal." "Seeming calamities may be real blessings." "Happiness and misery rather the result of prudence than of virtue in this life." These are headings which summarize the lessons of the ensuing chapters. Evidently, the book is a treatise on the art of life, as Fielding declared his own novels to be.[3] Goldsmith's didacticism is more pronounced because he has a definite dialectical object, a sound doctrine to put in the place of an erroneous one. But, essentially, it is the same intellectual realism, exhibiting the latent threads of causation, contrasting characters and opposite views of life, and reproving shortsightedness by showing into what ironical situations it leads. Like Fielding's, his fiction is self-authenticated,[4] it has the seal of general verisimilitude. The characters portray themselves, by

---

[1] For some specific borrowings, though several of those alleged must be accidental resemblances or the vague results of unconscious memory, see Sells, 125-132.

[2] Sells thinks Goldsmith's idyll must have been inspired by Rousseau's theories of primitive felicity. Goldsmith had considered the problem in the *Citizen of the World*, especially in Letters XLV. and CXIX., and his conclusions would have been endorsed by Mr Burchell. "Positive happiness is constitutional, and incapable of increase; misery is artificial, and generally proceeds from our folly." "An habitual acquaintance with misery is the truest school of fortitude and philosophy." "A life of pleasure is . . . the most unpleasing life in the world."

[3] See Volume IV. 133 and 160.

[4] *Ibid.* 191.

their speech, their actions, their gestures; their talk is so perfectly natural, so apparently unstudied, that it alone puts Goldsmith, not below, but beside the great four novelists of his day. Note, however, that the Vicar, writing the story himself, is able to tell us what he thinks, and hopes, and intends. This makes the lesson of his self-deception the more unmistakable. And that lesson corresponds with the moral of *Tom Jones*, as summed up in the little homily beginning, " Prudence and circumspection are necessary to the best of men. They are indeed as a guard to virtue, without which she can never be safe." [1]

In the age of sentimentalism there were fewer imitators of Fielding than of Richardson, fewer than even tried at greater or lesser distance to copy Sterne. Very few indeed ventured upon Fielding's elaborate architectonics; it was rather his comic wayside incidents, his racy characters, and above all his jovial spirits restrained by common sense, that took hold of younger writers and spurred them to observe, enjoy, and invent on their own account. Richard Graves (1715-1804), author of *The Spiritual Quixote*, had more of the Fielding high spirits than the Fielding technique, and if it had not come natural to him he might be thought to have caught them from living in the Fielding country, for Claverton, where he was rector, is about as far on one side of Bath as the house where part of *Tom Jones* was written is on the other.[2] Graves had been at Pembroke College, Oxford, at the same time as Whitefield, whom he never liked. At Bath, where he took his share in the social life and amusements and was one of those who used to drop their verses into Lady Miller's urn at Batheaston, he was disturbed by the excesses of the wilder sort of Methodist preachers and their converts in the West of England, and wrote this skit on Whitefield, mixed up with all manner of observations of places and people and disquisitions on such topics as dress, social observances, kindness to animals, beauties of nature, and of course religion. Often his leisurely digressions bring to mind the easy-going ways of Elizabethan novelists; his " Panegyric on Esquires," for instance, might have been by Nashe or Dekker.

Richard Graves and " The Spiritual Quixote "

[1] See Volume IV. 133.
[2] The house bears a tablet recording this probably veracious tradition ; but see also Cross, ii. 110-111.

Satire on the wilder Wesleyans   There is more fun than malice in the satire. An earnest clergyman might well have shown much more indignation at the spurious religiosity preached by some of the sectaries, often to the moral detriment of simple rustic folk. Graves was content to show how absurd they were, sometimes by parody, but oftener by quoting from Whitefield's sermons, with chapter and verse in the footnotes. He was the sort of person who took the world as he found it, and for his part he would have let sleeping dogs lie. For it is evident between his own lines that the vices and depravities of the time were justification enough for the efforts of the revivalists, as Hogarth's contemporary pictures of high life and low and Fielding's contemptuous characterization of the rabble also demonstrate. Like Fielding, he loved to sketch the tramps and tinkers, poachers and highwaymen, raw bumpkins and fuddled yokels, met on the highway and at village fairs and race-meetings; but, whilst Fielding is never more the moralist than when he stigmatizes the dangers of the doctrine of faith versus works, Graves is only lightly sardonic.[1]

Caricature of Whitefield   The burlesque knight-errantry assimilates the book somewhat to Smollett's *Launcelot Greaves*, published ten years earlier, but it is nearer akin to *Joseph Andrews*, that great picaresque story of the road. The young Gloucestershire squire Geoffrey Wildgoose is so uplifted by the popular doctrines that he leaves his comfortable home, enlists a Panza in the village cobbler Jerry Tugwell, and goes preaching in a travesty of the Whitefield style wherever he comes across a gathering of willing or unwilling listeners and a tub to stand upon. But his harangues are usually cut short by showers of missiles or a cudgelling, and in one scene he and his

---

[1] The chapter headed "Mr Wildgoose becomes a great Casuist" gives a foretaste of Maupassant's *Maison Tellier*. Mrs Placket, who, the Spiritual Quixote finds, keeps a "down-right bawdy house," consults him as to her spiritual situation. "I thank God, I have always had good custom, and have had twenty couple at a time, taking their recreation, in my house, yet (I bless God !) I never had any murder, or riot, or daggers-drawing, since I have been in business. Then I make my poor lambs read the Bible every Sunday, and go to church in their turn ; and, in short, though their bodies may be polluted, I take great care of their souls : and I hope God will wink at my poor lambs that sport themselves together." "Why," says Wildgoose, "without doubt, our outward actions are indifferent in themselves ; and it is the heart that God chiefly regards. God sees no sin in the elect. If we have true faith, that will sanctify our works." And he consoles her with Mr Whitefield's maxim, "The greater the sinner, the greater the saint" (Book VII., chap. xi.).

tub are blown up with fireworks. Then the two pilgrims move on to another village. The prime joke is that this caricature of Whitefield is in search of Whitefield himself, and at length he finds him, only however to be disenchanted: Whitefield is too much wrapped up in his creature comforts to be a saint or a martyr.

Mr Whitefield was sitting in an elbow-chair, in a handsome dining-room, dressed in a purple night-gown and velvet cap; and, instead of a Bible or prayer-book, as Wildgoose expected, he had a good bason of chocolate, and a plate of muffins well-buttered, before him.

This is very different from the accidental meeting with John Wesley, whose character and doctrines Graves treats with proper respect. Wildgoose is further undeceived. His mode of preaching has been all wrong. Instead of hurting people's feelings by denunciations of vice and drunkenness, he should have said " Down with your good works! " He learns that his favourite apostle " said little about repentance, but laid all the stress upon faith alone; so that if a man was, or fancied, or even said, that he was possessed of true faith, he was immediately pronounced a convert; and, whether he reformed his life or not, became a saint upon easy terms." [1]

After more adventures, some of the most amusing among giddy *Allusions* people of fashion at Bath, Wildgoose is shown the errors of *to other* Methodism and his own foolishness by the pattern clergyman *novelists* Dr Greville, returns to common sense and his home, and marries his Dulcinea, Miss Julia Townsend, who has furnished a sober measure of romance to relieve the satire. Other real persons besides Wesley and Whitefield come into the story, the Man of Ross, and Shenstone, for instance, the latter a great friend of Graves, who discovers him improving the landscape at the Leasowes and makes him the victim of a practical joke by Wildgoose, who cuts off the water supplying his fountains. What is still more surprising in a novel are the allusions to Fielding and Richardson; for instance, there is a flighty hoyden at Bath, a Mrs Booby, to whose advances Wildgoose plays Joseph,

[1] Book VII., chap. iii.

and a scion of the house of Grandison cuts a prominent figure. It is indeed a miscellaneous book, and so are the three that followed during the next twenty years. Except for the scholarly, good-humoured, and incisive prose, an accomplishment that links him again with Fielding, and for the pithy sketches of odd but not uncommon characters, there is not much to distinguish them. Shenstone reappears in *Columella, or the Distressed Anchoret* (1779). *Eugenius, or Anecdotes of the Golden Vale* (1785) is a trifle less unexciting as a story; *Plexippus, or the Aspiring Plebeian* (1790), shows best of the three his gift of portraiture.

Other disciples of Fielding   Bare mention must suffice for Charles Jenner, and his *Placid Man, or Memoirs of Sir Charles Beville* (1770), the title of which sufficiently describes a country novel modelled after Fielding, with glances at Sterne. Herbert Lawrence's *Contemplative Man, or the History of Christopher Crab Esq. of North Wales* (1771), might be characterized in the same general terms, save that the author aims rather at Sterne than at Fielding, whom, however, he regards as the first of novelists and almost unapproachable, a prevailing view which helps to account for the paucity of effort in such a difficult style for nearly half-a-century. George Brewer,[1] later on, tried to write another *Tom Jones*, in his *History of Tom Weston* (1791). But the only writer of any note who formed himself entirely on the Fielding model in fiction was the playwright and novelist Richard Cumberland.

Cumber-land   Richard Cumberland (1732-1811), whose temper and other foibles are twitted by Sheridan in the Sir Fretful Plagiary of *The Critic*, enjoyed a certain popularity in his time with his sentimental comedies, and had the distinction of being hailed by Goldsmith, in *Retaliation*, as " the Terence of England ":

A flattering painter, who made it his care
To draw men as they ought to be, not as they are.

His best play, *The West Indian* (1771), flimsy and conventional in plot, was evidently inspired by Fielding in the characterization. Belcour the foundling, adopted son of a rich Jamaica planter, but

---

[1] Brewer wrote another novel, *The Motto, or the History of Bill Woodcock* (1795), and got into trouble over his *Maxims of Gallantry, or the History of the Count de Verney* (1793), the licence of which met with such censure that he withdrew it.

eventually proved to be the son of Stockwell, is a good-hearted, sensual young fellow, of the same stamp as Tom Jones. Stockwell, the upright City merchant, is another Allworthy, though it must not be forgotten that these impersonations of all the virtues were a dramatic convention, and Lillo's Thorogood, in *George Barnwell*, is just such another. There are bits of autobiography worked into his *Arundel* (1789), a novel in letters, with a concluding one by the imaginary editor to supply the requisite happy ending. The story goes at a leisurely pace, so too in his second novel *Henry*; and it is a conventional, sentimental affair, but saved from mawkishness by a certain geniality which echoes Fielding.

Henry (1795) is a close imitation of *Tom Jones*, and if that "*Henry*" had never been written might be thought a very respectable achievement. Plot and the very manner and gait of Fielding are reproduced—at a perceptible distance. Henry, though not exactly a foundling, is the illegitimate son of a lady who is now the ill-used wife of a viscount; and the secret of his origin transpires some time before the general conclusion. Cumberland ushers in each successive book with a discursive essay, and no doubt flattered himself that he had caught the master's style. But of Fielding's irony he was sublimely unaware. This is conspicuous in the scenes where the hero's virtue is vainly assailed by three persistent wooers. For Henry doubles the part of Tom Jones with that of Joseph Andrews, and he rebuffs the seductions of pretty Susan the village girl, and also of the lecherous Mrs Cawdle, without having a Fanny to keep him straight, because there is more principle mingled with his natural goodness than was the case with Tom. These episodes in the scriptural mode of Joseph and Madame Potiphar are done in a loose and sensuous style beside which Fielding is restraint itself. Susan may be a pleasanter creature than Molly Seagrim; but she is a romantic figment compared with that piece of honest realism. Mrs Cawdle is a blend of Lady Booby and Mrs Slipslop, heavily spiced with religiosity. She rails at Lady Crowbery's "good works," and in the midst of her assault on Henry's chastity cries out, "I have a proper sense of your folly and impertinence in preaching to me, who am established by faith beyond the reach of guilt, or the possibility of falling." Fielding was lighter-handed in castigating those who held that faith weighed infinitely in the scale against the negligible element of works.

As to that flirtatious hussy Fanny Claypole, Henry is not guilty but only compromised by the affair into which she entraps him; in short, all this is padding, a simple pretence for thwarting for the present his hopes of the Sophia of the story, Miss Isabella Manstock. There are other coincidences with *Tom Jones*; for instance, the plot to get Henry out of the way through the agency of a press-gang, and the ensuing duel. Some of the by-characters are praiseworthy efforts in the Partridge vein, such as the rural practitioner Dr Ezekiel Cawdle, henpecked and made ridiculous by being soused in a mill-pond, not to mention that he has to put up philosophically with the knowledge that he is a cuckold. Though partly a butt, Ezekiel is a man of courage, sense, and loyalty, who does yeoman's service to Henry and Henry's unhappy mother. Another worthy who excites laughter with his militant Puritanism, his long prayers, and his genius for turning everything to edifying account, is Zachary Daw, another lampoon on Methodism, though he too is ranged with the hero's friends, and the sheep rather than the goats, when his mettle comes to be tested by events. *Henry* is planned on an ample scale, blocks of narrative in formal units, and it moves at an even tempo. This is not like Fielding, who can make time stand still when he pictures the calm of a long country boyhood, or sweep us off our feet when the plot thickens in the drama of manhood.[1]

[1] Cumberland wrote a third novel, *John de Lancaster* (1809), which I have not seen.

CHAPTER V

THE NOVEL OF SENTIMENT

RICHARDSON was not the only fount of sentimentalism from *The* which the minor novelists drew motives and encouragement; *vogue of* this is already clear. The other main influences will be scrutinized *Richard-* presently. But the rank and file for some time after *Sir Charles* *son :* *growing* *Grandison* (1753) went on plodding behind him, until they, and *demand for* probably their readers still more, cried out for variety and *more* more excitement. Among writers already considered, Sarah *excitement* Fielding and Charlotte Lennox, both brought up in the school of Richardson, yielded eventually to the taste for something less humdrum than domestic realism, and at the same time, far from renouncing or abating their fits of emotional indulgence and their pervading sentimentality, screwed up the tension, and dragged their lovers and heroines through stranger trials and more sensational adventures than could be counted among the ordinary contingencies. Realism was giving way to melodramatic romance. Cleland and Hill, be it also remembered, were contemporaries of Richardson, and wrote for people who no doubt read him, if not perhaps for those who took him most to heart. He was the great accredited novelist of the day, and even the scandal-mongering hack felt his influence directly or indirectly. A few other writers are worth a mention, as examples of the immense vogue of Richardson; otherwise their work is of no historical significance, although now and then an honest effort can be discerned at freshness of observation and serious thought.

There is significance in the mere title of the one novel of *Followers* William Guthrie (1608-1670), a scholar and miscellaneous *of* writer who collaborated with Johnson in the Parliamentary *Richardson* reports for the *Gentleman's Magazine*, and published a mass of work on politics, history, and classical subjects. *The Friends, a* *sentimental history, describing love as a virtue as well as a passion*

(1754), is called in the preface " An Epic in lower life, which ought to be stript of all the *Paraphernalia*, but not of all the *Properties* of Poetry; divested of *Numbers*, but not destitute of *Ornament*." Like Fielding, Guthrie thought fiction to be a very serious and exalted form of art. He proposes to tell a story from life introducing " *Events* that strike from the *Force of Probability*, and *Sentiments* that affect through the *Powers of Nature*, to keep in view one *moral Idea* and to inculcate one *import and lesson*." Obviously, he is every inch a Richardsonian, and he understands what is valuable in *Sir Charles Grandison*. " There is a character," he says, " which can be drawn from living Manners only, that, I think, is still imperfect, both in Comedy, and in Novel-writing; I mean the Character of a fine Gentleman." But Guthrie was no story-teller; fiction was not his sphere. Hence his endeavours to convince us that this is real life by making us very intimate with the leading characters are a failure. The laboured plotting results only in dullness, and the picture of life is not even recognizable.

The Misses Minifie

A humbler person but a better novelist in her homely way was Susannah Minifie (?1740-1800), of Fairwater, Somerset, who married John Gunning, brother of the beautiful sisters Gunning, and broke with her husband when he turned her daughter out for daring to love a man who was not his choice. She gave her account of this notorious " Gunningiad," as Walpole christened it, in *Memoirs of Mary* (1793). Her first novels [1] were written in collaboration with her sister Margaret, author of a sentimental novel, *The Count de Poland* (1780); they are in the Richardsonian form of letters, but put together in an involved and clumsy manner, and the style is affected and ultra-sentimental. *The Histories of Lady Frances A . . . and Lady Caroline S . . .* (1763) have little but a sickly tenderness to recommend them. *Barford Abbey* (1768) has at least the merit of eschewing melodrama and confining interest to the analysis of people in love, especially love at cross-purposes. Marrying in 1768, she left her *Anecdotes*

[1] Probably including *The Picture, Family Pictures*, and *The Cottage*. Maria Burney gives Fanny a charming account of "the very sweetest *Thatched Cottage*" at Teignmouth, and ends, "in short this Cottage would make a very great figure in Miss Minifie's hands and very much resembles the retreat of some heroine "—a thumbnail appreciation of their domestic fiction (*Early Diary of Fanny Burney*, i. 213, note).

of the Delborough Family (1792) to be finished after the separation from her husband. Then, in the *Memoirs of Mary*, she combined letters and narrative with some dexterity, and told a lucid story about characters who are not mere sentiments with a proper name attached.[1] Her daughter Elizabeth, occasioner of the domestic quarrel, also became a most industrious novelist, a fair sample of her work being *The Gipsy Countess* (1799), in letters more verbose and otherwise no better than her mother's. To write a methodical history of your life to your brother in India seems an arrant abuse of the epistolary device. But this was an expedient bound to be popular with the amateur novelist, especially when she had learned all she knew from Richardson. Two-score years after *Pamela*, during the decade 1760-1769, more than thirty novels were published in the form of letters.[2] There are two correspondents in *Letters between Emilia and Harriet* (1762), by Maria Susannah Cooper, author also of *The School for Wives* (1763) and *The Exemplary Mother, or Letters between Mrs Villars and her Family* (1769); all these are perfunctory as stories but resolutely edifying upon correct behaviour in the trying contingencies of life.[3]

One writer of this school, Mrs Woodfin, author of *The History of Sally Sable* (1758), was evidently tarred with the brush of Prévost. Here, a girl exposed to attempts upon her virtue, turns out to be the natural daughter of one of the rakes pursuing her. Such dallying with the incest theme was a weakness of the Prévost group; it is a prominent motive in *Cleveland*. Mrs Woodfin also wrote *The Auction* (1759), *The History of Miss Harriot Watson* (1763), and *The Discovery, or Memoirs of Miss Marianne Middleton* (1764), novels in which some touches of life and circumstance relieve the general mediocrity. The fraud of Thomas Hull the actor and playwright in trying to pass off his *History of Sir William Harrington* (1771) as, to quote the title, " written some years since, and revised, corrected, and improved, by the late Mr Samuel Richardson," has been alluded to. Story, chief characters, and of course the virtuous sentiments, are all lifted from *Clarissa*. But by this time the Richardsonian stock

[margin: Mrs Woodfin and others]

[1] She also wrote *Delves, a Welch Tale* (1796).
[2] G. F. Singer, *The Epistolary Novel from Richardson to 1800* (1933), p. 138.
[3] Much later she wrote *The Wife, or Caroline Herbert* (1812).

had been too much crossed with alien strains for many such slavish imitations to appear, or to have a chance with a public whose palates had been tickled with more pungent fare.

Hugh Kelly

A curious variant of the Clarissa-Lovelace formula, the man succeeding and then throwing the lady over, for motives approved by the author, is the novel of another playwright, Hugh Kelly,[1] *Memoirs of a Magdalen, or the History of Louisa Mildmay* (1767). A coxcomb, piqued by a lady's reputation for beauty and indifference, courts her successfully; but on the eve of the wedding, in an unguarded moment, she drops into his arms. She is no Clarissa, but an ordinary well-behaved but warm-blooded woman; and this conceited young rake is a very cheap imitation of Lovelace —although he deprecates comparison with that " contemptible blockhead." He argues that if she yields so easily to him and looks so innocent afterwards she may do the same with someone else. He treats her so contemptuously that the marriage is broken off, there is a row at the Mildmays', and she is driven from her home. A brother saves her from want; and presently the lover repents, and is on the point of doing her justice by marrying her. But the news arrives that Louisa has eloped. She has really been carried off by another Lovelace, to a house at Hampstead, where the second lover tries to force her to accept his hand, but abstains from proceeding to his prototype's extremities. One night, the house is on fire, and Louisa escapes. She is discovered by her friends, and the whole story comes out. Lovelace No. 1 is abroad, and now hastens home to make reparation. At Calais, by the strangest coincidence, he meets an affable gentleman who at supper tells him all about it. He has chanced on Lovelace No. 2. A duel is inevitable, and the less culpable of the two lovers dies like his great original. Then the estranged couple marry without any more fuss, and poetic justice is executed all round; missing relatives reappear with fortunes to bequeath, husbands and wives supposed to be deceased are restored to each other, and the wicked woman who had abetted the elopement is drowned in the Thames whilst trying to escape to foreign parts.

[1] Not the Kelly who wrote for a bookseller a continuation to Richardson's first novel, viz., *Pamela's Conduct in High Life* (1741), as Singer avers (p. 106 and index). Hugh was born in 1739, and even at that age was hardly capable of this " combination of pious and uninspired nonsense."

Apparently, Hugh Kelly wrote *Louisa Mildmay* as the masculine rejoinder to *Clarissa*, in which Richardson took the woman's side. His " wretched Louisa " is said to have shown " an uncommon turpitude of sentiment," and after her lapse the outraged lover tells his bosom friend, " O Melmoth! did these women but know how we worship them for refusing to gratify our wishes; did they but know how we doat upon the indignation of a fine eye, when fired into a blaze of conscious virtue, and striking an instant confusion upon the presumptuous addresses of a designing lover, how few of them would listen to an improper solicitation." The dedication to the Duchess of Northumberland explains that the book " is intended to support the interest of morality."

Richardson had founded the English novel of sensibility; but, after all, sensibility was not an object with Richardson, who wrote to inculcate prudence and self-control. His novels had a very definite purpose, edification; the long sub-titles of *Pamela* and *Clarissa* are clear advertisements of their moral and cautionary intent.[1] Sensibility was the predominant quality of himself and his favourite characters; but his themes were always the practical dilemmas of conduct and the formation of an estimable personality. Sensibility was invaluable as an endowment conducive to virtue; it is only by refining our perceptions and cultivating the utmost responsiveness to feeling that we attain the delicate balance and perfect control of our inner selves which makes possible a Clarissa or a Grandison. But sensibility soon became an object of engrossing interest and an end in itself; and then that hypertrophy of the emotional part of our being was inevitable which presently characterizes the post-Richardsonians. That amoral person Sterne cared nothing for edification, and if he pretended to moralize it was in a mocking, sceptical way that showed him to be a Gallio caring immoderately for something very different. He parodied the moralists in the honour of a Comic Spirit created out of his own impishness. He fondled his sensibility, he never tired of playing with it; he was a debauched sentimentalist, aware of his vice, and voluptuously enjoying all its sweetness and regarding those who disapproved with a sly and defiant leer. Mackenzie who followed and sometimes imitated Sterne was serious instead of

Sensibility becoming an end in itself

[1] See Volume IV. 21, for *Pamela*; 53, for *Clarissa*.

playful. Sterne in his sentimental rhapsodies often overstepped the borders of extravaganza; Mackenzie's mood was idealistic, almost utopian. But the seriousness even of Mackenzie must be discounted a little; for, after all, was he not a hard-headed and practical Scot, a successful lawyer, a thorough man of the world, who merely amused one half of his brain with his fairy-tales of superfine sensibility?

The reign of sensibility   But plenty of novelists appeared who were nothing if not in earnest, who were painfully, methodistically serious about it; and sensibility now becomes, not only the root of all virtue, but virtue itself, the indispensable quality, the hall-mark of the elect. It was adopted into the approved codes of behaviour; the refined congratulated themselves on their tenderness of heart, and affected the same modesty in dissembling their sensitive feelings and presenting an imperturbable face to the world as the generous person was expected to do in his acts of charity. Goldsmith had had enough sentimentalism in him to throw a charm over this trait in his Man in Black. Softness of heart, a fine gradation in our reactions to every appeal to our sympathy, and a readiness to be plunged at any suitable moment into orgies of emotion, were wellnigh universal qualities, held at least in universal esteem, and were the very thing to make the fortune of novelists who were of exactly the same frame of mind. Such were by no means lacking. Comedy was extinct, satire under a ban. Humour, cousin-german to sentiment, might fitfully survive. Wit and levity were a public scandal. Goldsmith and Sheridan might ridicule; their bantering comedies might enchant the town, but they could not kill sentimentalism, or set a fashion for further manifestations of such comedy on the stage or in the novel.

Richardson is gradually superseded   It would be inexact to say that the influence of Richardson was waning towards the end of the seventeen-sixties; if his novels were tending to go out of favour and to be superseded by new kinds of sentimental fiction, it was simply that he had established a cult and his devotees had gone beyond him. There were higher degrees to be attained by the faithful. The full-fledged novel of sensibility was to out-sentimentalize Richardson. This would probably have arrived here in some shape or form without the concurrence of external influences. The very English work of

Sterne and Mackenzie seems to mark the stages of transition, and Mackenzie owed little to foreign examples, at least in his first novel, beyond his mild interest in Rousseau's primitivism, whilst those to which Sterne was in debt belonged to an earlier day. But what may roughly but conveniently be distinguished as the novel of sensibility is as much French in character and origin as English. It was the French Richardsonians, pursuing a trend already observable in their own literature, who first outwent their acknowledged leader. They deepened his emotional colours with stronger pigments; they laid on thicker and more lurid tones.

For both sentimentalism and sensibility—they blend into each other and it would be safer not to draw a strict dividing line— were in no wise confined to this country. Here and abroad it was pre-eminently a sentimental age; and, naturally, there was interchange of products, free trade in literature. Richardson was translated into French, and so were his followers; the compliment was repaid to French novelists of the same persuasion. Indeed, it is often not easy to make sure whether a given novel appeared first in one language or in the other, the confusion being increased by the frequent fathering, or more often the mothering, of translated works by distinguished novelists who undertook the task out of pure admiration.[1] But before this concurrence, at any rate before it had its full effects, Sterne finished *Tristram Shandy*, or rather left it for ever unfinished, and wrote *The Sentimental Journey*, which, though inimitable, were not without literary offspring, and Mackenzie produced his three novels, which were imitable, and likewise not without issue. Meanwhile that odd personage Henry Brooke, author of the poem *Universal Beauty* and of the nondescript novel *The Fool of Quality*, enlarged the sentimental creed into a vague theosophy, and made it the basis

Relations with the French sentimentalists

---

[1] See Reynaud (p. 84) on *emprunts réciproques*. Nicolas Étienne Framéry's *Mémoires de M. le Marquis de S. Forlaix*, which appeared in French and in English (1770), is given to Mrs Frances Brooke, who only translated it, by the *D.N.B.*, the catalogue of the Bibliothèque Nationale, and that careful scholar Gustave Lanson (*Manuel bibliographique de la France*, 582). Prévost's version of Mrs Sheridan's *Sidney Bidulph*, under the title, *Mémoires pour servir à l'histoire de la vertu* (1762), is accepted by Servais Étienne as an original work of his; and another savant Joseph Texte (*Rousseau et les origines du cosmopolitisme littéraire*, 186) is quoted, who thought so too, and said it was only "une longue imitation de Richardson" (*Le Genre romanesque en France*, 123).

of an educational scheme like that proposed in *Émile*. These products of a cross between English and Irish or English and Scottish genius require some attention next as pointing the way to ulterior developments of sentimentalism.

Influence of Sterne's sensibility   Few of those who attempted the manner of Sterne were able to appreciate his humour or tried to echo it; only now and then did a lover of the facetious mimic the freakishness of his method. Most of his readers disliked all this, whilst they subscribed to his sentimentalism with an infatuation that would have amused their idol. "Where Sterne attempts the Pathos," writes Clara Reeve, " he is irresistible; the reviewers have well observed, that though he affected humour and foolery, yet he was greatest in the pathetic style.—His Maria and Le Fevre, and his Monk, are charming pictures, and will survive, when all his other writings are forgot." [1] Sterne was also a model as commentator on life. His sensibility privileged him to find enjoyment in the most melancholy circumstances; suffering and compassion were to him not pain but pleasure. Hence he was exempt from ordinary restraints, he need not observe the slightest reticence. Nothing was too sacred or too distressing. He invited all to look into his meditative soul and share the delicious pangs of his tormented bosom. Such a pose could be turned to account by any clever writer in fiction that took the form of observations by a critical spectator of the world's doings.

Followers of Sterne   It was remarked above [2] that Thomas Bridges, in his *Adventures of a Bank-Note* (1770-1771), tried to write like Fielding; his tears, however, his premeditated pathos, show a different master. The scheme is like that of *Chrysal*, but the manner more desultory and discontinuous; and he prefers a kind-hearted drollery to satire. The sketches of people and their very miscellaneous experiences as the note passes from hand to hand are mostly comic, a comedy often too broad for squeamish readers, but sometimes sad and affecting, to please the sentimentalists. It is Bridges who quotes the bookseller's protest that " a crying volume . . . brings me more money in six months than a heavy merry thing will in six years." A contemporary book, *Sentimental Lucubrations* (1770) by " Peter Pennyless," is made up of posturings and sentimental

---

[1] *The Progress of Romance*, ii. 31.   [2] Above, p. 52.

hyperbole outdoing even Sterne in extravagance, and must have been meant as a skit. On the other hand, one known as *The Koran*, or to give it its official title, *The Posthumous Work of a late celebrated Genius* (1770), pretends to be composed of materials left behind by Sterne himself.[1] Lawrence's *Contemplative Man* affects Sterne's humour but not his sentimentalism, and presents some rather dilute characterization after the same recipe.[2] *Fragments in the Manner of Sterne* (1797) by Isaac Brandon also feebly aspires to catch the accent of Sterne's humour, and brings in stage figures called Toby, Trim, and the like, who dialogue and ejaculate in clumsy mimicry of the original worthies. But other emulators, from Mackenzie, " Courtney Melmoth," Mrs Bonhote, and Jane Timbury, author of *The Philanthropic Rambler* (1790), to the ingenuous forgers of Sentimental Journeys and Yorick's Letters, could compete with Sterne only in sensibility and an occasional perception of some odd trait or affecting situation as they gazed at the passing show.

" Melmoth " and Mrs Bonhote, at any rate, deserve some further notice. Samuel Jackson Pratt (1749-1814), whose stage name " Courtney Melmoth " is attached to most of his novels, though he is as often known in literary history as " Benignus," is the man of many parts who long had an interest in a bookshop and circulating library at Bath, after he had resigned his Orders and failed as an actor. Lecturer, reciter, playwright, poet, and prose-writer on diversified subjects—these were his means of livelihood. And, not unnaturally, his first book profited by the fashion and availed itself of the miscellaneousness of Sterne, without going too far in copying his wilful eccentricities and literary acrobatics. It is a rambling, serial work in six volumes (1775-1777), with the bizarre title, *Liberal Opinions, upon Animals, Man, and Providence*, and in the second edition, *Liberal Opinions, or the History of Benignus*. So far as it is connected by a very tenuous thread of narrative, which grows a little more substantial as it proceeds, this is the autobiography of the young fellow

"Courtney Melmoth"

---

[1] It was probably by Richard Griffith, husband of the novelist Elizabeth Griffith, a disreputable man who was the author of a notorious book, *The Triumvirate, or the authentic memoirs of A[ndrews], B[eville], and C[arewe]*, but possibly by his son who bore the same name. *The Koran* was included in the collected works of Sterne in the 1775 and 1795 editions.

[2] See above, p. 88.

Benignus, his apprenticeship to the world, his startling contacts with the seamy side, and the whole course of his disillusionment, the philosophy so acquired being summed up in "Six Golden Rules of Oeconomy," inculcating prudence and discretion. Peripatetic meditations in prose and verse, anecdotes and dialogues in which figures of sensibility are opposed to the worldly, the wicked, and the hard-hearted, carry the tale placidly along to the hour when Benignus retires to his forest hermitage. *The Pupil of Pleasure, or the New System illustrated* (1776), undertakes a duty that a good many accepted about this date, to expose the de-moralizing tendency of the line of conduct recommended in the Chesterfield letters.[1] It is a lurid and harrowing story of illicit love and its consequences, and "Melmoth" had only himself to thank when he was censured for the licentiousness which he professed to condemn. *The Tutor of Truth* (1779) was a tame portrayal of one who cleaves to the opposite principle, rectitude and sobriety. *Travels for the Heart, or the New Paradise*, and *Shenstone-Green* (1779) both return to the sentimentality of Sterne, the ill-starred scheme of the philanthropist in the latter, with the jeers and horse-play that bring it to an end, anticipating Bage, who was to write *Mount Henneth* a couple of years later. *Emma Corbett, or the Miseries of Civil War* (1780), is described as "founded on some recent circumstances which happened in America," and fully lives up to its sub-title, the lovers finding themselves on opposite sides. It is perhaps not too sentimental, but certainly sentimental enough, and sold best of any of his works. In *Family Secrets* (1797) the flow of lachrymose sensibility runs copiously to the last, though some approaches must be acknowledged to natural character-drawing, or at all events to dialogue both racy and in character.

Mrs Bonhote and others Elizabeth Bonhote (1744-1818) followed in the well-worn footsteps in *The Rambles of Mr Frankly* (1773-1776), but adopted a different routine in her *Parental Monitor* (1788), *Olivia, or Deserted Bride* (1787), *Darnley Vale, or Emelia Fitzroy* (1789), *Ellen Woodley* (1790), and *Bungay Castle* (1797), the last a Gothic romance, pleasantly tinged with local feeling, for Bungay was her

[1] A contemporary story in *The Lounger* (No. 35) has the same object, and may be compared with the "History of a Wife seduced by her Husband (*Lounger*, 75).

home. Only the first of these properly belongs to the consanguinity of Sterne. Beside it may be grouped such chronicles of sentimental journeyings as *The Philosopher in Bristol* (1775) by William Combe,[1] author of the erstwhile popular *Tours of Dr Syntax*, James Thistlethwaite's *Man of Experience* (1778), George Keate's *Sketches from Nature, taken and coloured in a Journey to Margate* (1779), the *Philanthropic Rambler* (1790-1791) of Jane Timbury, who also put *The Story of Le Fevre* into verse (1787), and many others, often anonymous. Joseph Cradock, author of *Village Memoirs* (1775), and Thomas Cogan, author of *John Buncle Junior, Gentleman* (1776), a memoir of Buncle's son by Miss Dunk, were both sentimental travellers; and their novels are an outlet for their philosophic or moralistic views, with the merest adumbration of a story. The former consists of letters, which are simply disquisitions or sermons written by a country parson to his son in London, and the soundness of his advice is borne out negatively by the daughter who disregards it and comes to grief. John Williams (1761-1818), well known as a journalist and satirist under the style of "Anthony Pasquin," ventures in *The Curate of Elmwood, a tale* (1795),[2] to wield the pen of Sterne and voice the sentiments of Yorick, Mr Shandy, Uncle Toby, and Dr Slop, upon scenes illustrating War, Justice, Religion, Missions, and other vexed topics. Keate was perhaps the only one among those named who did catch some gleams of the master's subtle impressionism; his intuition of all that was going on in the minds of his curiously sensitive characters, and of himself, the most sensitive of all; his rendering of the finest shades, the almost imperceptible significance of a sensation or the quiver of an emotion. All made a cult of feeling for its own sake, but they rarely came within measurable distance of Sterne's sentimental virtuosity. But Keate was a painter, a man of keen perceptions and versatile accomplishments, with personality enough to be an intimate friend of Voltaire. In the sketches of his tour through Kent, he set down what he himself saw, thought, and felt, of places and persons, incidents and conversations, and in assuming the manner with a

---

[1] Combe wrote sentimental fiction, including two epistolary novels, *Letters between two Lovers and their Friends* (1781) and *Original Love Letters between a Lady of Quality and a Person of Inferior Station* (1784).
[2] Afterwards entitled *Julia, the Curate's daughter of Elmwood*.

grace of his own proved himself something more than a mere second-hand Sterne.[1]

Henry Mackenzie   The one successor of the great sentimentalist who counts historically, however, was Henry Mackenzie (1745-1831), who disliked Sterne's buffoonery, which he described as "the bathos of wit."[2]   He hated to be told that he had imbibed his sensibility, or his skill at portraying the character, from that source: "An imitation of Sterne had been early objected to me; yet certain it is that some parts of *The Man of Feeling* which bear the strongest resemblance to *The Sentimental Journey* were written, and even read to some of my friends, before the publication of that ingenious performance."[3]   But Mackenzie may be relieved of the imputation that he expressly imitated either *The Sentimental Journey* or those chapters of *Tristram Shandy* which were virtually a first draft for parts of that book, and be recognized as none the less a disciple of Sterne.   He was well read in the literature of sensibility; and, whilst his chief enthusiasm was for Richardson, Rousseau, and Marmontel, after all, *Tristram Shandy* was coming out at the time he was engaged upon *The Man of Feeling*, "some time between 1766 and 1768,"[4] and it is incredible that he should not then have read a book, read by everyone indeed, with which he showed himself familiar later on, as in the criticism already quoted. Incredible too that he could otherwise have assumed Sterne's airs and graces so felicitously.   He was in London, reading English law, a knowledge of which was necessary in the Exchequer business in Edinburgh which he was presently to take up, when he conceived the idea of the novel.   It was to have little plot or incident, the purpose being to sketch "the life and sentiments of a man of more than usual sensibility," a martyr to shyness like the young Mackenzie himself, a humanitarian repelled by what he sees of the world, and, like Mackenzie again, one who felt disgust "at some parts of the legal profession," in which he fails to make

---

[1] Fanny Burney depicts Keate as an inordinately conceited poetaster (*Early Diary*, ed. A. R. Ellis, i. 315-316).   He manœuvres, clumsily and transparently, for a chance to read his worthless Ode to the company, and except when he was the topic of conversation sat mute, waiting for an opportunity to drag it in again.

[2] *Anecdotes and Egotisms*, ed. H. W. Thompson, 182.

[3] H. W. Thompson, *A Scottish Man of Feeling*, 127.

[4] *Ibid*. 107.

a career. To sum it up, the author afterwards spoke of *The Man of Feeling* as " a real picture " of his London adventures.[1]

Mackenzie affects a whimsicality like Sterne's, and finds a *The* pretext for the disjointed nature of his sketches in the account of *Man of* the sporting curate, who rolls bits of the manuscript telling the *Feeling*" story into wads for his fowling-piece. Thus it is less a continuous novel than a series of glimpses of life from one point of view, that of a benevolent, deeply compassionate man, who, whether he knows it or not, finds his supreme bliss in ecstasy of feeling; and, grief and pity being the most spontaneous of all emotions, is happiest when his heart is wrung with anguish. It might be said that sensibility is his plaything, though he regards it with such seriousness, and though there is a genuine nobility in the exercise of even an impure unselfishness. But the analogy with Sterne is obvious, and in that case sensibility became a vice. Harley, the Man of Feeling, at any rate, has his heart in the right place, though it is only the extreme, the perhaps morbid, softness of that heart which entitles him to Mackenzie's strange form of hero-worship. He makes himself a spectator of the follies and disorders, the injustices and the crimes of the underworld of London. He goes with a party of sightseers to Bedlam, and indulges freely in " the luxury of tears." He risks scandal and ridicule by befriending a prostitute, whose story of her betrayal by a man of the world is a comment upon an upbringing in which the romantic idea of soldierly honour was put before religion. He restores her to the broken-hearted parent, and urges him not to be enslaved by the names the world affixes to motives and actions, but to look beyond.

A familiar device, a sketch of the characters in a stage-coach, *Harley's* with their exchange of views, affords opportunity for a survey of *view of* the world. Shrewd and often caustic comments are neatly put in *social* Johnsonian antitheses. Harley's opinion of the state of society *his* *conditions:* is gloomy enough; it is a time of corruption, " when not only is *melancholy* virtue declined, and vice prevailing, but when the praises of virtue are forgotten and the infamy of vice unfelt." The country shows him scenes like Goldsmith's deserted village. Where is the old schoolhouse, and the benches full of little cherubs, and the green

[1] *Anecdotes and Egotisms*, 186 and 190.

on which they sported? "The squire has pulled it down, because it stood in the way of his prospects."—"What! how! prospects! pulled it down!" cried Harley. "Yes, to be sure, sir; and the green, where the children used to play, he has ploughed up, because, he said, they hurt his fence on the other side of it." Society was the scene of those affectations which are so caustically scourged in Fanny Burney's *Cecilia*. "But we take our ideas from sounds which folly has invented: Fashion, Bon-ton, and Vertù, are the names of certain idols, to which we sacrifice the genuine pleasures of the soul; in this world of semblance we are contented with personating happiness; to feel it, is an art beyond us." Mackenzie's manner is different; though the feeling is not so very remote from the satire of the virulent Johnstone and Churchill, or the brooding and outraged soul of Cowper. But, instead of shafts of ridicule and sarcasm, tears gush incessantly, and not solely from the eyes of Harley. The lachrymatory glands seem to be in a state of chronic inflammation. But that is a philistine remark, for it is not the arch-sentimentalist, the mountebank Sterne, that is in question, but a man of very different stamp, whose sincerity at all events is not to be sneered at. He believed that he was telling a story "uniformly subservient to the cause of virtue."[1] It was an elaborate eulogy, fortified by examples from real life, of Benevolence, the natural and instinctive virtue approved by philosophy as the foundation-stone of morals, and he coupled with this the melancholy which is the corner-stone of high-mindedness. For the truly benevolent man can make only others happy; he is too acutely conscious of realities to find satisfaction for himself in this lower sphere. The world, Harley has realized, is "a scene of dissimulation, of restraint, of disappointment. I leave it to enter on that state, which I have learned to believe is replete with the genuine happiness attendant upon virtue." "The world is in general selfish, interested, and unthinking; and throws the imputation of romance or melancholy on every temper more susceptible than its own. I cannot think but in those regions which I contemplate, if there is anything of mortality left about us, that these feelings will subsist; they are called— perhaps they are—weaknesses here, but there may be some

[1] Letter quoted by H. W. Thompson, 112.

better modifications of them in heaven, which may deserve the name of virtues."[1]

Harley's is highly conscious virtue, and such consciousness is "*Con-* foreign to the spirit of other ages. Harley and those worthy to be *sciousness*" his friends wear their hearts on their sleeves; they seem to be always holding these organs up for the admiration of themselves and of others, and, in this last passage for instance, as claimants for the approval and special favour of heaven. The beauty that his contemporaries saw in the book can be appreciated only very dimly, except by such as do not perceive anything absurd in the fragment recounting how a wealthy man tries to do a good turn to a needy old friend by giving him the charge of his son.

"I have a favour to ask of you, my dear Mountford," said my father, "which I will not be refused: You have travelled as became a man; neither France nor Italy have made any thing of Mountford, which Mountford before he left England would have been ashamed of: my son Edward goes abroad, would you take him under your protection?" He blushed—my father's face was scarlet—he pressed his hand to his bosom, as if he had said, My heart does not mean to offend you. Mountford sighed twice—"I am a proud fool," said he, "and you will pardon it;— there!" (he sighed again)—"I can hear of dependence, since it is dependence on my Sedley."—"Dependence!" answered my father; "there can be no such word between us; what is there in £9000 a-year that should make me unworthy of Mountford's friendship?"—They embraced; and soon after I set out on my travels, with Mountford for my guardian.[2]

It is the consciousness of the natural man, so we are assured, which the conventions of an artificial social life make us conceal and repress. Through the accidents of circumstance, Harley was left very much to himself in boyhood, and so received something like the natural education preached by Rousseau and approved by Mackenzie. In the fragment just quoted, some unknown person remarks, "But as to the higher part of education, Mr Harley, the culture of the mind;—let the feelings be awakened, let the heart be brought forward to its object, placed in the light in which nature would have it stand, and its decisions will ever be just." There are passages to the same effect upon this crucial problem

[1] *Man of Feeling*, lv. [2] *Ibid.*, "The Pupil, a fragment."

of education in the next novel also. But the problem is implied in the general tenor of both stories, the issues of which might be interpreted as the results of the right or the wrong treatment applied to the original instincts. At this stage of his experience Mackenzie was in agreement with Rousseau in wishing to encourage the natural sensibilities in both sexes. Later he seems to have had some misgivings, and to have perceived the risks of a system that relied too exclusively on the development of that which is innate in the individual.

A hero of sensibility   The last scene of all must be read with similar allowances not to sound extravagant and even absurd. Accept the gospel of sentimentalism, and Harley will be recognized as a hero. He is that paradox, a hero of sensibility. A willing martyr to his creed, he endures scoffs, hardships, the bitterest privations, without a murmur. He is also a lover, and in that character again shows himself a hero. Too poor, and perhaps needlessly modest, he loves Miss Walton but does not confess his love. But in looking after one of the unfortunates whom he has befriended, Harley catches a fever, and the heiress visits him on his deathbed. At length he may pardonably avow his affection for that kindred spirit, and she entreats him to have better hopes.

" Let not life be so indifferent to you ; if my wishes can put any value on it—I will not pretend to misunderstand you—I know your worth—I have known it long—I have esteemed it—what would you have me to say?—I have loved it as it deserved." He seized her hand—a languid colour reddened his cheek—a smile brightened faintly in his eye. As he gazed on her, it grew dim, it fixed, it closed. He sighed and fell back on the seat—Miss Walton screamed at the sight. His aunt and the servants rushed into the room. They found them lying motionless together. His physician happened to call at that instant. Every art was tried to recover them ; with Miss Walton they succeeded—but Harley was gone for ever !

" The Man of the World "   *The Man of the World* (1773), in which Mackenzie drew an ugly picture of the antithesis to his Man of Feeling, is a longer story, and many things happen in it, but most of them had happened already to other people in other novels. It is, in short, a story competently told according to the rules, but with little to distin-

guish it from the average story, except that it is also a commentary on life with some odds and ends of wisdom characteristic of the author.   It may be divided into two halves, two distressful tales; a dissolute baronet, the Man of the World, playing in the first the part of Lovelace to the innocent daughter of a poor clergyman, and in the second the part of Mr B. to a Pamela who turns out to be his own illegitimate child.   He is only too successful in his first abominable enterprise; the Clarissa of this portion dies, not before her father.   In the second he is foiled; and, mortally wounded by the lover of the young lady whom he was about to ravish, he repents of his misdeeds and expires in the odour of forgiveness.[1]   His wickedness, however, is too cold-blooded and too complete for any such easy redemption, except in the eyes of a sentimentalist.   But, happily, it is impossible to believe in such a monster.   After all, there are no real people in the fiction of this period, except in the novels of Goldsmith and Fanny Burney. Novels may be interesting and lively; but characterization is only two-dimensional, devoid of the flesh and blood, the living strokes of idiosyncrasy that make every syllable and gesture of even the minor figures of a Fielding or a Scott recognizable realities. Speeches and sentiments may be unexceptionable; as dialogue they lack the personal touch.   Mackenzie writes gracefully; but his characters always talk like books, and many of his episodes and anecdotes are bookish.

This criticism applies to the incidental story of the young man *The* who is a failure in the Old World, in spite of his university *Noble* education and his father's caution against the inadequacy of mere *Savage* book-learning.   Going in disgrace to America and serving with the colours, he is captured by the Cherokees, and living with the tribe learns the wisdom of nature and the virtue of nature's children. He finds happiness in the woods, and only when the aged chief who has been his protector and teacher dies does he feel it his duty to return to his native land.   Mackenzie was evidently interested in the redskin, who was now coming to the fore in romantic literature; there is a brief glimpse of one in the preceding novel; but here he portrays the savage at full length, and endows him

---

[1] The narrow escape from incest is similar to that in the *Cleveland* of the Abbé Prévost (see below, p. 128) which Mackenzie must surely have read.

with the primordial virtues discerned by sentimentalism. When the exile turns homeward he says:

Though there wanted not some rekindling attachment to a people amongst whom my first breath had been drawn, and my youth spent, yet my imagination drew, on this side, fraud, hypocrisy, and sordid baseness; while on that seemed to preside honesty, truth, and savage nobleness of soul.

It was not the first appearance in English fiction of this new birth. Not to mention Oroonoko, Shebbeare had imported his Cannassetego into this country; but Cannassetego was a preposterous creation. The *Cleveland* of the Abbé Prévost had been Englished in 1734, and had introduced readers to his primitive but not irredeemable Abaquis. Mackenzie was the first English novelist of distinction to take up the thesis of the Noble Savage with any seriousness. Had he read *Cleveland*, and was it that novel which suggested also the idea of the narrow escape from incest in the second part of *The Man of the World*? [1]

"Julia de Roubigné" What prompted Mackenzie to write *Julia de Roubigné*, the most romantic of his three novels, is related by Sir Walter Scott.

A friend of the author, the celebrated Lord Kames, we believe, had represented to Mr Mackenzie, in how many poems, plays, and novels, the distress of the piece is made to turn upon the designing villainy of some one of the dramatis personæ. On considering his observations, the author undertook, as a task fit for his genius, the composition of a story, in which the characters should be all naturally virtuous, and where the calamities of the catastrophe should arise, as frequently happens in real life, not out of schemes of premeditated villainy, but from the excess and over-indulgence of passions and feelings, in themselves blameless, nay, praiseworthy, but which, encouraged to a morbid excess, and coming into fatal though fortuitous concourse with each other, lead to the most disastrous consequences. [2]

The scene and characters are French, and the story is in the form of letters. Julia sacrifices her feelings, and for the sake of

---

[1] H. W. Thompson (98, note) says that he probably knew Marivaux and Prévost, "but he seems not to have been influenced by them." This seems a risky conclusion.

[2] *Lives of the Eminent Novelists and Dramatists*—"Henry Mackenzie." "In tragic life . . . no villain need be," says Meredith, in *Modern Love*, "we are betrayed by what is false within." But a comparison must not be pressed too closely.

her widowed father who has lost the family estates consents to marry the rich Count de Montauban, who is much her senior. She settles down loyally to a life of chastened happiness; but the news arrives that the young man whom she had loved is not married to another, as she had been led to believe, but is actually coming home from Martinique with a fortune which he has won in order to win her. Julia is reluctantly prevailed upon to meet him at the cottage of her old nurse to bid him farewell. But the jealous count hears of the assignation, believes the worst, and plots vengeance upon both. By an accident Savillon escapes; but Julia drinks the poison prepared by her husband, who hears from her dying lips that, although she loves Savillon, she is innocent of any act of disloyalty. He kills himself in despair.

The likeness of the situation to that of *Othello* has naturally been pointed out, and also the probability that recollections of the *Nouvelle Héloïse* must have left their traces, for like Rousseau's Saint-Preux Savillon had loved and been loved when he was the girl's tutor, though he had abstained from declaring his passion.[1] Yet this, at the same time, is the one among Mackenzie's novels most analogous to Richardson, in the moralistic presentment of a conflict between love and duty, and, it may be added, in a certain fundamental sophistry in the sentimental attitude. Julia loves Savillon; but Montauban would never have killed her for a mere disloyalty of the heart; being a man of feeling he would have admitted that she was impotent to control her affections. The decisive factor when it comes to business is that of the divorce court: have the lovers been guilty in the material sense? The sentimentalists talk at large about the things of the spirit; but, more than many of those who are less self-righteous, they are really thinking of the flesh, harping on the strings of sensuality. Hence the disgust of Coleridge, who cannot help seeing through the deep-seated if unconscious hypocrisy of Richardson and his school.[2] The implied grossness conflicts with the professed idealism. Apart altogether from this aspect of the question, moreover, there is the obvious charge that Richardson and Mackenzie were sentimentalists themselves and accordingly always took sides with their martyrs of sentiment. Catastrophes really due to the

Sensibility and sensualism

[1] H. W. Thompson, 148-149.   [2] See Volume IV. 45, note.

excess which they theoretically acknowledge to be a fault are still presented as falling upon the innocent, and they exalt the beauty of the sentimentalism which has brought down the tragedy. This incurable propensity to a false view of life becomes more and more glaring in the French and English Richardsonians who will soon claim attention.

Signs of Gothic tendencies   Some beginnings of the romantic scene-painting soon to be a marked characteristic of Gothic fiction are observable in *Julia de Roubigné*, and may reasonably be credited to the example of Prévost, who loved to set the stage gloomily for the experiences of his ill-starred lovers. Montauban's château, where Julia finds herself buried, is " a venerable pile, the remains of ancient Gothic magnificence." She felt, as she drove up between two rows of lime-trees, that "There was a presaging gloom about this mansion, which filled my approach with terror; and when Montauban's old domestic opened the coach-door, I looked upon him as a criminal might do on the messenger of death." She tells her correspondent, "My dreams ever since have been full of horror, and while I write these lines, the creaking of the pendulum of the great clock in the hall sounds like the knell of your devoted Julia." This inoculation with the sensitivity to the sombre and fearful, which was presently to arrive at fever-pitch in Charlotte Smith and Mrs Radcliffe, is the more interesting in Mackenzie from the fact that, eleven years after the publication of *Julia de Roubigné*, it was his lecture at Edinburgh on German drama which was to be the signal for the advent and growth of a more sensational kind of romanticism.[1]

Mac-kenzie's short stories   Some of the narrative pieces in those Edinburgh periodicals *The Mirror* (1779-1780) and *The Lounger* (1785-1786) show that Mackenzie's sentimentalism outlived his youth. As moral tales of this particular cast they are little masterpieces.[2] They were also very popular, especially four of the most sentimental: "The Effects of religion on minds of sensibility—Story of La Roche," " Inefficacy of guilty pleasure to confer happiness—

---

[1] See F. W. Stokoe, *German Influence on the English Romantic Period* (1926), pp. 19-32. Mackenzie's paper was responsible for Scott's early enthusiasm for the German romantics.

[2] They are miniatures even in comparison with Marmontel's *Contes moraux*, in which Dr H. W. Thompson finds the germs of several.

Story of Louisa Venoni," "Father Nicholas," and "Nancy Collins,"[1] all four replete with pathos and deliberately calculated to rouse humanitarian feeling and admiration for virtue. Let "Louisa Venoni" suffice as example. It is the pretty little tale of a rich Englishman travelling in Italy who runs away with the innocent but too susceptible daughter of a peasant, thus mortally injuring an old man who had been his own rescuer in an accident. He takes her to England, where she pines with grief for her father, who she believes had died broken-hearted. One day they hear an organ-grinder playing an air that she knew of yore. It is her father, who has begged his way across Europe in search of his child. Sir Edward, already weary of the emptiness and falsity of worldly life, marries Louisa, and swears to return and seek in the humble Italian cottage the peace and innocence not to be found elsewhere.

Both his novels and the periodical essays that won him the name of the Scottish Addison contain a great deal of social criticism, ranging from manners in general and the vagaries of fashion, with the usual sprinkling of anecdote, and of course the moral predicaments of everyday life, to such subjects as the effect of plays and novels on character and conduct, methods of education, economic problems; much of it is of the kind soon to form the staple of Bage's fiction. And Mackenzie is surprisingly liberal in his outlook. He has an ineradicable grudge against the rich, and seems to have made a mental classification of mankind into two divisions, the wealthy, egoistic, and unscrupulous, and the good people, who are always poor. The philanthropic Mr Rawlinson, in *The Man of the World*, the exception which proves the rule, is the only rich man that cuts a decent figure in any of his stories. Mackenzie held enlightened views on education, on the game laws,[2] which before long were to be exposed in all their ferocity by Crabbe, and on slavery. Yambu, in *Julia de Roubigné*, is a second Oroonoko, a prince who is a noble savage and a victim of white brutality, and who furthermore shows that if a negro is treated with kindness and confidence, he

His dis-cussions of social questions

---

[1] *Mirror*, 108-109, 42-44, and 49, respectively.
[2] The English game laws would hardly win the approval of an Edinburgh gentleman, a century before the time when Scottish deer-forests were to become a national grievance.

will work better as a servant than as a slave. Whatever the
absurdities of sentimentalism, it was on the side of civilization
in an age guilty of much barbarity.

Of senti-
mentalism
and
sensibility

In his discursive papers in *The Lounger* on the subject of
novels and plays, Mackenzie makes it clear that he did not think
his own glorifications of sensibility in the least excessive or likely
to have risky effects upon unreflecting readers. It was a question
that stared him in the face, for moral improvement was decidedly
the chief end that he envisaged in estimating the value of fiction;
in other words, he takes exactly the same view as Dr Johnson
and most other critics of that day. Some may be prone to " the
enthusiasm of sentiment," which is as dangerous as any other
sort of enthusiasm, by which he means an emotionalism exceeding
all rule of restraint. But he omits to provide any determinate
check. When emotions are equally balanced, what is to decide
between them? At what point does emotionalism become excessive? When does sensibility cease to be a virtue? Mackenzie's
lucubrations suggest these questions, and leave them unanswered.
He talks eloquently about duty and benevolence, and sometimes
refers to the arbiter conscience; but conscience seems to be only
sensibility again, coming in at another angle. He is more to the
point on the unconscious hypocrisy of many if not most sentimentalists. " In morals, as in religion," he says, " there are not
wanting instances of refined sentimentalists, who are contented
with talking of virtues which they never practise . . . who open
their minds to *impressions*, which never have any effect upon
their *conduct*, but are considered as something foreign to and
distinct from it." Yet good works are of infinitely more value
than visionary feelings. He has no patience with that " sickly
sort of refinement " which creates imaginary evils and distresses,
and "inspires a certain childish pride of our own superior delicacy,
and an unfortunate contempt of the plain worth, the ordinary but
useful occupations and ideas of those around us." [1]

His
criticisms
of the
novels of
sensibility

This and more to the same wholesome purpose may well cause
us to open our eyes wider, and ask, can it be the author of *The
Man of Feeling* and of that novel of inordinate sensibility *Julia
de Roubigné* who talks so much like ourselves? But, apparently,

[1] *Lounger*, xx.

he did not class his own novels with that dangerous " species
called the *Sentimental*." " These have been borrowed from our
neighbours the French, whose style of manners, and the very
powers of whose language, give them a great advantage in the
delineation of that nicety, that subtilty of feeling, those entanglements of delicacy, which are so much interwoven with the
characters and conduct of the chief personages in many of their
most celebrated novels." Here Mackenzie was right. There is
a difference of degree, but a difference also of kind, in the sensibility that was now coming in, under French encouragement, a
difference not entirely subsumed under the epithet erotic, although
this was the interest that almost monopolized the attention of
French novelists. The Scottish sentimentalist, if he would have
accepted that description, was afraid of passion, which in one of
his essays on tragedy he identifies with the " weaknesses of men." [1]
The sentimentalists whom he censures rarely if ever succeeded
in portraying that noble infirmity; but they were always trying
to. Mackenzie's eye discerned their failings, but had not the
width of focus to see that his own was a very inadequate view of
life. Hence he could not forgive Sheridan's sweeping satire on
the school, and accused his and other comedies of a licentiousness
" more dangerous than the indelicacy of the last century."
" Those," he goes on, " sometimes violated decency, but these
attack principle; those might put modesty to the blush, or
contaminate the purity of innocence; but these shake the very
foundations of morality, and would harden the mind against the
sense of virtue." [2]

Mackenzie's novels, *The Man of Sentiment* especially, con- *Mac-*
tinued to be very popular in England and Scotland, and also in *kenzie's*
the United States, down to the first decade of the nineteenth *influence*
century. What influence they may have had upon other novelists
is not to be easily disentangled from other influences, even of
the French exponents of sensibility whom he condemned. A
novel here and there may have the look of being an imitation of
Mackenzie, particularly if it is conspicuously lacking in humour.
Mr Bently, or the rural Philosopher (1750), might.well have

[1] *Lounger*, 67.
[2] *Ibid.* 50. The French too " have assumed the like pernicious licentiousness.
Figaro, though a less witty, is as immoral a play as *The School for Scandal.*"

had such a genesis; and, later on, *Wanley Penson, or the Melancholy Man, a miscellaneous history* (1791), *The History of Ned Evans* (1796), and Mary Robinson's *Walsingham, or the Pupil of Nature* (1797), may more or less debatably be assigned to the Mackenzie tradition, despite the fact that they are by no means exempt from the animadversions quoted from him above.

Henry Brooke

At a time when the sentimentalists regarded fiction as so important an influence upon morals, one of them was sure sooner or later to write a novel embracing divine as well as human things. And it might have been predicted that Henry Brooke (1703-1783), the Irish enthusiast who, in his poem *Universal Beauty* and elsewhere, had fused the benevolent deism of Shaftesbury with the mysticism of Jacob Böhme,[1] was the likeliest man to do it. In due time, Brooke turned aside from poetry, plays, and political writing, and brought out the five volumes of his strange novel, *The Fool of Quality, or the history of Henry Earl of Moreland* (1765-1770).[2] Another, not less strange even in that age of shapeless amalgams of fiction and personal revelations, *Juliet Grenville, or the history of the human heart* (1773), was written when Brooke was almost in his dotage, though still visited by gleams of his old enthusiasm. John Wesley was so impressed by the spiritual fervour and exalted moral ideals of the former book that he obtained the author's permission, and published it again, abridged of about one-third of its original bulk, under a new title, *Henry, Earl of Moreland* (1781), and this long passed with many of his followers as a work of his own.[3]

"The Fool of Quality"

The Fool of Quality[4] is the first of the pedagogic novels in English; *Sandford and Merton* was to appear the year that Brooke died, and to follow the same mixed plan of story and illustration, if plan it can be called in the earlier case. Rousseau's *Émile* had been published in 1762, and was evidently read and

[1] There is much more of Böhme's mystical interpretation of Christian doctrine in the later poem *Redemption* (1772).

[2] The first volume appeared at Dublin (1765); see bibliography of Brooke (*Fool of Quality*, ed. E. A. Baker, 1906). Charles Kingsley's introduction to the edition of 1859 is also reprinted there.

[3] Wesley laid himself open to criticism by not mentioning the author either on the title-page or in his own preface.

[4] The title, *The Fool of Quality*, is analogous to that of *The Idiot* of Dostoevsky. Brooke alludes to the contrast between the simplicity of nature and the artificial product of fashionable education.

digested by Brooke, who agreed with Rousseau that the basic principle of education should be to bring out the healthy original instincts, to foster and develop the spontaneity and probity of nature. The book describes the whole course of the upbringing of an ideal nobleman; and, since nothing is omitted, since everything that happens to Harry Moreland is thrown into it, along with the experiences of all who cross his path, and the instances from ancient and modern history, the fables, anecdotes, and sermons, with which his imagination is fed, the result almost outdoes *John Buncle* in heterogeneousness.[1] Everything is made to yield edification and an inspiration to noble living, often in a manner beyond all praise. Thus the excellence of the book is in the parts, and in the spirit of universal goodwill and abnegation of self informing every incident, every utterance; it is a transparency, a shadow-picture, in which the soul of the lovable Henry Brooke is the shining light.

Since the intention of Harry's self-appointed tutor is to make him learn from his contacts with life, the story is a succession of episodes; and Brooke's quixotic idealism pushes these nearly every time beyond the utmost margin of probability. Everything is in excess, the hero's natural goodness and sensibility most of all. His Alcides exploits and deeds of boyish charity are absurdly overdone, and the calamities of the blameless unfortunates are exceeded only by the marvellous turns of the wheel by which innocence is at length rewarded. There is no measure, no regard for common sense. The goats are jet-black, the lambs snowy white; if this is nature, it is not human nature. Mackenzie, if read in proper chronological order after Brooke, as he should be, will seem reticent, in comparison; his sentimentalists do try to repress their emotions, not to make themselves a public exhibition. Brooke's hero and his friends burst into tears alike in sympathy with grief and at any example of human affection or of nobility of soul. This " passionate and tearful sensibility " seemed to Charles Kingsley, who republished the book when it was nearly a century old, not an English but a French or Irish trait. It surpasses all the extravagances of English and French sensibility,

Its extravagant sensibility

---

[1] " A strange extravagant novel then much admired " (Mackenzie, *Anecdotes and Egotisms*, ed. H. W. Thompson, 81).

and there is nothing to prevent its being put down to Brooke's Irish temperament. At any rate, it is not sentimentality of the morbid kind. And, in spite of the floods of tears, this is not an effeminate but a manly book. Harry's mentor plays upon his sensibilities in order to keep him at the right heroic pitch, to inspire emulation of the greatest examples in history. And he does it deliberately. Brooke is providing an object lesson in education through the emotions. Damon and Pythias, in one of the inset stories, having chanted their duet of conscious virtue, Dionysius, who had been " confounded and awed by the dignity of these sentiments, and by the manner (still more sentimental) in which they were uttered," when Pythias offers to die for his friend, now is overwhelmed. " His heart was touched; his eyes were opened; and he could no longer refuse his assent to truths so incontestably approved by their facts. He descended from his throne. He ascended the scaffold. Live, live, ye incomparable pair! he exclaimed. Ye have borne unquestionable testimony to the existence of virtue; and that virtue equally evinces the certainty of the existence of a God to reward it. Live happy, live renowned! and, O form me by your precepts, as you have invited me by your example, to be worthy of the participation of so sacred a friendship."

Stories for the young In retelling the story of the burghers of Calais, Brooke strikes an epical note; and, although when Queen Philippa intervenes, she appears in the guise of a sentimentalist and addresses the king in the well-known phraseology, this cannot ruin the magnanimity of that great episode: it is a trumpet-call to the heart of a boy. One can keep a dry eye, however, but hardly a grave face, over the tale of the sentimental lion, who goes into paroxysms of tenderness at the death of the overfed lap-dog. " For five days he thus languished, and gradually declined, without taking any sustenance, or admitting any comfort; till one morning he was found dead, with his head lovingly reclined on the carcase of his little friend. They were both interred together, and their grave plentifully watered by the tears of the keeper and his loudly lamenting family." But it is only fair to remember that these stories are told for the edification of a boy, and a boy would not perceive the ridiculous side. And whatever may be thought of the system of education propounded, the study of boyhood itself is admirably done; this is, in fact, the first full-length of a boy in English fiction, and the first to be thoroughly sympathetic and in the main natural.

All this could be utilized by a Wesley, but only after cautious *The* expurgation; when Charles Kingsley greeted Brooke as a kindred "*Mystic* spirit in the next century, it was because his extravagances had *Divinity*" become merely the quaintnesses of another day and were now *in it* harmless.[1] Wesley did not object to the sentiments, which he thought "generally very just"; but he excised "great part of the Mystic Divinity, as it is more philosophical than scriptural." This Divinity develops the idea, already elaborated in his most ambitious poem, that the beauty of the universe is the expression of the divine immanent in all creation, a beauty which,

> mimicked in our humbler strains,
> Illustrious, through the world's great poem reigns.

The universe is organized on sentimental principles; the supreme Governor regards His creatures with infinite sensibility, and " imparts to them also a perception and relish of the beauty with which He has formed them," a " sentimental beauty " as Brooke calls it, " for universal nature can exhibit no single grace or beauty that does·not arise from sentiment alone." The feelings and instincts, even of Turks, even of " the wild Indians, who never listened to the toll of a bell, nor ever were called into any court of civil judicature," are beautiful and good because of their divine origin. " The truth is, that people live incomparably more by impulse and inclination than by reason and precept. Reason and precept are not always within our beck; to have their due influence, they require frequent inculcation and frequent recollection; but impulse and inclination are more than at hand; they are within us, and from the citadel rule the outworks of man at pleasure." After the Fall, God employed what Browning afterwards calls " this blessed evil " to turn us back to the true goal of our existence. Brooke was a sincere Christian, and he satisfied himself that these sentiments were consistent with orthodoxy,

---

[1] Kingsley must have read *The Fool of Quality* before writing *Westward Ho!* —his Vindex Brimblecombe is obviously founded on Brooke's Mr Vindex, the brutal schoolmaster.

at the same time finding their analogues in non-Christian teachers, for instance, in Zoroaster, "the illuminated philosopher." But for " all sorts of sectaries, all persons of selfish and little minds," who " would make a monopoly of the Saviour," he has only a mild rebuke, and would recall them to that benevolence on which God "builds the happiness of all his intelligent creatures." [1]

"Juliet Grenville" Brooke was sixty years old when *The Fool of Quality* began to appear, and by the time the last volume was published he was a broken old man. He had married his cousin, then under his guardianship, when she was at school, a girl of thirteen, and they had lived together happily for nearly fifty years. She died in 1773, and the blow reduced him for a length of time " to a state of almost total imbecility." " The powers of his mind were decayed, and his genius flashed only by fits." [2] It was in these circumstances that his second novel, *Juliet Grenville* (1774), appears to have been written. More emotional and incoherent and even more extravagant than *The Fool of Quality*, it tells the story of a pair who fell in love when at school together; and in the fond picture of family life in the country, as rich in good deeds and as happy as his own, Brooke had the best possible inspiration. His theme is a variant on that of the other novel, the education of the heart, which is purified and annealed in the furnace of sorrow and strife. There is tenderness, there are beauties in it, there are passages admirably true to human nature; but they are buried in a complication of episodes ringing fantastic changes on the old motive, and wearisome except to the confirmed sentimentalist.

Wesley on sentimentalism Wesley's derisive remarks on the word " Sentimental " in Sterne's *Sentimental Journey* have been often quoted [3]; and it is the more amusing to catch him in the act of appropriating for his own evangelical uses one of the most sentimental books ever penned. But his attitude towards sentimentalism was sane enough, as a letter to his sister in 1772 shows. " Happy are you to whom

---

[1] Brooke's " Divinity " is set forth in many dialogues and disquisitions by chosen characters throughout the story (see *Fool of Quality*, 1906, especially pp. 134-135, 223-224, 336-338, 367-369 and 393-396).

[2] Quoted from family papers (see Introduction to *Fool of Quality*, 1906).

[3] *E.g.*, by Leslie Stephen (*English Thought in the Eighteenth Century*, xii. 114): " Sentimental! What is that ? It is not English; he might as well say Continental. It is not sense. It conveys no determinate idea ; yet one fool makes many. And this nonsensical word (who would believe it ?) is become a fashionable one."

it is given," he writes, " both to do and to suffer the will of God! It is by this means that He will confirm your soul against too great sensibility. It is then only too great when it hurts the body or unfits you for some part of your duty. Otherwise it is a blessed thing to sorrow after a goodly sort."[1] He was nearer to Mackenzie than to Brooke, nearer still perhaps to Dr Johnson. In truth, Wesley's belief in the essential goodness of human nature, his serene optimism, and his faith in the good will of a Creator with whom the human soul may be in direct communion, link him with the sentimentalists.

[1] *Letters of John Wesley*, ed. J. Telford, v. 320.

CHAPTER VI

THE NOVEL OF SENSIBILITY

Difference Too much must not be made, as the foregoing chapter has noted,
between of the rough distinction between the novel of sentiment and the
the novel of novel of sensibility. The phrases are not much more than con-
sentiment
and the venient labels, and it would certainly be risky to try to fit them to
novel of national differences and distinguish between an English character-
sensibility istic or tendency and one that is mainly French. Yet French
mainly one influences did as time went on react more and more perceptibly
of degree on English novelists, and the general effect was an intensification
of what is indicated by the second of the two terms. English
sentimentalism met with a warm response from French sentimentalists, for, as already remarked, it chimed in with feelings
and tastes that were neither new nor strange; and when French
fiction went to further extremes there were English novelists
ready to follow. He would be a bold critic who would dare to
say which went furthest.

Senti- Sentimentalism of various tints and shades is, of course, plenti-
mentalism fully visible in the recent French novels of gallantry, and earlier
in French in the pastoral and heroic romances. The idealization of philander-
novels and
romances ing nymphs and swains or of sophisticated adventurers in the
Pays de Tendre, the expatiation on feeling, the analysis and fond
comparison of states of the heart, in two words, the sentimental
metaphysics—all this was woven into the very texture of the
fiction most enjoyed by the seventeenth century.[1] But it was
no real world that was thus portrayed, but one wholly ideal, an
exercise of poetic fancy; no realism here, nor very much
imaginative seriousness. It was all play-acting, a release from
the troubles and deformities of life. The high-bred habitants of
d'Urfé's Arcadia willingly submitted to a refined code of manners,
self-repression, and impeccable virtue; love was a duty, sympathy

[1] See Volume III., chap. i., " The Revival of Romance," pp. 26-27 and *passim*.

a noble feeling, not yet because it was a source of pleasure to oneself, for it was not yet confounded with the self-regarding impulses, but for the sake of its supreme social value. These generous fancies, far from being in any contradiction thereto, were a refinement upon the classical canons of order, good taste, and restraint that were universally acknowledged. Sensibility accepted the rule of reason.[1] Hylas the libertine and other lawless individualists lay under censure. The reign of sensibility, the absolutism of feeling and instinct, was still in the distance; fundamental revaluations had to take place before its divine rights could be admitted.

In the later romances, though fiction came by various stages *The cult of* nearer to life, sensibility was forced like a hot-house plant, and *sensibility* grew more and more artificial, affected, pretentious. Now high-flown emotionalism is a disguise for baser impulses, " fiddling harmonics on the strings of sensualism "; and now the cult of sentiment and of the beautiful soul leads to an absurd preciosity. But by this time the anti-romancers and realists were bringing their artillery to bear on extravagances and affectations, and ravaging these paradises and fairy palaces. Literature was ceasing to be exclusively an aristocratic amusement; the middle classes, as in England, were beginning to take a hand, with similar results. And very soon French sentimentalists discovered and began to assimilate the popular philosophy which in England claimed the authority of Locke and Shaftesbury; and they found its ethics more congenial than the strict legislation of their own Grand Siècle, age of the Classical and Catholic supremacy.

Whether the ridicule of Sorel, Scarron, and Furetière [2] and *Influence* their appeals to reality and common sense had any direct effect *of realistic* or not upon the writers of romances, these did presently orient *fiction :* themselves in a new direction. The last of the school, Madame *Madame de la* de la Fayette, returned from Arcadia to the realm of actuality, *Fayette* and at the same time exchanged mere sentimental fancy for an *and others* imagination that stripped the heart bare of all disguise. In her *Princesse de Clèves* (1678) [3] the missing factor was brought into

---

[1] " La raison est humaine, la sensibilité est individuelle " (Louis Reynaud : *Le Romantisme, ses origines anglo-germaniques,* 1926, p. 114).
[2] See Volume III., chap. ii., " The Anti-romances, etc."
[3] See Volume IV. 69-70 and note.

the equation again, natural feeling, suppressed passion, "noble strength on fire," masked and shut down but only in time to save an explosion. Already there had been something of the sort in the *Lettres portugaises* (1669),[1] that premature outbreak of irrepressible ecstasy and despair. Madame de la Fayette gave her story some circumstantial solidity, by bringing in historical personages, and making them talk and conduct themselves in character. Here, and in *Zayde*, is enounced in concrete terms the sentimental doctrine of the omnipotence of love. It is a fatal thing, not to be withstood, only to be suffered, if possible with dignity. Passion overwhelms, without our complicity or power to avoid it. Sensibility is thus installed as the basis for pathetic emotion, not only inaugurating the novel of sensibility, but also bringing into sight the dramatic treatment of passion in *Manon Lescaut* and the *Nouvelle Héloïse*. Madame de la Fayette maintained the seventeenth-century tradition of decorum and self-command, which contributed in no small degree to the fineness of the tragedy. But, in all these four instances, mere sentimentalism is transcended. To the mere sentimentalist love is a passive emotion, a thing to prize and cherish, to brood over and idealize; not a convulsion of the whole being that comes out in acts, determines events, and reshapes personality itself. The author of the *Princesse de Clèves* brought sensibility to earth, without bringing it low; the new realists were to rob it of its ideality in every sense, and in protesting that it was the most natural and virtuous of human impulses were to vulgarize it.

Realism of Count Anthony Hamilton, Courtilz de Sandras, etc.   Realism at this date was appropriating older forms of fiction, such as the picaresque story and the romance of adventure, as well as preparing to stand on its own base as a simple portrait of reality. The former was the field chosen by Le Sage, the most searching realist of the day. Count Anthony Hamilton, in his witty *Mémoires du comte de Gramont* (1713), made what is largely fiction pass for true biography, by an intuitive anticipation of the arts of the modern historical novelist. Madame la Comtesse d'Aulnoy (1650-1705) in like manner mixed invented facts and valid experience so ingeniously as apparently to take in Defoe,[2] just as he took in his contemporaries with his pretended histories

---

[1] See Volume III. 83-84 and note.   [2] See Volume III. 223.

and books of travel. But the past master in this fraudulent art was the Courtilz de Sandras who has already been briefly mentioned as a precursor of Defoe.[1] Between the dates of the *Princesse de Clèves* and of *Gil Bas*, he poured forth a stream of alleged memoirs, histories, military journals, and narratives of diversified adventure, composed of matter from the news-sheets, personal experience and confidential information, barrack-room gossip and drawing-room scandal, which was so lively and entertaining, and not in the broader sense untrue, as to be in no small part responsible for the legion of memoirs and letters published soon after by known and unknown writers who are usually accepted as authentic witnesses to what they relate. That he gave such an incentive in the following century to Dumas, who accepted the memoirs of Monsieur d'Artagnan as trustworthy, is a more familiar fact. The importance of Courtilz de Sandras at this point of time, however, is that he was the chief artisan in a fashion of writing, simulating not only realism but also a considerable measure of historicity, which was taken over by the Abbé Prévost, and formed the principal link between the French and the English groups of sentimental novelists.

The particular claim of the Abbé Prévost to attention in the history of English fiction is not that he was the author of *Manon Lescaut*. This, it has been said often enough, was inimitable, and few have been so rash as to try to imitate it. But in the enormous mass of his writings, which rivalled Goldsmith's in miscellaneousness, three novels intrinsically inferior stand out as having exercised such an influence on French and also on English writers as cannot easily be over-assessed. That it was he who afterwards translated Richardson, and so was instrumental in bringing another most important influence to bear upon the French novel, and that in his periodical *Le Pour et contre* he applied himself manfully for seven years to the task of interpreting the one nation to the other, are further not irrelevant facts. A. F. Prévost d'Exiles (1697-1763) was a runaway Benedictine who returned more than once to the cloister, at last making his peace with the Church; and whilst in exile spent enough time in England, and employed it to

The Abbé Prévost

[1] See Volume III. 178-179 and note; see also A. le Breton : *Le Roman français au 18ᵉ siècle* (1898), 135-138.

such effect, as to earn the reputation of an Anglomaniac. What sort of a person he was in himself may be gathered from his writings better than from the scanty records that have survived independently. His was largely a clandestine life. He was under the cloud of some obscure affair or affairs of the heart, and of one offence that brought him within the clutches of the law.[1] Having quarrelled with his superiors, or, as he maintained, been treated with signal injustice, he had taken French leave, and even re-criminated in a defiant way. He was a restless, discontented, unhappy being, the typical man of sensibility, the romantic in-dividualist, that curious product of his age of which he has left the monotonous impress in the protagonists of his novels—to call them heroes would in his case be peculiarly incongruous. He can be pictured as an amiable and affectionate person, rather effeminate in his lack of courage and self-reliance, though he could retaliate from a safe distance, always a prey to haunting anxieties, a man who was afraid of life. Like his protagonists, he was easily impressed, easily tempted, easily overwhelmed by disappointments, slights, or misunderstandings. Like them, he brooded over his wrongs, and saw himself as one evil-starred from birth and pur-sued by the special malignity of heaven. In his Man of Quality and the unfortunate marquis, his Cleveland, the brother and sister of his Dean of Coleraine, and in the Chevalier des Grieux who is known to everyone, he went on putting counterparts of himself into situations corresponding, with a good deal of imaginative licence, to his own outer and inner experiences, in the last instance corresponding perhaps very nearly, but that is only for conjecture. Thus he gave his stories a poignancy which was infinitely agreeable to the sentimental reader.[2]

His principal novels   The first of the three novels, all of which were enormously popular and were quickly translated into English, was the *Mémoires et aventures d'un homme de qualité qui s'est retiré du monde* (1728-1731), the seventh and last volume of which consisted of his

[1] Details concerning his arrest for forging a promissory note, his examination by a justice, and his discharge, will be found in Mysie E. I. Robertson's intro-duction to an abridged *Adventures of a Man of Quality* (1930); see pp. 15-22. The case remains somewhat obscure, like other episodes of his career.
[2] " Sans doute Prévost n'est jamais absent de ses œuvres d'imagination " (Pierre Trahard : *Les Maîtres de la sensibilité française au 18ᵉ siècle*, tome i. 108).

masterpiece *Manon Lescaut*, or as it was entitled in full, *Histoire du chevalier des Grieux et de Manon Lescaut*, which was tacked on to a completed story with which it had next to nothing to do. There was an English translation of the *Mémoires* in 1738, but this was probably by no means the first; and later editions bore the title of *The Memoirs of the Marquis de Bretagne*. A favourite in this country was his next novel, *Le Philosophe anglais ou histoire de M. Cleveland, fils naturel de Cromwell* (1732-1739), which began to appear in English at least as early as 1734. The third was *Le Doyen de Killerine : histoire morale, composée sur les mémoires d'une illustre famille d'Irlande* (1735-1740). Of this there were English editions in 1742. *Manon Lescaut*, which is incomparably superior to the rest, appeared repeatedly in English, as well as in French, as a separate work. Other novels of Prévost were translated, but, though of the same general character, they are of minor importance.

Prévost wrote for those as sensitive as himself, and it was the history of his own heart that he unfolded in these protracted and complicated stories of thwarted lives and tortured sensibilities. *Self-revelation in Prévost's novels—introspective fiction* They are all histories of blighted love, of love frowned upon by earth if not by heaven. Love is the agent of fatality driving his martyrs of sensibility to perdition; it is the cause of strife between kindred, of unholy intrigues, abductions, duels, murder, disasters that neither foresight nor experience can avert. Pathos is piled upon pathos by a writer who strives to be tragic, but succeeds only in being violent, sensational, terrifying. No detail too gruesome for his scenes of horror. He racks his readers with fear and anxiety, plunges them in nightmare gloom, wrings them with pity. But the would-be tragic history is, after all, only a funereal kind of picaresque, a loose-knit melodrama. The mental experiences, however, of his victims of their misplaced affections are undeniably moving. In spite of the glaring improbability of incidents and situations, the artless realism gives the effect of a personal record, as if Prévost himself had lived through these scenes of tenderness and uncontrollable passion, and been wrung by these betrayals, jealousies, bereavements, paroxysms of heartbreak and unappeasable regret. But he never knows where to draw the line; he relieves his soul by pouring out all its agonies, he seems to beseech his reader's compassion. And this very effusiveness acted like a spell on the sympathetic. It was all so transparently sincere. Prévost was the founder of the novel of introspection.

General character of his novels— unrestrained sensibility

"If tears and sighs are not to be described as pleasures," writes the Man of Quality, whose memoirs are in the main an agonized spectator's account of the wild love affairs and consequent disasters of those whom he most cares for, "it is true nevertheless that they have infinite sweetness for a person in mortal affliction. The moments that I devoted to my grief were so dear to me that to prolong them I abstained from sleep."

"Mémoires d'un homme de qualité"

This was a sentiment soon to be echoed by Madame de Tencin, Baculard d'Arnaud, and even the sardonic Crébillon fils, and by Marivaux in the latter part of *Marianne*. It is a tale of strange and unforeseen accidents chequering and thwarting the course of ardent and insensate love, and some of the scenes are of a sanguinary and atrocious nature. If the artists who illustrated Prévost are any guide, these episodes were among those best appreciated by his readers. One sensational incident follows another as fast as in the stories of Courtilz de Sandras' bravoes, and half the countries in Europe provide the stage, from Spain and Portugal to Adrianople and Constantinople. The episodes in England which were written after the first two volumes had appeared, and after Prévost's rupture with the ecclesiastical authorities, make effective use of what he had seen and the guide-book knowledge that he had read up of manners and persons and recent occurrences in this country.[1] He gets his semi-historical background by dating his recital some fifteen years earlier, and he was well informed enough to be guilty of few anachronisms or other inaccuracies. Among several portraits, that of the Duchess of Marlborough was acknowledged as very true to life, and the general picture of English manners was as good as any yet done by a foreigner. Thus the book appealed to more than one class of reader, and was well able to compete with the current story of adventure. The novelty and the compulsive interest for the more discriminating was, however, in the way Prévost lays bare

---

[1] This is the portion reproduced in the edition by Mysie E. I. Robertson (1930).

those intense though abnormal and undefinable feelings which
he himself, no doubt, had experienced, and in the terrors and
lacerating griefs that extort sympathy for these lovers seemingly
predestined to ruin. Worn out with sorrow but maintaining his
dignity till the end, the Man of Quality at last retires to the
peace of an abbey, where Prévost says he came across his papers.
He tells us that the real name is suppressed, though it is well
known to many, and the man himself is still alive and well. This
show of authenticity is kept up in *Cleveland* and the *Doyen de
Killerine*.

So it is in *Manon Lescaut*, which is too familiar to need any "*Manon
summary*. In that immortal story, Prévost excelled himself. We *Lescaut*"
have to remember in reading the other novels, as a critic [1] has
pertinently said, that they are by the man who was capable one
day of writing *Manon Lescaut*; but it is often difficult to do
so. In that jewel attached to a necklace of inferior metal he
somehow produced a gem of the first water, and there is much
to be said for the possibility that he quarried it out of his own
most intimate and poignant experiences. At any rate, here he
let Nature have her own way, and gave the world one of those
dramas of impassioned life that seem to enact themselves, reducing
the dramatist to a mere spectator and scribe. We can only
wonder if he was not indeed the protagonist.[2]

In *The Man of Quality*, love is presented in conflict with "*Cleve-
worldly wisdom, and flouting experience and the counsels of a land*"
loyal and anxious friend. *Cleveland* shows philosophy itself
worsted in the conflict with unruly passion. Cleveland is the
philosophe anglais, and his colloquies with the Count de Clarendon
gave the book a special distinction.[3] Once more there is a show
of historicity. Cleveland and Bridge are illegitimate sons of
Cromwell, who is depicted according to the French idea of him
as a base usurper and regicide. Brought up by his mother in the

---

[1] Servais Étienne.

[2] Such a view cannot be substantiated, though it receives some colour from
recent research. It is safest to be content with Sainte-Beuve's dictum : " Sous
la généralité de sa morale et la multiplicité de ses récits, il est aisé de saisir les
traces personnelles d'une expérience bien douloureuse. Sa vie, en effet, fut
pour lui le premier de ses romans et comme la matière de tous les autres "
(*Portraits littéraires*, i. 270).

[3] Recognized, *e.g.*, by Sainte-Beuve (*Ibid.* 281).

dark recesses of Rumney Hole,[1] to escape persecution by the tyrant, he receives an admirable education, based of course on nature and instinct, and so acquires a " perfect knowledge of the world." It leads, however, to disillusionment, for in his actual contacts with his fellow-men Cleveland is duped and cheated; yet he stands by his ideals and refuses to disobey the voice of heart and conscience. It is a bizarre story. Cleveland is harried by misfortune, like his compeers, and wanders all over the world in pursuit of Fanny Axminster, whom he loves when he and she are directed by parental authority to marry others. After many adventures, he finds her in the American backwoods. They are united, but jealousy divorces them. Further adventures supervene, all distressing; he is wellnigh reduced to madness. In one episode, his daughter is burned to death by savages before his eyes, or so it appears. This, however, is one of several horrible incidents which are eventually explained away. His daughter is not dead; and in the sequel Cleveland falls deeply in love with a girl Cécile, only to find that she is the daughter whom he believed he had seen die. Prévost gives full rein to his tragic sensibility in picturing Cécile's unhappy passion for her father. As to Cleveland himself, it is no wonder that he loses his philosophy, only however to find another in the mixture of self-admiration and self-pity which was the privilege of the sentimentalist. " My name," he says, " was inscribed in the blackest and most fatal page of the book of destiny; accompanied by a multitude of terrible sentences that I was condemned to suffer one after the other." But his sensitive heart is precious to him, melancholy is his element, sadness he ranks among the felicities of a lofty soul. Hence autobiography, pouring out one's confidences, is as pleasurable as commerce with a faithful friend. Sensibility, dear and delectable sadness,[2] is the distinction marking off Prévost's heroes from the common herd; they form an aristocracy of the blasé and disillusioned: each thinks himself unique, singled out for suffering and sorrow, and thus excepted

---

[1] Another cave figures also, near Reigate, said by Prévost to have been the refuge and council-room of the barons in the time of King John. This cave still exists, and the description is not incorrect; probably our novelist had some authority for the legend too.
[2] " Chère et délicieuse tristesse."

by the Author of his being from the common law, from that, for example, which forbids self-slaughter.[1]

Prévost shows the mind of the deist better perhaps in his third novel, translated as *The Dean of Coleraine*, than in the others.[2] *" Le Doyen de Killerine "* It is noticeable that he calls it a moral history, and in the preface explains that his dean proposed to show how far a Christian could with impunity abandon himself to the world. There is a significant allusion to the *morale naturelle* as distinguished from Christian ethics; the leading characters, in truth, have no other morality, and are typical embodiments of that obedience to instinct, feeling, passion, which is justified by the assumption that man's nature is fundamentally good. Strong passions are the sign of greatness of soul. They lead to disaster; but Prévost regards them with complacency and even admiration; and his autobiographer, though troubled like the Man of Quality by the excesses of those who are dear to his heart, pities instead of correcting them, and resigns himself to the inevitable. The time is just after the battle of the Boyne, when the forests of this part of Ireland are infested with Catholic malcontents and outlaws. There is mysterious talk about a Jacobite treasure buried in a forest. All this provides the vague historical setting and the stage properties for the theatrical romanticism that Prévost loved.

The dean is not much more than a recorder of the ill-regulated *Patrice,* conduct of his half-brothers and their sister, all three creatures *type of* of acute sensibility. Rose is a susceptible girl with little know- *romantic melancholy* ledge of the world, who has to be rescued from compromising relations with various lovers. But the leading figure is her brother Patrice, whose furious craving for he hardly knows what leads him into peril and adversity, and leaves him a prey to desolation and despair. To such as he and Rose, love and gallantry are all that makes life worth living; love is the most sacred of the rights of man. Helpless in the grip of passion, they are carried

[1] Rousseau's Saint-Preux is another such, and puts the case in a nutshell : " Je ne prétends pas que tout le genre humain doive s'immoler d'un commun accord, ni faire un vaste tombeau du monde. Il est, il est des infortunés trop privilégiés pour suivre la route commune, et pour qui le désespoir et les amères douleurs sont le passe-port de la Nature " (*Nouvelle Héloïse*, 1764, iii., lettre 1).

[2] Physically, the dean was a very unprepossessing man ; yet Fanny Burney says she fell in love with him (*Early Diary*, ed. A. R. Ellis, i. 45). " The piety, the zeal, the humanity, goodness and humility of this charming old man have won my heart."

from land to land, from creed to creed, from one deadly crisis to another. This sounds exciting, and there is no stint of adventure, coincidence, and the usual surprises of melodrama. But Prévost was not a first-class story-teller; the tension is continually relaxed, the incidents are monotonous, and his readers must have had plenty of leisure and patience to wait contentedly for the next thrill.

Ancestor of Saint-Preux, Werther, René, and the Byronic heroes

Doubtless, he had other spells for readers of the right temperament, in the atmosphere of dread, brooding melancholy, and sheer horror that invested the ancient castles and abbeys, the vast forests and mysterious caverns, in which he loved to set his stage. But the more powerful attraction for the sensitive was in the mental experiences of his fated heroes and heroines, whose moods of self-abandonment and self-torment Prévost analysed with a perception of what lies below the threshold of consciousness acquired from his own sentimental adventures. Hence Cleveland and Patrice fascinated all other *âmes sensibles*, and quickly reappeared under new names in the works of other novelists, French and English. Types of romantic melancholy, they were ancestors of the race recognizable later in Rousseau's Saint-Preux, Goethe's Werther, the René of Chateaubriand, and in the Byronic heroes if not in Byron himself. That melancholy was nothing else than the obverse of the sentimental optimism. Vague trust in the general benevolence of things, the cult of emotion, repudiation of reason and prudence, leave the man who suffers shipwreck with no defence against disillusionment and despair. The transition to utter pessimism and the claim of these lofty souls to the right to suicide is paradoxical but not obscure.

Beginnings of Gothic romance

The novels of Prévost contain all the materials for the novel of sensibility. They also have in them a good part of the material that was soon to be utilized in what came to be nicknamed the Gothic novel. His gloomy scene-painting: the grim shades of Rumney Hole, the catacombs of Paris where Patrice, chasing a girl he has fallen in love with, finds himself when the Protestants are holding one of their secret meetings to inter their dead, and he is in danger of his life; the forest that feeds his reveries, and the Benedictine abbey, near Orleans, where he immures himself; the sinister castle of Corogne, in Spain, where Fanny Cleveland

sees a spectre, which, it transpires, is the person of an injured
man done up in white bandages; the Jacobite business in *The
Dean of Coleraine*, the fighting with redskins in *Cleveland*, the
murders and carnage, and miscellaneous adventure, here is the
raw stuff of Gothic romance.[1] Even those tiresome explanations
which were to be a concession to sense and a dubious passport
to credibility appear already in Prévost, as in the case of the
spectre, of Fanny Cleveland's escape from the redskins, or, to take
a different sort of example, the hairbreadth evasion of incest and
other narrow escapes from a too ghastly catastrophe. Prévost
at an early date also had that earnest belief in the perfectibility
of the savage which attained such ludicrous developments later.
Cleveland in the course of his peregrinations falls in with a race
of American Indians, and becomes their king. He is too pleasantly
impressed by their natural mode of life to run the risk of corrupt-
ing them by the arts of civilization; but he does convert them
to a Christianity simplified into a sentimental deism.[2]

Prévost was less than half a realist, and much more than half *Contrast to*
a romancer, the romanticism of his fabulous adventures over- *the realism*
shadowing the honesty and unreserve with which he emptied out *of*
for all to see the contents of his palpitating heart or those of his *Marivaux*
sentimental kindred. He was too deeply immersed in what he *Crébillon*
was describing to be very clear-sighted; he could not see the *fils*
forest because he was one of the trees. Marivaux and Crébillon
fils, on the other hand, were comic realists, standing not inside
but outside the picture, holding themselves aloof, neutral, critical,
sardonic. They too, however, dealt with the over-sensitive
nerves and ill-regulated feelings of the votaries of sensibility, and
with the half-pretences of the sensualists who accepted the sentimental punctilio as a game that brought the ball right into their
hands. And, though they looked on as at an entertainment, with

---

[1] Servais Étienne noticed this when he referred to "le roman noir dont
l'essentiel était déjà dans Prévost" (*Le Genre romanesque en France*, 1922,
p. 361).
[2] The historian of the French novel, André le Breton, devotes 90 pages, nearly
a quarter of the book (*Le Roman français au 18e siècle*, 1898), to a glowing
appreciation of Prévost, agreeable to read but not too critical. Sainte-Beuve
wrote two notices of the abbé (*Portraits littéraires*, i. and iii.), the first and
longer of which should perhaps be a little discounted by the reflection that
Sainte-Beuve was the author of that modern novel of sentimental introspection
Volupté, which is very much like a *Cleveland* purged of its sensational features

mockery in their eyes, their covert satire did not check those who took the game seriously. Marivaux was older and Crébillon younger, but they were writing about the same time as Prévost; Marivaux and Prévost died the same year, the youngest of the three a decade and half later. Marivaux' *Vie de Marianne* came out in 1731-1741, Crébillon's *Sopha* in 1741, and the rest of his stories a little before or after. Prévost's very free translations of Richardson were also appearing now: *Paméla* (1742), *Clarisse Harlowe* (1751), *Sir Charles Grandisson* (1754-1758). And the fresh fuel and the damping down had much the same effect, to keep the fire burning more and more vigorously.

Marivaux and Crébillon fils Marivaux knew more about sentimentalism than the sentimentalists themselves knew; he was a connoisseur with a touch of malice in his appreciation. Hence the beauty and the wit of his diagnosis of sentimental states and situations in *Marianne*. He took the straightforward path of a realist studying the commonplace characters, circumstances, and events of the life everyone knew; he rejected the romantic and everything extraordinary. His Marianne is simply a young thing of extremely acute insight and ability to look after herself, who keeps her eyes open and seizes by intuition the thoughts and motives of those who have designs upon her or who merely happen to be close at hand and able to affect her interests. Marivaux penetrates as easily as Prévost to the more impalpable feelings that lurk at the bottom of the heart, and those that we disguise even to ourselves. Prévost had lost more truth by his sentimentalism than he had gained by his candour. Marivaux is able to contemplate his admirable Marianne dispassionately; nothing in the book is finer than her involuntary response to admiration or to the attentions of those whose motives she sees through. Crébillon fixed his stage in other social spheres, and on it with an unconcern next-door to cynicism he presented the comedy of libertinage. Not a syllable of comment is vouchsafed; the reader can draw a moral or not according to inclination. The writer simply presents the spectacle of moral corruption as he sees it going on, and with a refined artistry makes the polite rakes of both sexes analyse themselves without the least consciousness that they are doing anything but behave as usual. Sometimes the comedy is not unlike Sterne's flirting with sentimentalism; at other times a withering contempt brands the ugliness of these lascivious revellers in promiscuity. But it is we who read contempt into the picture. The clear, cold scrutiny of the novelist is more deadly in its neutrality than the most indignant satire. Marivaux and Crébillon remain amused spectators of the comedy of manners, and, on the whole, the most penetrating witnesses of what underlay the affectations of the age of sensibility. They were both unlike Richardson, Marivaux about as far from him on one side as he is from Crébillon on the other; but all three bear witness in their several ways to certain unanimities of attitude and feeling in the social world of that day.

The successor, or rather the pretender, to the chair so long *Baculard* and so acceptably held by Prévost was his understudy Baculard *d'Arnaud* d'Arnaud, whose motto was to out-Herod Herod, and who was recognized as the great master of *le tenebreux*. There were other professors, the accomplished Madame Riccoboni, for instance; but most of them may be left out of account as not being well known or much imitated in England. François-Thomas Marie de Baculard d'Arnaud (1716-1805), with his novels, and especially with the manifesto introducing his play *Comminge*, gave a great impetus here both to the novel of sensibility and to its offspring the Gothic novel, in spite of his crudity and sensationalism, if not because of it. He exaggerated the melodramatic element in Prévost, and tried to outdo his pathos by sheer gush and bombast, the insincerity of which did not entirely escape detection.[1] Yet his devotees put him beside Prévost and Richardson and Rousseau, as one of the great painters of virtue and sentiment, and found his stories heart-rending, thrilling, and full of inspiration to the elect.

Love defying all laws, human and divine; love which can be *His emo-* felt only by the virtuous heart and loftiest soul: this is the un- *tionalism* ending theme. Invariably, it brings the self-devoted to ruin and *and love of* misery. No matter. The soul that has proved itself capable of a *terror* *grande passion* rejoices in its distinction from the common herd, and finds a delicious ecstasy in tears and suffering. It is the extravagance of Prévost and Prévost's disciples served up again and

---

[1] The verb "bacularder" for his emotional rant, and the byword "darnauderies" for his hysterical sentimentality, were coined by modern critics, hte latter, in fact, by Servais Étienne (*Le Genre romanesque*, 332).

again; and from the same quarter is introduced the lurid, terror-striking, funereal scenery—vast, mysterious forests haunted by birds of ill omen; gloomy caverns, vaults, and places of the dead, where the visitant gropes his way between rows of corpses; castles, abbeys, dungeons, painted in more sombre and more blood-curdling tints, as Baculard explains, from his reading in the *Inferno*, in *Paradise Lost*, and in the *Night Thoughts* of his beloved Young.[1] He bequeathed a large collection of hoary, sinister, and awe-inspiring museum specimens for use by the Gothic romancers.

His novels, and the drama, "Comminge"   In Baculard's first story, *L'Époux malheureux* (1745), there is no mistaking the family features of Patrice in the melancholy La Bédoyère, hating the world, believing himself hated by it, and experiencing a fearful joy in loving and being loved by Agathe, a joy the more intense in that their union is forbidden by a father's veto and the tyranny of society. All for love, and the world—nay, even heaven—well lost, might be his watchword. Baculard's first play, *Les Amans malheureux, ou le comte de Comminge* (1765), is a stage adaptation of a story by Madame de Tencin, *Les Mémoires du comte de Comminge*,[2] contained in her *Malheurs de l'amour* (1735), a glorification of the delights of grief, of the sensibility that luxuriates in tears and the contemplation of its own misery. In the famous preface, Baculard announces pity and terror as supremely the subject, and one requiring drama to make it fully impressive. In order to give proper effect to that favourite element *le sombre*, he has staged the piece in the austere monastery of La Trappe, the very walls and corridors of which fill one with *horreurs délicieuses*. And, he goes on, the writer, especially the poet, who can invest our imperfections with the seductive interest of sentiment is the sovereign magician; to that end, he must by illusion raise us above ourselves, even out of the sphere of humanity. Those whom a sort of natural predilection seems to distinguish from the rest, long, according to Shaftesbury, to find everywhere the noble simplicity that inspires themselves, their morals, their actions. Terror and compassion have not yet been utilized adequately on the stage; hence *Comminge* marks a new epoch. Some have objected to the monks, the grave, the grave-diggers, intro-

---

[1] *Discours préliminaires* to *Comminge*, see below.
[2] Translated as *Memoirs of the Count Comminge* (1773).

duced upon the stage. These features have been criticized as too sensational, too distressing. But our lethargy to-day requires such violent shocks. It is necessary to bring before our eyes the great picture of death, to familiarize us with the terror pertaining to that image, to teach the worldly how to die. Why not a sacred theatre? The Germans, Klopstock for instance, have one. After his *Messias*, we cry, with Rousseau: "O sentiment, sentiment, sweet life of the soul! what is the heart of iron that you have not touched? From what unhappy mortal have you never drawn tears?" The story is as monstrously far-fetched as the characters are monsters of sentimentality. The father of Comminge shuts him in a dungeon to force him to give up the woman he loves. She marries a hateful person, who dies; and, Comminge having entered La Trappe, she follows him there. It is years before Comminge discovers that the young monk Euthime for whom he has conceived such an affection is a woman, his lost Adelaide.[1]

Besides six tomes of short stories named collectively *Les Épreuves du sentiment* (1772-1780),[2] Baculard wrote a set of *Nouvelles historiques* (1774-1784), in which the tendency to lay the events of a story in the past is pushed further, and some real or fictitious incident is developed into a sentimental and semi-historical tale. It is remarkable what a large proportion of the contents of these two collections have English subjects. The heroine of *Fanny, histoire angloise*,[3] brings back to proper ways of feeling the demoralized English lord who had artfully seduced her. This tale was afterwards dramatized, as also was *Anne Bell*, under the new title of *Clarisse*, after some new complications had been added to the plot. It is in *Makin, anecdote angloise*, that two

(marginal note:) "*Épreuves du senti- ment*" and "*Nouvelles historiques*"

[1] Here again he expounds his object—"de nourrir et de fortifier cette sensi-bilité qui élève l'homme au-dessus des autres créatures. Le raisonnement ne suffit point pour nous distinguer de la foule immense des êtres: nous devons encore éprouver cette sensation si chère et si touchante qui nous approprie les malheurs de nos semblables. La pitié étend nos rélations: l'inhumanité nous isole." Thus the ancients loved to give way to their feelings ; we have Achilles shedding tears, etc., etc. (*Épreuves du sentiment*).

[2] *The Tears of Sensibility* (1773) by John Murdoch gives four stories from this series—viz. *The Cruel Father* (*Anne Bell*), *The Rival Friends* (*Adelson et Salvini*), *Rosetta, or the Fair Penitent rewarded* (*Clary*), and *Sidney and Salli* (*Sidney et Volsan*).

[3] Translated as *Fanny, or Injur'd Innocence* (1767), and as *Fanny or the Happy Repentance* (1777). Other stories with English subjects are *Le Comte de Strafford, Salisbury*, and *Nancy, ou les malheurs de l'imprudence et de la jalousie*.

eloping lovers are shipwrecked on an unknown shore, and find themselves threading their way in impenetrable darkness between files of dead bodies of gigantic stature. In *Liebman* (1775), the story of a youth of eighteen who adopts an infant with a view to rearing her to be worthy of such a passion as he alone perhaps could rise to, and experiences an almost irresistible ardour at the touch of her childish caresses, is taken from an earlier novel by M. de la Solle.[1] *Clary, ou le retour à la vertu recompensé, Nancy, Sidney et Volsan*, and *Adelson et Salvini*, are other tales with an English setting. *Varbeck*, one of the *Nouvelles historiques*, was translated into English by Sophia Lee (1786), author of *The Recess* (1783-1785), that pioneer of historical romance in the Gothic style; it is a semi-historical tale modelled on *Cleveland*. In *Warbeck, a pathetic tale*, history is made to turn on a stormy love affair, and is embellished with the gloom and horrors of Baculardian fiction. Translations of several other of his stories were published in the *Ladies' Magazine* and elsewhere.

Traces of Prévost and Baculard in Mrs Sheridan and Mrs Brooke   Baculard's influence will appear more importantly later, in many of the characteristic features of Gothic romance; but that is not the whole story. Even such superior work as Mrs Sheridan's *Sidney Bidulph* shows his impress, in the heaping of catastrophe upon catastrophe, of tragedy upon tragedy, although in detail it is evident that she was following after Richardson and Madame Riccoboni. Frances Brooke's *Lady Julia Mandeville*, again, though directly patterned on Madame Riccoboni, shows the trail of Prévost if not of Baculard in the effusiveness of the sensibility and in the violence and horror of its abrupt close. A number of third-rate novels of the time have revealed the same imprint, and if it were worth while no doubt a long catalogue might be compiled of popular novels imitating or borrowing from Prévost and Baculard d'Arnaud. A good many of those in Polly Honeycombe's list would have to be included, and the indebtedness of Sarah Fielding, Sarah Scott, and others has been indicated already.

Madame Riccoboni   A change of tone is felt in opening the pages of Madame Riccoboni (1714-1792), who, although she learned the elements of her art from Crébillon fils and found her subjects in the same social sphere, never repels with the profligacy and cynicism of a

[1] Servais Étienne, 334, note.

life abandoned to indiscriminate love-making or harrows with the brutal pathos of Prévost and Baculard d'Arnaud. It is true, she explains, that in this high society " l'usage est d'avoir un amant " ; but the majority of her lovers seem, or may easily be supposed, to be legitimate husbands and wives, or at least aspiring to be such. Many of her scenes and characters are English, and she has something akin to the moralistic spirit of the English sentimentalists ; but this is more probably a legacy from the *Princesse de Clèves* with its lofty conception of love than derived from Richardson, to whom her resemblances are superficial. Madame Riccoboni prided herself that all her best people have that " *noble fermeté* " distinguishing generous hearts from the small souls which are always ready to receive whatever impression may be given them. She wrote a *suite* to *Marianne*, with Marivaux' acquiescence, and a whole series of epistolary novels, modelled, it seems, to begin with on Crébillon's *Lettres de la marquise de M . . . au comte de R . . .* (1732). There is not much variation in the story she tells. It is always that of the woman who loves too well, and who is the one to suffer. But the finer quality of woman's feelings is brought out much better than Prévost could do it, though not with the subtlety of Marivaux ; and Madame Riccoboni shows a loyalty to her sex that would have been more praiseworthy had she been fairer to the men.

The best is her *Histoire de M. le marquis de Cressy* (1758), in which the conflict of motive happens to be in the mind of a man. The middle-aged marquis has engaged the affections of a young girl, and for a moment hesitates between the charm of her youth and the worldly advantages of marriage with a beautiful widow who will second his ambitions. He writes one of those sophistical letters in which Madame Riccoboni excelled, explaining to the unfortunate girl that although his heart burns for her he must sacrifice his dream of happiness. She feels that for her life is over, and takes the veil, bidding her perfidious lover adieu. She loves him yet, though she knows now that she has loved an illusion : it is not the lover that is most regretted, but the sentiment, the enchantment that has flown, the bliss of loving. That is the consolation of the sentimentalist. But the winning lady and her complacent husband are also persons of sensibility ; they are

" Le Marquis de Cressy "

overwhelmed by the pathos of the situation. It is a feast of pathos and pity, the pity which is, in reality, centred on oneself. There was an English translation in 1765.

" Lettres de Fanny Butlerd "   Elegant feelings overflowing in an elegant style characterize another epistolary novel,[1] in which the items are dated from London, Hampstead, Canterbury, and other English addresses; this is the *Lettres de Mistriss Fanny Butlerd à mylord Charles Alfred, duc de Caitombridge* (1759). Fanny Butlerd is a woman who believes in giving all, and accepting the risks of ingratitude and desertion. But she learns that men can look back upon a liaison with pleasure, as a victory, a triumph; women can think of it only with shame and regret. Her first letters are a crescendo of amorous hyperbole; but the key changes to the minor when mylord marries someone else. Can she go shares in her forsworn lover's heart? She decides that it is impossible. After which debate she writes: " Adieu, mylord; may you never feel such an affection for one resembling yourself." Here again the woman has the worst of it; but, as in the case of the virginal Adelaide and the Marquis de Cressy, ideally she is the one that scores.

" Lettres de Juliette Catesby "   Frances Brooke translated the *Lettres de milady Juliette Catesby à lady Henriette Campley, son amie* (1759); and her own novel, *Lady Julia Mandeville* (1763), was the direct result. Married at sixteen and widowed two years later, Lady Catesby is sought by a number of suitors, but decides upon Lord Ossory, whose strong, reserved personality marks him off from the crowd. But Ossory goes away in a hurry, and she receives a letter mysteriously alleging some inexorable reason why he cannot fulfil his vows. Wounded, perplexed, but still loyal, Lady Catesby pours her heart out to her correspondent. Others court her in vain, even when she hears that Ossory has married a Miss Montfort. Then she learns that a daughter is born, and has been christened after herself; lastly, after two years, it is announced that Lady Ossory is dead. The errant lover presently tries to renew his addresses, but Lady Catesby returns his letters unopened; and even when by a trick he induces her to read one she still declines to receive his explanation. But an *éclaircissement* is merely delayed. It comes out at

---

[1] Her elegance, however, does not extend to punctuation, the use of italics, and the like. She might have varied " Female punctuation forbids me to say more " to " enables me to say more."

last that Lord Ossory, in a fit of semi-intoxication and through a strange set of circumstances, had compromised the sister of a friend, and had been bound in honour to give her his hand. The issue of this not very probable story is a happy one; the interest is in the sensibilities of the dramatis personæ. Tenderness and delicacy of feeling, the sentiments that touch the heart, the way we bear our sorrows, the grandeur of soul that comes out more sublimely in the disasters of love than in those of fortune: these are the things to prize. Lady Catesby has suffered; but at the end of it all she feels that it has done her a world of good: it has developed her sympathies and her magnanimity. Lord Ossory is not guiltless. What he regarded as a peccadillo would have been an unpardonable dereliction on the part of a woman: the sexes have different codes of behaviour, alas! But now she can pity the hapless Jenny, whose lot as her own lover's wife she had thought so enviable. Had but Ossory confessed the whole situation to her, she might have been friends with his wife, perhaps that wife would have been living still. " L'amitié nous eut liées de ces chaînes douces, si chères aux cœurs bien faits." But mylady Ossory is dead. Was her husband in fault? Is he so still? That is the difficult point. " His reasons for keeping his secret from me were so slight; such a lack of confidence . . . but, after all, it was his wife! Oh! how am I to decide? " It cannot be said that she resolves all the points of her casuistry; but she cuts the knot by marrying him and receives the felicitations of her correspondent and bosom friend.[1]

[1] A good example of Madame Riccoboni's sentimental dialectic is this letter, *A typical* quoted by Lady Catesby, from Lady Sunderland in answer to the addresses of *piece of* a lover. It is the custom, she says, to have a lover, and Lord Sunderland's *a* indifference might excuse her. But she thinks it more dignified not to show *senti-* contempt for the man whose name she bears. She continues :   *mental*

" Livrée à mes réflexions, j'ai long-tems considéré le monde, les différens *analysis* âges de la vie, la durée des choses, ou pour mieux dire, leur perpétuelle variété. Mon étude la plus sérieuse a été d'examiner mon sexe, ses vertus, ses écarts ; j'ai cherché les ressources qui nous étoient données pour nous aider dans les positions difficiles où nous nous trouvons, soit dans l'éclat de la jeunesse, soit sur le retour de nos ans. J'ai vu, Monsieur, que la coquetterie, la foiblesse et la vanité, étoient le partage des deux sexes, mais particulièrement celui du mien. La vanité bien entendue et tournée vers le grand, fait des femmes vertueuses. La coquetterie ménagée fait des femmes agréables ; la foiblesse en fait de deux sortes, dont les unes sont malheureuses, et les autres méprisables. Notre goût nous range indispensablement dans une de ces classes ; le mien m'a décidée, j'ai de la vanité. Celle qui n'a estimé que le frivole avantage d'être belle, passe une partie de sa vie à s'applaudir de ses charmes ; et l'autre, à en regretter

Other novels of sensibility English again in personages and setting is *The History of Miss Jenny Salisbury, addressed to the Countess of Roscommon* (1764), but not so *Lettres d'Adelaïde de Dammartin* (1766) or the *Comtesse de Sancerre*, which appeared as *Letters from the Countess of Sancerre to the Count de Nancé, her Friend* (1767). Later came the brief *Histoire d'Ernestine* and the novel translated as *Letters from Elizabeth Sophia de Valière to her friend Louisa Hortensia de Canteleu* (1772). A follower of Madame Riccoboni was Madame Élie de Beaumont,[1] from whom were Englished two novels in letters, *The History of the Marquis de Roselle* (1765), and *The History of a Young Lady of Distinction* (1766). The catalogue of similar translations from the French could be easily extended.

Madame de Graffigny's "Lettres d'une Péruvienne" An early enunciation of the gospel of nature ought to be mentioned here, which is also a remarkable anticipation of Bernardin de Saint-Pierre in its ecstatic word-painting of tropical scenery; this is Frances de Graffigny's *Lettres d'une Péruvienne* (1747), which appeared at once in English as *Letters wrote by a Peruvian Lady* (1748).[2] Here sentimentalism tries to compete with the *Lettres persanes*, in disparaging civilization and more particularly French manners, institutions, and what are branded as prejudices, from the point of view of a child of nature. The Princess Zilia, daughter of the sun, is betrothed to her brother Aza, according to the custom of her race. But the Spaniards take the city of Cuzco

tristement la perte. Quel personnage joue une coquette, lorsqu'elle n'a plus de cet état, que le ridicule d'y prétendre encore ? Les femmes foibles sont à plaindre : le plaisir que leur a donné la sensibilité de leur cœur, est un écueil pour leur raison. Trop souvent elles conservent l'habitude d'aimer, long-tems après qu'elles ont perdu le don de plaire. Elles deviennent le jouet des ingrats, et l'objet de la risée d'une jeunesse vile, intéressée, qui recherche, les trompe et les déshonore.

"La vanité n'a aucun de ces inconvéniens ; elle jouit du passé, du présent, de l'avenir ; a toujours les mêmes plaisirs, l'âge ne les détruit point ; elle s'aime, s'admire dans tous les tems. N'est-on pas plus heureux, Monsieur, par un sentiment qu'on est sûr de conserver, que par ceux qui assujettissent nos goûts, et font dépendre notre bonheur du caprice et de l'inconstance des autres ? De quelque façon que vous pensiez sur mon choix, croyex que rien ne peut m'y faire renoncer. Si mon amitié vous est chère, abandonnez pour jamais l'inutile projet de troubler la douceur de ma vie ; et par une conduite conforme à mes principes, rendez vous digne de ma confiance et de mon estime."

[1] There was also a Madame Le Prince de Beaumont, who wrote *La Nouvelle Clarice* (1767), translated in *The New Clarissa* (1768).

[2] Fanny Burney knew the book. Mrs Rishton got her husband to read from it (*Early Diary*, ed. A. R. Ellis, 255).

and carry her off, and in a sea-fight she falls into the hands of a Frenchman, the Chevalier d'Eterville, who brings her to Paris. Eterville loves Zilia to distraction, and would fain marry her. But even when she learns that Aza is wedded to another she will consent only to a philosophic friendship. Such is the story. The letters begin at Cuzco, where she sentimentalizes and philosophizes for the benefit of the unresponsive Aza ; they are continued at Paris, approximating more to the caustic style of Montesquieu. On their more interesting side, they are an impassioned plea for the worship of instinct, sensibility, the simple virtues ; the doctrines that had spread from England to the Continent now being transplanted to the forests and mountains of Peru. There Zilia meditates and rhapsodizes on the spectacle of the universe, which fills the contemplative soul with rapture and self-forgetfulness. It is all very incoherent and devoid of any tangible intellectual idea, and could hardly have seemed pregnant with meaning even in the days of revolutionary speculation sixty years later ; though a new translation, *The Letters of a Peruvian Princess* (1809), came from the pen of William Mudford, afterwards one of Canning's ablest supporters.

The most distinguished English novel in line of descent from *Mrs Richardson*, which shows unmistakable traces of some infusion *Frances* of blood from Madame Riccoboni and more from Prévost and *Sheridan* Baculard d'Arnaud, is that novel by Mrs Frances Sheridan, *Memoirs of Miss Sidney Bidulph, extracted from her own journal* (1761), which made Johnson wonder if an author had the right to make her readers suffer so much.[1] Frances Sheridan (1724-1766), mother of the dramatist and statesman, has already been mentioned out of due chronological order, as author of that engaging piece of Orientalism *Nourjahad* (1767). Among other titles to fame, she was the creator of Mrs Twyfort, the amusing figure in *A Journey to Bath*, written in her last days at Blois, which her son

[1] Boswell speaks of it as containing " an excellent moral, while it inculcates a future state of retribution ; and what it teaches is impressed upon the mind by a series of as deep distress as can affect humanity, in the amiable and pious heroine who goes to her grave unrelieved but resigned, and full of hope of ' heaven's mercy.' Johnson paid her this high compliment upon it : ' I know not, Madam, that you have a right, upon moral principles, to make your readers suffer so much ' " (Boswell's *Johnson*, 1763). Nothing could better illustrate on what canons English novels were assessed at that time.

converted into the peerless Mrs Malaprop. But her fame ought truly to rest upon *Sidney Bidulph*, the extreme example in English of pathos for the sake of pathos, of a banquet of woe deliberately provided for the epicure of sensibility. The story goes that it was written for the express purpose of upholding the doctrine of the tragic end, in reply to criticism of Home's *Douglas*. This would hardly account for such a long-drawn chronicle of misery; pushed to such extremes, the argument tends rather to confute the doctrine.

"*Sidney*   Miss Bidulph is loved by her brother's dearest friend, the rich
Bidulph" and accomplished Mr Faulkland, and is on the point of being married when it leaks out that Faulkland has seduced and deserted a young girl. In spite of the remonstrances of the brother, Sidney and her mother will not even look into the circumstances, which might have exonerated Faulkland from any baseness. The match is broken off, and shortly after Sidney marries Mr Arnold, a gentleman of moderate fortune and moderate worth and attractiveness. She dutifully accepts her lot, and settles down to be an affectionate if not a happy wife. But, after she has borne him two children, Sidney finds that her husband is intriguing with a Mrs Gerrarde. This is actually the disreputable woman who had sold her niece Miss Burchell to Faulkland, or rather, entrapped him with her as the reward for having paid her own gambling debts. Arnold craftily puts Sidney in the wrong by insinuating that she has encouraged Faulkland in illegitimate addresses. Submissively, far too submissively, Sidney bows to her husband's censure, leaves her children, and goes to live in retirement. But in no long time Mr Arnold's affairs are found to be embarrassed; soon the household is threatened with ruin.

Meanwhile, however, a brilliant stratagem of Faulkland's clears Sidney's good name and also detaches Arnold from the adventuress. He runs off himself with the handsome Mrs Gerrarde, who is easily persuaded that he has fallen a victim to her seductions. But, as soon as he has extracted from the siren a letter bidding Arnold farewell and admitting that the imputations she had made against his wife were groundless, he shows his hand, and leaves her in France married to his former valet. This episode is a comic interlude as well related as it could possibly be in the epistolary style. But it does not end Sidney's trials; they are indeed only begun. She loses her children, she loses her worthless husband, she loses the last shreds of her fortune. Yet, like Lady Catesby in Madame Riccoboni's novel, she still resists Faulkland's renewed courtship, and bids him marry the injured Miss Burchell. He obeys, and a new chapter of calamity opens. Ill follows close upon ill, as in the ordeals through which Baculard conducts the sensitive heart; Faulkland and Sidney are wrung like Prévost's sufferers, and pour out their misery in similar accents. Miss Burchell, innocent and merely imprudent as she had appeared to Sidney, is one of those dreadful beings " a female rake." Sidney's brother had known it all along, and now the whole train of machinations that had snared Faulkland comes to light.

But before the upshot which the reader now foresees, a pleasanter episode seems to promise relief. A forgotten kinsman arrives from the West Indies, rolling in riches. Dressed as a beggar, he solicits charity from Sidney's brother and his stingy wife, and is scornfully repulsed. Then he applies to Sidney, who, poor as she is, offers him her last crown. He throws off the mask, having thus tested the character of his relations, and proceeds to set her up in affluence, to the bitter chagrin of her sister-in-law. But her good wizard cannot ward off the nemesis resulting from the original error of judgment. News arrives that Faulkland has caught his wife in the act of adultery, and in shooting her paramour has accidentally killed her. He throws himself on Sidney's mercy, and urges her now that both are free to become his wife. His prayers are supported by all who love her, and Sidney gives way. They flee to the Continent. But the erring wife is not dead; the catalogue of disasters has a final entry. Faulkland in despair commits suicide, and Sidney is left truly desolate. Mrs Sheridan added a sequel carrying on the story to the next generation.[1] *A climax of tragedy*

The likeness to Richardson is obvious. Sidney is of the Clarissa type; Faulkland, whose frailties are minimized, of the Grandisonian. Like Richardson and Madame Riccoboni, Mrs Sheridan throws her weight on the woman's side. In the frank exposure of a woman's heart, the scruples, revulsions, apprehensions, and all the tenderness that she feels but dare hardly confess even to herself, there is an insight that had perhaps been rendered more acute by *Debts to Prévost and others*

[1] This was included in the posthumous edition in five volumes (1770-1777).

the example of Prévost. The mode of narration, through a young lady's confidential letters to her best friend, a sort of epistolary journal, with enough allusion to the replies to let us glimpse the other side, is less cumbrous than Richardson's plurality of correspondents. There is also some humour, unforced and good-natured, especially in the incidental sketches of character: the sorry husband, the munificent uncle, one of nature's worthies, the intriguing Mrs Gerrarde who so egregiously overreaches herself, and the lickerish Miss Burchell. Here is the pompous Lady Grimston:

> She is always dressed out. I believe she sleeps in her clothes, for she comes down ruffled, and towered, and flounced, and fardingaled, even to breakfast. My mother has a very *high* opinion of her, and says she *knows more of the world* than any of her acquaintance. It may be so; but it must be of the old world; for Lady Grimston has not been ten miles from her seat these thirty years. . . . There is an austerity about her that keeps me in awe, notwithstanding that she is extremely obliging to me, and told my mother, *I promised to make a fine woman.* Think of such a compliment to one of almost nineteen.

In its naturalness, this has points of superiority even to the pungent but too deliberate caricaturing of Fanny Burney, who was now a girl of ten, and had hardly begun the stories which she had to burn before she started upon *Evelina*. Prévost's *Mémoires pour servir à l'histoire de la vertu* (1762) were an adaptation rather than a strict translation of *Sidney Bidulph*.

Mrs Frances Brooke: " Lady Charlotte Mandeville "

A summary is necessary also of the principal novel of Mrs Frances Brooke (1723-1789) to exhibit her French affinities. She had Englished Madame Riccoboni's *Letters from Lady Julia Catesby* (1760), and *Lady Charlotte Mandeville* is in the same genre. But in her own novel there is no happy issue from doubt and disappointment; on the contrary, a love affair which has fought its way through obstacles that look formidable if not desperate, right on the eve of happiness is turned to blackest tragedy by a mere accident. This is more like Prévost, whose influence can be traced in her later novel also, *Emily Montagu*. Here is the story. Henry Mandeville is brought up like a lord by his rich kinsman the Earl of Belmont, in the same house as that nobleman's daughter, and in spite of conscientious scruples loves her and knows that his love is returned. He is sanguine enough to determine to win fame and wealth by his own efforts, and in every way he conducts himself honourably and loyally towards his benefactor. But he is informed that Lady Julia is to marry the more eligible young Lord Melvin. In a wild fit of jealousy, he attacks his supposed rival, and is mortally wounded. Julia dies of a broken heart. And, all the time, the over-wise Lord Belmont had destined Julia for Henry, who was to succeed to his peerage; disaster results from a mistake, and is the matter of the last ten pages. *Sidney Bidulph* was far better planned.

In construction and in motivation this is perfunctory work, and *An* does not bear comparison with the models Mrs Brooke must have *appeal to* had in her mind's eye. Its success with her readers, no doubt, *sensibility* came from " the voluptuousness of sorrow " in which, the final letter puts it, the survivors are left. This is from the pen of Lady Anne Wilmot, the one gay and lively, yet by no means the least serious and intelligent, of the band of sentimentalists. Her raillery is almost a corrective to Henry Mandeville's high-flown solemnity; but no satire of that lofty trait is intended. Lord Belmont writes to another suitor that it is not likely Lady Julia would " approve the pretensions of a man who professes being above those tender affections which alone can make happy." Yet the catastrophe is due to Lord Belmont's mistake of judgment in keeping his intentions secret. Lady Anne, too, though she wears her sensibility lightly, suffers at heart from being unable, through her dead husband's jealous will, to marry her lover: this is a position characteristic of Madame Riccoboni's trials of feminine endurance. She is the cheerful martyr who smiles at grief. If there were any real character-drawing in the book, she would be the most lifelike. But that is an element almost entirely suppressed in the novel of sensibility; community of feeling does not make for the emergence of idiosyncrasy or the development of a strong character. Mrs Brooke is too intent on the heart and feelings, the sensations on which the select few, the over-refined aristocracy, play such luxurious tones. " At a certain time of life," again it is Lady Anne who writes, " there is no pleasure without the heart; where that is untouched, and takes no part in your amusements, all is still-life and vegetation." In short, all concerned talk about and think about nothing but their sensibilities; they never tire of the word. The best people make it the first article in their children's education; it is the sole foundation for sound principle and virtuous conduct. And it reduces human nature to a dull dead level.

"Emily Montague" and her other novels   Mrs Brooke spent some years of her life in Canada, her husband being chaplain of the forces at Quebec, and in *The History of Emily Montague* (1769) she was able to follow Rousseau's lead and infuse local colour from first-hand knowledge. Not that she shared his deep feeling for nature. She simply reproduces the striking spectacle that she had seen with the eyes of a wondering stranger. She describes the St Lawrence and the falls of the Montmorency in the grandiloquent terms appropriate to the middle of the eighteenth century; even her effusive sentimentalism does not betray her into the pathetic fallacy. The story, adjusted to the setting in a foreign land, is yet another of various persons endowed with too much sensitivity for their peace of mind; but in this case, without any exciting events to stir the quiet current of domestic life, Mrs Brooke manages to bring her pairs of lovers through all misunderstandings and antagonisms into the spiritual haven which too many miss. *The Excursion* (1777) is a still quieter story, of two sisters, one of whom aspires to be a poetess. It is told soberly and naturally, and the correction of the young enthusiast is done without satire. This is the novel into which, as Fanny Burney remarks, she put Garrick, " but said afterwards that she regretted it." [1] *The History of Charles Mandeville* (1790), the sequel which she wrote to her first novel, seems to have disappeared, and presumably did not add to her renown.[2]

[1] *Early Diary*, ed. A. R. Ellis, 284. Fanny described Mrs Brooke, " the celebrated authoress of *Lady Julia Mandeville*," as " very short and fat, and squints ; but has the art of showing agreeable ugliness " (*Ibid.* 283).

[2] Mrs Brooke translated *Memoirs of the Marquis de Saint-Forlaix* (1770) from N. E. Framery (see above, p. 97, note), and the book has frequently been taken for her original work. It consists of the letters of two lovers and their friends and relations. A young lady depicts in scandalized terms the corruption of a world where love-making is the only business, and exchanges the most private confidences with the sister of a man who says he would like to find himself in the lively circles that shock her friend. It is rather surprising to find Mrs Brooke taking the trouble to reproduce complacent portraiture of the fast life presented, not quite with the same complacency, by Crébillon fils and Choderlos de Laclos, especially of the unbridled eroticism of the women. In one episode, Julie is

At this point it is easier to appreciate the French tendencies in *A glance back at Mackenzie* the post-Richardsonians already noticed; the reader can now see what was meant by the filiation of many of them to Prévost. To go back only to Mackenzie: it is difficult to account for his change of tone and manner from the quiet sentimentalism of his first novel to the melodrama and forced tragedy of his second and third, except by putting it down to his study of Prévost, if not of Baculard d'Arnaud. Not only his choice of French scenes and French characters in *Julia de Roubigné*, but also the dire conclusion and the awe-inspiring accompaniments, corroborate the supposition. Listen to the agonized accents of Julia, when she feels herself caught in the tragic dilemma, even before she begins to forebode the tragic solution:

The daughter of Roubigné, the wife of Montauban! I will not bear to be pitied. No; I will stifle the grief that would betray me, and be miserable without a witness. This heart shall break, this proud heart, without suffering a sigh to relieve it.

Alas! my friend, it will not be. That picture, Maria, that picture! Why did I not banish it from my sight?—Too amiable Savillon! Look there, look there! in that eye there is no scorn, no reproach to the unhappy Julia: mildness and melancholy! We were born to be miserable! Think'st thou, Maria, that at this moment—it is possible—he is gazing thus on the resemblance of one, whose ill-fated rashness has undone herself and him? Will he thus weep over it as I do? Will he pardon my offences, and thus press it? I dare not: this bosom is the property of Montauban. Tears are all I have to bestow. Is there guilt in those tears? Heaven knows I cannot help weeping.

And she has the premonitions of one of Prévost's or Baculard's predestined victims.

What a situation is mine! to wear the appearance of serenity, while my heart is wretched; and the dissimulation of guilt, though my soul is unconscious of a crime! There is something predictive in my mind, that tells me I shall not long be thus; but I am sick of conjecture, as I am bereft of hope, and only

eized by *lettre de cachet*, at the instance of an enamoured lady of quality, who wants to separate her from Saint-Forlaix and have him in her own clutches. *Lady Charlotte Mandeville* was translated into French by Bouchaud (1674), *Emily Montague* by Robinet (1770).

satisfy myself with concluding, that, in the most fateful lives, there is still a certain point, where the maze of destiny can bewilder no more ! [1]

Treyssac de Vergy   Now the Prévost inspiration was in the ascendant, and now that of Madame Riccoboni, the latter especially in the work of the women novelists, and the majority of circulating-library novels now were written by women. When, however, men took a hand, they often went to lengths of sheer sentimentality such as the other sex could not exceed. Perhaps the meretricious Treyssac de Vergy hardly comes into the question, for he simply trimmed his sails to the wind that happened to be blowing. Pierre-Henri Treyssac de Vergy [2] was a Frenchman loosely connected with the French embassy, continually reviled by the critics as a venal purveyor of the abandoned sentimental eroticism which was the vulgarized legacy of Crébillon and Riccoboni. No doubt, he did far less harm than he was charged with; and his worst offence was the unblushing way in which he made free with current scandals and reputations easy to identify. Except when he was primed with this sort of material, his stories are uneventful chronicles of states of the heart, the theme love and virtue, the latter being extolled, the former always getting the best of it. Memoirs or confidential letters were the forms he affected, and he did not scruple to pretend that he was merely the editor. At his best, de Vergy possessed a Gallic ease and sprightliness, which made his impudent meddling with the manners and morals of his adopted country the more exasperating to his reviewers. *The Lovers* (1768-1772) contains two stories, *The Memoirs of Lady Sarah B . . . and the Countess P . . .*,[3] and *The Memoirs of Lady Mary Sc . . . and the Hon. Miss Amelia B . . . The Mistakes of the Heart, or the memoirs of Lady Caroline Pelham and the Lady Victoria Nevil* (1769) also had a sequel (1772). *Henrietta, Countess Osenvor, a sentimental novel in a series of letters* (1770), is one of the least interesting and most harmless.

---

[1] Letter XXXVIII.

[2] In Watt's *Bibliotheca Britannica* (1824) his works are put under the name of Louis de la Vergne, Comte de Tressan, and include *The Mistakes of the Heart* (3 vols., 1769); whilst under " Treysac, M. de Vergy," appear *The Mistakes of the Heart* (4 vols., 1772). Such is the bibliography of our period.

[3] This is the scandal-mongering novel alluded to above, p. 50.

The Palinode, or the triumphs of virtue over love (1771), is pointedly sub-titled " a sentimental novel, in which are painted to the life the characters of some of the most celebrated beauties of England." He was responsible also, according to suspicious reviewers, for some other anonymous or pseudonymous fiction, including *Memoirs of the Countess de Barré* (1770), *The Nun, or adventures of the Marchioness de Beauville* (1771), and *Memoirs of an Hermaphrodite* (1772).

A novel that followed in the wake of *The Man of Sentiment* *John* and outdid it in lachrymose emotionalism was *The Sorrows of the* *Heriot* *Heart* (1787), by John Heriot, known also as author of *An* *and* *Historical Sketch of Gibraltar.* He was a naval officer who had a *William* hard time after the peace of Versailles, when he was put upon *Renwick* half-pay, and he concocted a piteous story out of his own troubles in *The Half-pay Officer* (1789). Another unprofessional novelist was William Renwick, a naval surgeon ill-treated by fortune and by those in authority, who set forth his grievances in *Misplaced Confidence or Friendship Betrayed* (1777), and wrote two epistolary novels, in the current sentimental style, *The Unfortunate Lovers, or the genuine distresses of Damon and Celia* (1772), and *The Solicitudes of Absence* (1788).

Of Elizabeth Griffith (?1720-1793), whose novels, not un- *Mrs* deservedly, had a vogue far superior to these occasional writers, *Griffith* Miss Reeve says: " Mrs *Griffith's* novels are moral and senti-mental, though they do not rise to the first class of excellence, they may fairly be ranked in the second, they are very unexception-able and entertaining books." She was a follower of Madame Riccoboni, and could handle conflicts of feeling with restraint and delicacy, as in the well-named novel in letters *The Delicate Distress* (1769), an affecting study of marital fidelity. A young wife subdues the temptation to protest and to reproach an erring husband, and by tact and silent forbearance wins him from the old passion into which he had relapsed.[1] Another trial of loyalty in which the wife is the one tempted is the more tragical *History*

---

[1] *The Gordian Knot* (1779) by her Irish husband Richard Griffith is described as a companion work to *The Delicate Distress.* They had published together *A Series of genuine Letters between Henry and Francis* (1757), composed of select letters, highly sentimental, of course, that had passed between them before marriage.

of Lady Barton (1771). It was criticized by the *Monthly Review* as devoid of romance and content to portray everyday life, despite the curious situation of a mother in love with the aspirant to her daughter's hand packing the latter off to a convent and pretending that she is dead.[1]

The Story of Lady Juliana Harley (1776) is the tragic history of such a marriage as that of a Clarissa and a Solmes. Mrs Griffith's characters are all cast in one mould, that of her own sentimental self; but this detracts little from the truth and poignancy of the inner conflicts and domestic discords which are her theme. She wrote or adapted some plays for Garrick from French and Italian originals, and was an industrious translator of novels, letters, and memoirs. The French influence on her own work is not a matter of internal evidence only. She was also the editor of *A Collection of Novels selected and revised* (1777), from the hands of Mrs Behn, Mrs St Aubyn, and Eliza Haywood.[2]

Mary Robinson and Helen Maria Williams

Two perfervid exponents of the sentimental theme were the poetesses, Mary Robinson,[3] that is, the unwise and unfortunate " Perdita," and Helen Maria Williams, who is often vaguely associated with the Della Cruscans. She actually preceded them; but " Perdita," or " the British Sappho," did probably belong to the coterie. Mary Robinson (1758-1800) is at her most romantic and most glowing in her Spanish novel *Vancenza, or the dangers of credulity* (1792), which she describes, however, as " an interesting yet simple picture of Human Nature, unadorned by the extravagant flatteries of romantic enthusiasm, and divested of the dark shades of prejudice." She comes appreciably closer to the

---

[1] Miss Husbands notes this criticism.

[2] If Mrs Griffith was good second-rate, an indifferent specimen of the third-rate was Mrs Cartwright, whose best work was perhaps *Retaliation, or the history of Sir Edward Osborn and Lady Frances Seymour* (1787). It was in letters, and so were the four following : *The Generous Sister* (1779), *Letters Moral and Entertaining* (1781), *The Duped Guardian, or the Amant malade* (1786), and *The Platonic Marriage* (1786). The tag of French in the last title but one, the epistolary form of the whole batch, and their ultra-sentimentality, indicate, not erroneously, their French affinities. The form was in great favour at this period, and does not always mean Gallicism or sentimentalism. Charlotte Palmer, for instance, in her *Letters on several Subjects from a Preceptress to her Pupils who have left School* (1797), was conscientiously didactic ; though her earlier novel, *Female Stability, or the history of Miss Belville* (1780), was not more so than the average novel protested itself to be.

[3] *The Shrine of Bertha* (1794) was by her daughter, M. E. Robinson.

normal, and her liberal ideas are more persuasively conveyed, in such novels as *The Widow, or a picture of modern times* (1794), *Walsingham, or the Pupil of Nature* (1798),[1] and *The False Friend, a domestic story* (1799), the last-named an effort in letters obviously after Fanny Burney. Helen Maria Williams (1762-1827) made some stir in her time, especially when in France during the Revolution she entangled herself with Madame Roland and the Girondists, was imprisoned in the Luxembourg by Robespierre, and narrowly escaped the guillotine. She wrote poems, novels, history that was suspect of mendacity, and inflammatory accounts of countries, people, and politics, French especially. She had just published *Edwin and Eltruda*, a legendary tale in verse (1782), when Fanny Burney met her in a drawing-room and bridled at her airs—" a pretty girl rather, but so superfinely affected that, tho' I had the honour of being introduced to her, I couldn't think of conversing with her." [2]   She had also published *Anecdotes of a Convent* (1771), which is almost a novel in letters. But it is in *Julia, a novel interspersed with some poetical pieces* (1790), that the poetess lets herself go, not only in the verses. The tragic story of Julia's love for the man whom she did not meet till too late, of his death through his impassioned response to her more sober affection, followed by that of his wife, is told with a certain power; and, if the sentiments are excessive, they are at any rate sincere, and, further, Helen Maria could bring out character. The scene is laid in fifteenth-century Spain and so a quasi-historical colour is imparted. Among other things, she translated *Paul and Virginia* (1796), and from Xavier de Maistre *The Leper of the City of Aoste* (1817). Another tale which she must have adapted from the French was *The History of Perourou, or the Bellows-maker* (1801), said to be a sketch from life; Lytton's *Lady of Lyons* was based upon it.

Mary Wollstonecraft paid a heavy tribute to sensibility when she stressed the value of passion in her novel of purpose *Mary, a Fiction* (1788). This need not be put down exclusively to the influence of Rousseau, of whose works, including *La Nouvelle Héloïse*, *Émile*, and the *Confessions*, translations were

Rousseau-ism and Werther-ism

---

[1] See also above, p. 114.
[2] *Early Diary*, ii. 302.

plentiful.[1] *Werther*, which appeared in 1774, was translated through the French as *The Sorrows of Werter* (1779), the rendering being attributed to Richard Graves, and was imitated in a number of works, not all of them of native authorship; for example, in *The Letters of Charlotte during her connection with Werter* (1789), *The Female Werter* (1792), " from the French of M. Perrin "; and *The Confidential Letters of Albert, from his first attachment to Charlotte to his death* (1793).[2] One of Goethe's characters is the heroine of *Eleonora, from the Sorrow of Werter* (1785). This influence and that of Rousseau, not to mention Bernardin de Saint-Pierre, coalesced agreeably enough with the ·prevailing sentiments, giving a distinct and recognizable tinge. After all, it was nothing foreign. Rousseau had absorbed so much from Richardson and Prévost, and Wertherism was such a blend of Prévost and Baculard d'Arnaud, that all this came very natural to the English sentimentalists.

Other votaries of sensibility Lady Hawke's *Julia de Grammont* (1788) is considered by Miss Husbands to be probably the identical *Mausoleum of Julia*, extolled by the rather stupid Lady Saye and Sele for its elegance, and compared with *Evelina*. " Like yours," she tells Fanny Burney, " only yours is the prettiest." [3] Fanny describes the book later : " It is all of a piece—all love, love, love, unmixed and unadulterated with any more worldly materials." [4] George Monck Berkeley's *Héloïse, or the Siege of Rhodes, a legendary tale* (1788), and the richly caparisoned novels of the learned but ultra-romantic antiquary Sir Samuel Egerton Brydges, affiliate themselves to the Gothic strain. Brydges with his worship of the past invokes its imaginary splendours and virtues in a novel of the present, *Mary de Clifford* (1792), in which hyperbole of sentiment and enthusiastic word-painting of ancestral parks and woods and ancient halls combine in a tawdry romanticism. He idealizes himself in the hero of *Arthur Fitz-Albini* (1798), which is embellished with the

---

[1] *Eloisa, a series of original letters* (1761) was followed by *The New Eloisa* (1784), *Emilius and Sophia, or a new system of education* (1762), *The Solitaries, being a sequel to Emilius* (1783), *The Confessions, with the Reveries of the Solitary Walker* (1783, new and complete edition 1790), etc.

[2] There were also : *Werter to Charlotte* (1785) and *Charlotte to Werter* (1788), *Werter, a tragedy* (1786), and a number of poems, sequels, etc.

[3] *Diary and Letters of Madame d'Arblay*, ed. C. Barrett and A. Dobson, ii. 61.

[4] *Ibid*. iii. 500-501.

same highly coloured landscapes and other trappings. His theme here is ancient blood and long-descended worth contending with upstart riches for the heroine, who with her lover is sacrificed to the demand for pathos. Mrs Radcliffe never approached his extravagance.

It was about now that Beckford wrote his two skits : *Modern Novel Writing, or the Elegant Enthusiast, and interesting emotions of Arabella Bloomville : a rhapsodical romance, interspersed with poetry* (1796), by " Lady Harriet Marlowe "; and to this fictitious lady is inscribed the other, *Azemia, a descriptive and sentimental novel, interspersed with pieces of poetry,* by " Jacquetta Agneta Mariana Jenks," " to which are added, Criticisms anticipated " (1797).[1] *Modern Novel Writing* was suspected to be by Robert Merry, the Della Cruscan, and *Azemia* was taken for a " servile imitation " of the other burlesque. The lady who was the particular object of these parodies of a style that had become epidemic seems to have perused them with the same good faith as the housekeeper at Fonthill accepted the *Memoirs of Celebrated Painters*. It was pert and clever stuff, sauced with indecencies that hit at *Pamela,* and probably also at scandals that were nobody's secrets at the time.

Beckford's antidotes to sentimentalism

[1] See also above, p. 72. Miss Jenks is duly catalogued as the veritable author by various standard bibliographies.

CHAPTER VII

FANNY BURNEY

Fanny Burney's very mild senti-mentalism FANNY BURNEY provides an interlude of natural comedy in the long monotone of solemn and pretentious sentimentalism. She was not entirely immune from the chief foible of her time. But she was aware of that foible, she laughed at its aberrations in others, and she usually succeeded in checking it in herself. Fanny Burney, at any rate, was never an affected person. Effusions of tears occur in her pages such as other periods would have thought unseemly. She was a warm-hearted, sympathetic creature, of normal sensibilities; and, if she dwelt more tenderly upon a pathetic scene than is the wont in less demonstrative times, it was simply because this was the habitual tone of her society. In comparison with her fellow-novelists she was an anti-sentimentalist. If she is compared with such men and women of her own world as Walpole, Mrs Delany, or Mrs Montagu, the attitude in this respect is much the same in her novels and their letters. All were still under the sway of the didactic spirit, prone to moralize, apt to drop into a sentimental mood. Sane as they were, it did not take much to melt them. In the days of Fanny's youth, everybody was expected to go into tears at any affecting news, at a signal act of magnanimity or show of fine character. What Fanny quietly thought of it may be read between the lines in many a passage in her diaries. There is the great traveller Mr Bruce, for instance, " the Abyssinian giant." When he hears about the young lady at her first concert, who " sighed and groaned, and groaned and sighed, and at last she said, 'Well, I can't help it!' and burst into tears. 'There's a woman,' cried Mr Bruce, with some emotion, ' who could never make a man unhappy! Her soul must be all harmony!' "[1]

There were, of course, all this time sets of people who had no patience with the absurdities of the sentimental school. Fanny

[1] *Early Diary*, ii. 20.

Burney was a natural girl who did not rush to either extreme. *and a*
She was anti-sentimentalist to the same extent as Dr Johnson, but *moderate*
not more consistently so than Goldsmith. Read the passage in her *anti-senti-*
diary where she reasons with a flighty young lady who has evidently *mentalism*
drunk deep of the literature reviewed in the foregoing chapters,
and who is suffering from all the romantic obsessions : pessimism,
misanthropy, despair of ever finding anyone to understand her,
belief in suicide as her only refuge.

" How you amaze me ! " cried I ; " I have met with mis-
anthropes before, but never with so complete a one ; and I can
hardly think I hear right when I see how young you are."

She then, in rather indirect terms, gave me to understand
that she was miserable at home, and in very direct terms, that
she was wretched abroad ; and openly said, that to affliction
she was born, and in affliction she must die, for that the world
was so vilely formed as to render happiness impossible for its
inhabitants.

Yet, on a little cross-examination, her woes appear to be
unsubstantial at bottom. Fanny is baffled, and asks her :

" Are you sure that some real misfortune would not show
you that your present misery is imaginary ? "
" I don't know," answered she, looking down, " perhaps it is
so,—but in that case 'tis a misery so much the harder to be cured."
" You surprise me more and more," cried I ; " is it possible
you can so rationally see the disease of a disordered imagination,
and yet allow it such power over your mind ? "

" A disordered imagination " ; that is exactly what was the
matter with the sentimentalists, and an intellect thrown out of
gear by uncritical reading in the philosophers and others. It is
from Hume, the young lady admits, and yes, from Bolingbroke,
" the divinest of all writers," that she has picked up these dreadful
notions. So Fanny piously recommends her to peruse the Bible,
which she says she has read till she was " sick to death of it," and
then Beattie on the Immutability of Truth and Mason's " Elegy
on Lady Coventry." [1] This was in 1780, when Fanny was twenty-
eight ; and here and in other such episodes one can easily see her,

[1] *Diary and Letters*, i. 394-399.

a rather prim young woman, admirably brought up, not too intelligent and not intellectual at all,[1] frightened and embarrassed by such glimpses into a state of mind altogether outside her comprehension, and yet having a sound intuition of the weak point in someone's principles or character. Fanny did not often need to repress her own inclinations to sentimentalize, for she was not given to excessive self-abandonment; nor were her feelings likely to blind her eyes to the mannerisms and oddities of those about her.

Her direct transcript of life   Fanny Burney's importance in the history of the novel is not, however, that she broke with sentimentalism, nor is it that she extended in any way the scope of fiction; it is, rather, that she came so near to what may be called a direct transcript of life. The impressions of a sharp-eyed observer went straight into literature with a minimum of the simplifying, ordering, or interpreting process implied in such realism, for instance, as Fielding's.[2] At her best, she seems to reproduce what she sees. There is only, as it were, a narrow and vanishing margin between literature and life. Scores of pages in her diaries may be put side by side with pages from her novels to illustrate this. Contrary to what has been repeatedly alleged, she was an omnivorous novel-reader. But she learned less from others than she knew by instinct of how to reproduce the movement and sparkle of social commerce and the singularities of individuals. Her indiscriminate reading—and she was not a good critic—was responsible for the conventions and artificialities that marred her simple truthfulness. She was best when story and all the regulation framework of fiction was lost to sight in the vividness of a scene apparently written down exactly as she saw and heard it. It was an innate faculty that she was gifted with, and her very first novel published shows that gift fully developed. But she had had to develop it; she had gone through her course of training, although this first novel came out when she was only twenty-six. The story is familiar of " that

---

[1] She was backward though not a dunce. " Even in her backward childhood, there is no sign that Fanny was ever thought a dunce by any one who knew her well " (A. R. Ellis, in the preface to the *Early Diary*, lxxviii.).

[2] Her fiction was simply a mirror; Fielding's had been a mirror with a philosophy of life; *Rasselas* is an example of the philosophy without the mirror.

piteous bonfire of her works in prose and verse, in the paved court in Poland Street,"[1] which took place ten years before *Evelina* was finished. Poems, tragedies, and more than one novel, consumed in the conflagration, represent the first stage of her training; the diaries which then began and the draft of *Evelina* upon which she worked in secret for some unknown period before 1778 represent the final stage.[2]

There is no need to go over the old story of the life of the Burneys in Queen Square and afterwards in Newton's old house in St Martin's Street; of Fanny's desultory schooling, her literary hobbies, and the providential discipline she had in writing and observing under the kindly eye of her adopted uncle " Daddy Crisp." Everybody went to Dr Burney's; the house of the distinguished master and historian of music was a meeting-place for those prominent in letters, art, and society, and also of many who were treasure trove to the " character-monger " as Johnson called her. And Fanny was writing out the conversations she listened to and jotting down her portraits all the time, in her journals and in her letters to Daddy Crisp. " A very able portrait painter,"[3] he calls her, and in another letter he says, " The pen, as well as the pencil, sometimes exhibits pictures with such strong marks of nature, that one instantly pronounces them like, without having seen the originals."[4] He also lectures her on the best style of writing in the genre which was so obviously hers. He tells her what are her failings, and goes on: "There is no fault in an epistolary correspondence like stiffness and study. Dash away whatever comes uppermost; the sudden sallies of imagination, clap'd down on paper, just as they arise, are worth folios, and have all the warmth and merit of that sort of nonsense that is eloquent in love. Never think of being correct when you write to me."[5] Then again he repeats himself almost in the same words, and reminds Fanny, "You cannot but know *that trifling, that negligence, that even incorrectness,* now and then in familiar epistolary

(margin note: Her continual observation of the people about her)

---

[1] Preface to *Early Diary*, lxv.-lxvi.
[2] " I burnt all up to my 15th year—thinking I grew too old for scribbling nonsence, but as I am less young, I grow, I fear, less wise, for I cannot any longer resist what I find to be irresistible, the pleasure of popping down my thoughts from time to time upon paper " (*Ibid.* 314).
[3] *Early Diary*, i. 268.   [4] *Ibid.* ii. 101.   [5] *Ibid.* i. 268.

writing, is the very soul of genius and ease; and that if your letters were to be fine-labour'd compositions that smelt of *the lamp*, I had as lieve they [travelled elsewhere]." [1] Sound advice this, not only for letter-writing, but also for novels. The more unstudied the latter, the more Fanny's genius shone.

Power of reproducing conversations

Fanny astounded everybody with her power of reproducing a long conversation, even if it had no particular point or brilliancy.[2] Her long talk with Mr Seaton on the nature of women and on the novels of Marivaux and Richardson is a good instance, especially as she evidently did not quite know what he was driving at.[3] She was very young then, and only seventeen when she gives that lively account of the dance at South Street which seems like a preliminary study for a famous incident in *Evelina*, and corroborates the suspicion that she drew her first heroine from herself.[4] One would like to quote the whole of that scene a few years later when Garrick arrived " in a most odious scratch wig, which nobody but himself could dare be seen in," and ravishes the Burneys with his playfulness.

He would not be prevailed with to lengthen his visit. We all followed him [instinctively] down stairs; though he *assured* us he would not pilfer anything! " Here is a certain maid here," said he, " whom I love to speak to, because she is *cross*: Egad Sir, she does not know the *Great Roscius*: but I frightened her this morning a little. Child, said I, you don't know who you have the happiness to speak to! Do you know I am one of the first Geniuses of the Age? Why, child, you would *faint away*, if you knew who I am!"

In this sportive way he continued, till the door was shut. He is sensible that we all doat on him; but I believe it is the same thing wherever he goes, except where he has had a personal quarrel, which, I am sorry to hear, is frequently the case with those who have been his best friends. He promised he would often call in the same sort of way, *to plague us*; we assured him we would freely forgive him if he did. In truth, I desire no better entertainment than his company affords.[5]

All that part of her diary recounting the disclosure of her authorship of *Evelina* to the different members of the Burney

[1] *Early Diary*, ii. 41.   [2] *Ibid*. i. 39, note.   [3] *Ibid*.
[4] *Ibid*. 78-82.   [5] *Ibid*. ii. 31.

family and one friend after another, Fanny's shyness and alarm, and her embarrassment at the eulogies of Dr Johnson, Mrs Thrale, and others, is as good comedy as the novel itself.

The characters are hit off in a few pithy phrases as the talk *Impromptu* goes on. In the entertaining account of the dance at the Debiegs', *character-* a dozen gentlemen and ladies are sketched in less than a page. *sketching*

Mrs Pringle *chaperoned* us, and we were almost the first in the room; but I will mention the whole party by name, for indeed they well deserve it. To begin, *as I ought*, with the women. Mrs Seaton, a very engaging woman, about twenty-three, widow of Major Seaton, an elder brother of our acquaintance—she is rather handsome, extremely elegant in her manners, and mild and sensible in her conversation. Mrs Pringle, who was as gay, chatty and clever as usual. Mrs Debieg herself, who is always charming. Miss Peggy Adams, *an old flame of Mr Seaton's* she is called: she is about twenty-six or seven, ugly in person, and too reserved in manners to permit me to judge of her, but I will imagine she has some remarkable qualities to have engaged Mr Seaton's attention, though I cannot wonder he has transferred it to another object, when I see how striking is the difference between them: nevertheless, I am concerned to find this additional proof of the fickleness of his disposition. Miss Stuart, she is about nineteen or twenty, has a fine face in spight of the small pocks, is modest, well-bred, and very silent. Miss Dalrymple, who we have frequently seen at Mrs Pringle's. She too, is reported to be an old flame of Mr Seaton's—she is about twenty-eight or nine, rather handsome, lisps affectedly, simpers designedly, and looks conceitedly. She is famed for never speaking ill to any one's face, or well behind their backs. Miss Burney and Miss Fanny Burney—sweet charming young creatures!—I need not describe. Now to the men. I must begin with Mr Debieg, for whom I have conceived a great regard: he was all spirits and sweetness, and made, with the other half's assistance, all his company happy. Sir Harry Seaton, the eldest brother of Mr Seaton and Mrs Debieg: he is very unlike either; grave, reserved, silent, yet perfectly well-bred, and very attentive; and there is something in his manners *prévenant*. Mr Dundas, to whose successful election we owe this meeting, almost the same words I have used for Sir Harry Seaton would suit him, save only he was less reserved, rather. Major Dundas, his younger brother, very unlike him;—conceited, talkative, coxcombical. Mr John Dundas, a Cousin to these gentlemen, a well-behaved man, nothing extraordinary. Mr Adams, very sensible, very polite, and very agreeable,—the most so, Mr Debieg excepted, of the whole party. Mr —— Adams, his younger brother, a well-behaved good sort of young man. Mr Farquar, he is . . . very droll and a favourite rather of Hetty's for his pleasantry. Mr Robinson, a very handsome young man, and also . . . agreeable,—tolerably, at least. Captain Pringle, who has lately rather risen in my opinion, as he has forebore giving himself the airs he formerly did: he seems less conceited, and speaks less in a rhodomantide (*sic*) manner, and is also less liberal of flattery and compliments. Mr Alexander Seaton, I need not give his character—indeed I could not—I once thought I knew it—I now am sure I am ignorant of it. I believe I have mentioned the whole party; and though my account may be very faulty, it is such as I think.[1]

Her realism purely superficial Such an impromptu bit of charactery—and there are very many such—shows her strength and her weaknesses, the superficies that she sees, the inwardness that is often concealed from her; and it shows how Fanny was roughing out studies for the more finished portraits all the time she was preparing for or actually at work upon her novels. It was an intensive application of one part of the Fielding method, a more minute observation of the passing show, a closer actualism, keen enough to detect originality and eccentricity in the most familiar types met with in the most familiar world. But the inner world, the deeper life of human beings, the springs, the hidden machinery, remained invisible. Fanny understood behaviour but not action; she was no dramatist, and her attempts to write a play were complete failures. When she tried to make a novel dramatic, she scamped the inherent difficulties and fell back upon melodrama.

" Eve- lina " *Evelina, or a young lady's entrance into the world* (1778), is a novel in letters; but, although Fanny Burney would not have liked the comparison, the letters are used more as in Smollett's *Humphry Clinker,* to bring out the humour of different points of view, than for disclosing thoughts and feelings in the most agitating crises. Her aim was modest: " I have only presumed to trace the accidents and adventures to which a ' young woman ' is liable. I have not pretended to show the world what it actually *is*, but what it *appears* to a girl of seventeen :—and so far as that, surely

[1] *Early Diary*, i. 91-93.

any girl who is *past* seventeen may safely do." [1] But she was not content to do simply this: it was incumbent upon her, at least she thought so, to arrange the accidents and adventures in the conventional order now required of a novel. There must be a plot, and of course a chequered love affair; and she fulfils these obligations by putting her young woman under a cloud, providing all the due episodes of tragic tension, and ending with an act of recognition that dissipates the cloud, and brings satisfaction to all that deserve it. Fanny Burney had long ago noted in her diary what was her own idea of a good novel. " I cannot be much pleased without an appearance of truth; or at least of possibility —I wish the story to be natural though the sentiments are refined; and the characters to be probable though their behaviour is excelling." [2] Her first approximates to this better than her later novels; yet the conventional secret marriage and the conventional problem, whether the wicked baronet who is Evelina's father will recognize his daughter and restore her rights, detract from the proper interest of the book, which is in the jostling together of a crowd of oddly-matched characters.

A juvenile novel destroyed in the famous bonfire supplied a *Sequel to* starting-point, a framework, and some of the dramatis personæ. *an early* This was *The History of Caroline Evelyn*, and the heroine was *novel that* Evelina's mother. She had eloped with Sir John Belmont, who *she burned* deserted her and refused to acknowledge their child. A large proportion of the letters in the new novel are from Evelina to her guardian Mr Villars, who is too deeply devoted to the memory of Caroline Evelyn to be willing to entertain the proposals of Evelina's friends and deliver her over to " *him,* who had so basely betrayed the mother." A legacy from the former story is Evelina's grandmother, the barmaid with whom Caroline's father had misallied himself, who had married again, and now after many years abroad figures, rather inconsistently, as a foreigner speaking bad English. This Madame Duval is a thorn in the flesh to Mr Villars and Evelina, since she suddenly arrives in England and insists on asserting her rights over the young girl. She is one of the leading vulgarians, and she forms the link between Evelina and her friends in the polite world and that most magnificent set of vulgar people,

[1] *Early Diary,* ii. 212.   [2] *Ibid.* i. 9.

the Branghtons, connexions of her own.   Before this event,
Evelina has been happy in the society of Mrs Mirvan, and her
worst adventure has been to be badgered and mortified by the
importunities of a fop at a ball, through her ignorance of the rules,
and more grievously tormented by the rakish addresses of another
bad baronet, Sir Clement Willoughby, a scion of the Lovelace
and Pollexfen family.   Fortunately for her, there is a Grandison
at hand in the person of Lord Orville, who repeatedly arrives in
the nick of time to rescue Evelina from awkward situations,
and who, apparently, is in love with her, but, perplexed by her
equivocal position, shows no signs of paying her serious attentions.
The end which has to be contrived is the union of the heroine
with this immaculate type of gentility when the question of her
paternity has been fully cleared up.   But all this is of minor account
in comparison with the scenes of comedy that intervene, when
Evelina cannot escape from Madame Duval and the Branghtons,
and through their low tastes not only has to put up with their bad
manners at home, but also finds herself in dreadful scrapes when
they take her to the shilling gallery at the opera, to Vauxhall,
and to Marylebone Gardens.   The last straw, on each occasion,
is that she has to be rescued by Lord Orville, who is perplexed
by her being mixed up with people like the Branghtons, or by
Sir Clement Willoughby, who seizes the opportunity to make
violent love.   Fanny Burney manages the situation admirably
when she brings these polished members of the fashionable
world and Madame Duval with the ill-mannered Branghton
family on the stage together, although her own prudishness[1]
and a tinge of the snob are evident in the way she puts the
emphasis.

Satire of
vulgarity
—the
Brangh-
tons
Vulgarity was not a new thing in novel or play; but no one
had made it the principal theme as Fanny Burney did in the central
chapters of *Evelina*.   The squabbling of the Branghton sisters,
the pinchbeck gentility of the City beau, Mr Smith, the uncouth
attentions of the one and the ill-bred sneers of the others, their
conceited airs and their prostration when confronted by a real
baronet: it is all first-class comedy.   Mr Smith, the Branghtons'

---

[1] "But I suppose you must not tell her," said her father.   " Poor Fan's *such*
a prude " (*Early Diary*, ii. 222).

odger, was rightly the favourite character in the book to Dr
Johnson and to Hazlitt.[1]

"O fie, Tom,—dispute with a lady!" cried Mr Smith.
"Now, as for me, I'm for where you will, provided this young
lady is of the party,—one place is the same as another to me,
so that it be but agreeable to the ladies,—I would go anywhere
with you, Ma'am" (to me), "unless, indeed, it were to *church*;—
ha, ha, ha,—really, ladies, I beg your pardon, for being so rude,
but I can't help laughing for my life!"

Sir Clement Willoughby, too, although not quite free from
exaggeration, is drawn with consummate skill and goes through
his difficult part with magnificent address. Madame Duval would *Madame*
have been better but for some uncertainty on the part of her *Duval*
creator, who seems to have meant her chiefly as a butt for ridicule,
a vulgar and uneducated Frenchwoman, which, of course, she was
not. But as often happens with low-comedy figures, Madame
Duval proved too much for the author's intentions, and shows
herself not a bad sort of woman at all. She turns the tables on
the formidable Sir Clement in one scene, to the general applause.
Nor was Fanny successful with her salt-water captain; a young *Captain*
lady of her propriety could not be, as she conceived him, like one *Mirvan*
of Smollett's brutal seamen. "I can only give you a faint idea of
his language," she says, "and, besides, he makes use of a thousand
sea-terms, which are to me quite unintelligible." Hence she was
handicapped in the one talent, for lifelike speech, that served her
with the most intractable of her other oddities. No wonder that
Captain Mirvan was regarded as a libel on his profession. The
horseplay perpetrated on the unlucky Madame Duval is, for
reasons not dissimilar, another blot on the story. Then there is
the unfortunate episode in which Fanny slips into the rôle of the
contemporary novelist of sensibility. The melancholy and suicidal *The senti-*
Mr Macartney, the desperate man of sentiment, is as bad as *mental*
Mackenzie's Harley at his worst, who was to be a spectacle to *Mr*
the world three years later. But Fanny's attitude in this and other *Macartney*

[1] "'Oh, Mr Smith, Mr Smith is the man!' cried he, laughing violently.
'Harry Fielding never drew so good a character!—such a fine varnish of low
politeness! such a struggle to appear a gentleman! Madam, there is no character
better drawn anywhere—in any book or by any author'" (Dr Johnson, quoted
in the *Diary and Letters*, i. 72).

scenes of artificial pathos, in *Cecilia*, for instance, ought to be compared with such a passage in her diary as that of the misanthropic young lady already cited.[1] She was delineating all sorts of life, now sympathetically and now with satire, and when she touched upon sentimentalism it was always with some respect.

"Cecilia" Fanny Burney's second novel was a more ambitious and a more elaborate production; the subject again is a young lady's entry upon life, and again the comic delineation of character is adapted to the expectations of readers at the circulating library by means of an absorbing love affair and the problematical issues of a plot. But the plot is both more complicated and more far-fetched; it is at once an intricate scheme for the display of a large and diversified crowd of characters, and a means of providing an ample allowance of excitement, suspense, and surprise. Novelists had yet to learn how characters can be left to show themselves off spontaneously, without such an artificial framework as can have very little interest for thoughtful readers. The nature of the plot is hinted in the title: *Cecilia, or Memoirs of an Heiress* (1782). Cecilia Beverley inherits £10,000 from her father, and is left £3000 a year by her uncle, the dean, on the condition that her husband, if she marries, shall take the name of Beverley. Ere long Cecilia and Mortimer Delvile fall in love. But the young man comes of a very ancient family, and the Delviles hotly oppose a match coupled with such a proviso, their head, Mr Delvile, that stickler for pedigree, most of all. The question is much debated by all their connexions and friends—needless to say, it was much canvassed by readers when the book appeared, and important authorities took the side of Mr Delvile, although changes of manners render it difficult for the modern reader to sympathize even poetically, with the conflicting motives.

Melo-dramatic scenes But, whilst the champion of ancestral pride remains implacable, his wife is gradually melted when she comes to know Cecilia better. She is torn different ways, by her husband, her enamoured son, and the fascinating girl; and the general anguish, intensified by misunderstandings between the lovers, culminates in several dramatic scenes for which Fanny Burney laboriously prepared. Presently, Cecilia and young Delvile settle their private differences

[1] See above, p. 155.

and, after terrible struggles between natural affection and the
prejudice which she shares with her husband, Mrs Delvile
consents to a secret marriage. The young couple part at the
church door. But the embarrassing sequel is that Cecilia's fortune
from her uncle is forthwith claimed by the next heir; she has
forfeited it under the will. Distressing scenes ensue, a further
motive, jealousy, being rather superfluously imported. At one
moment, Cecilia goes insane and disappears.[1] Earlier occurrences
have added to the main perplexity. Before falling in love with
young Delvile, Cecilia had been staying with the Harrels, a friend
of her girlhood and her fashionable and spendthrift husband. This
episode had introduced the inexperienced young woman to fast
life in London and brought her into embarrassments parallel to
Evelina's experiences. Mr Harrel was one of her guardians; and
when in a highly theatrical scene he commits suicide at a soirée
at Vauxhall—a scene greatly admired by some—it comes out that
Cecilia's £10,000 has disappeared in helping to pay off his debts
on the turf. Thus new trouble arises when at length Mr Delvile
would have agreed to his son's marrying the heiress with her
£10,000, but without the £3000 a year and the change of name.
This Harrel underplot and the rest of the subordinate complications are ingeniously attached to the main business; it is a piece
of clever melodrama, but mechanical, not truly motived. Fanny
Burney does not understand the fundamentals of character;
her concern is with the differences and oddities of human nature,
not with that which is universal. Hence, apart from a few scenes
of concentrated comedy, her novels are inferior to the diaries in
the very characteristics which are her strength.

It was, however, the Delvile affair and the harrowing struggle *Moralistic*
between the claims of family and those of love that riveted the *elements*
attention of most of her contemporary readers; and next to this
the Harrel episode, which was regarded as a tragic and powerful
illustration of the nemesis waiting upon folly and vice. The latter
is didactic through and through, and for moralizing was not to be
outdone even by Maria Edgeworth, who at this time was writing
or translating educational tales under the eye of her pedagogic

---

[1] Perhaps the first appearance of the agony column in literature is the notice
inserted by her finders in the *Daily Advertiser* : "MADNESS : Whereas a crazy
young lady, tall, fair-complexioned," etc. (see Book X., chap. viii.).

father.[1] Cecilia's behaviour in these trying emergencies is so angelic that she seems far too faultless for an imperfect world. And her propriety is more impeccable even than the innocent Evelina's. All this was warmly approved ; see the famous discussion of *Cecilia* by those queens of the bluestockings, Mrs Delany, Mrs Chapone, and the Duchess of Portland : " The Harrels !—Oh, then the Harrels ! " cried Mrs Delany. " If you speak of the Harrels, and of the morality of the book," cried the Duchess, with a solemn sort of voice, " we shall, indeed, give Miss Burney her due : so striking, so pure, so genuine, so instructive."

The prize scene   Fanny said herself that the scene between the mother and son, in which Mrs Delvile is so frenzied with " grief and horror " that she suddenly cries " My brain is on fire " and breaks a blood-vessel, was the very scene for which she wrote the whole book, " and so entirely does my plan hang upon it, that I must abide by its reception in the world, or put the whole behind the fire." [2] People took sides in the controversy. Mrs Delany reminds the Duchess of Portland of her earnestness when she came to this part : " Down dropped the book, and just with the same energy as if your Grace had heard some real and important news, you called out, ' I'm glad of it with all my heart.' " [3] But Fanny herself also took sides : no author so incapable of detachment. " I never meant to vindicate old Delvile, whom I detested and made detestable ; but I always asserted that, his character and situation considered, he did nothing that such a man would hesitate in doing." [4] She had the satisfaction of knowing that she had secured the effects she aimed at, and made the impression upon her most esteemed readers that she desired. " *Cecilia* sends us into people's houses with our eyes swelled out of our heads with weeping," writes one of her sister Susan's correspondents. " We take the book into the carriage, and read and weep. . . . During Cecilia's delirium, anyone coming into the room would have been surprised. . . . The children wept and sobbed aloud ; my heart was bursting with agony ! and we all seemed in despair." [5] Nor was this her only concession to the claims of sensibility. The history of the

[1] *Diary and Letters*, ii. 201.   [2] *Ibid.* 71.   [3] *Ibid.* 201.   [4] *Ibid.* 125.
[5] *Early Diary*, ii. 325, note.

unfortunate carpenter and his family, reduced to poverty because Mr Harrel had neglected to pay his bills, and the death of the little boy, would have done honour to the contemporary *comédie larmoyante*.

Yet the excellence of *Cecilia* lies elsewhere. Its true merit is in *Satire of the many* scenes, too many unfortunately, in which the character- *contem-* monger makes her fops and eccentrics exhibit their mannerisms *porary* and idiosyncrasies. Goldsmith had glanced at the "paltry *affectations* affectation, strained allusions, and disgusting finery," which are too frequently "the badges of ignorance, or of stupidity," and made his Chinese visitor seize his hat and leave the room because he aimed "at appearing rather a reasonable creature, than an outlandish idiot."[1] But by Fanny Burney's time these extravagants had become a social plague, and admirable sport for the satirist. Of course, they figure in the diary. Fanny does not repine at being placed on a sofa next "the thin quaker-like woman" Mrs Aubrey, when it enables her to evade Miss Weston, "for the extreme delicacy of Miss Weston makes it prodigiously fatiguing to converse with her, as it is no little difficulty to keep pace with her refinement, in order to avoid shocking her by too obvious an inferiority in daintihood and *ton*."[2] But she makes a select muster of such exquisites and grotesques in *Cecilia*; our only complaint is, not that there are so many, but that she makes them perform the same antics too often; the same situation is so often repeated that she exhausts the possibilities of her creations, and all but exhausts the reader's enjoyment of them. This is what the old criticism implied, that they speak too much in character. After all, Fielding did not keep on giving us Partridge at the play, and Goldsmith's Mr Burchell was not always saying "Fudge!" Fanny Burney was not a mistress of the art of handling bores.

There are so many of them that they have to be drawn up *The In-* in ear-marked groups, each representing some folly that will *sensibilists,* soon be driven out by a new affectation. "The present race of *Jargonists,* Insensibilists" are still on speaking terms with the followers of *etc.* Miss Larolles, head of the Voluble tribe, and the Supercilious, led by Miss Leeson. But they are threatened by the sect of the Jargonists, and are hard put to it to maintain their pre-eminence.

[1] *Citizen of the World*, Letter XXXIII.   [2] *Diary and Letters*, i. 381.

Mr Meadows, " since he commenced Insensibilist, has never once dared to be pleased, nor ventured for a moment to look in good humour ! "[1] But " he is now in the very height of fashionable favour: his dress is a model, his manners are imitated, his attention is courted, and his notice is envied." " And by what wonderful powers has he acquired such influence? " Cecilia asks the caustic Mr Gosport. " By nothing but a happy art in catching the reigning foible of the times, and carrying them to an extreme yet more absurd than anyone had done before him. Ceremony, he found, was already exploded for ease, he therefore exploded ease for indolence; devotion to the fair sex had given way to a more equal and rational intercourse, which, to push still farther, he presently exchanged for rudeness; joviality, too, was already banished for philosophical indifference, and that, therefore, he discarded, for weariness and disgust."[2] Mr Meadows, with his vacant smile, does it very well, if a little too often. " You are right, ma'am, extremely right; one does not know what in the world to do with one's self. At home, one is killed with meditation; abroad, one is overpowered by ceremony; no possibility of finding ease or comfort." He and the voluble Miss Larolles are an excellent contrast when they get together. " Do you love the country? " he asks her, not to open his mouth for nothing.

" Yes, vastly; only I'm so monstrously tired, I can hardly stir a step. Do *you* like it? "

" The country? O no! I detest it! Dusty hedges, and chirping sparrows ! 'Tis amazing to me anybody can exist upon such terms."

" I assure you," cried Miss Larolles, " I'm quite of your opinion. I hate the country so you've no notion. I wish with all my heart it was all under ground. I declare, when I first go into it for the summer, I cry so you can't think. I like nothing but London.—Don't you? "

" London ! " repeated Mr Meadows, " O melancholy! the sink of all vice and depravity. Streets without light! Houses without air! Neighbourhood without society! Talkers without listeners !—'Tis astonishing any rational being can endure to be so miserably immured."

" Lord, Mr Meadows," cried she angrily, " I believe you would have one live nowhere ! "

[1] Book IV., chap. ii.   [2] *Ibid.*

" True, very true, ma'am," said he, yawning, " one really lives nowhere; one does but vegetate, and wish it all at an end. Don't you find it so, ma'am ? " [1]

The supercilious Miss Leeson and the Jargonist Captain Aresby, *Mr Briggs* who is always *abîmé*, or *assommé*, or *au déséspoir*, are amusing at the same rate. The vulgar but shrewd Mr Briggs, who infuriates Mr Delvile by referring to him as " Don Pedigree," if he seems to exceed even the bounds of farce, was authenticated for those who prefer possibility to probability by the " poor little mean City man," who jumped up when there was a dispute whether such things as a Mr Briggs exist, and said, " But there is though, for I'se one myself! " [2]

If Mr Briggs is possible, what about Albany, whose wild elo- *Albany* quence and stilted denunciations made him one of Dr Johnson's first favourites ? Most of Fanny Burney's characters, however eccentric, had their origin either in individuals or in some prevalent characteristic. Was Albany perchance drawn more or less freely after the lineaments of " that worthy, good, half-mad " James Hutton, the Moravian, who makes divers appearances in the diary, and of whom Fanny says, " There is something in his flightiness which speaks so much goodness of heart, and so much ignorance,—or *contempt* (I know not which) of the world, that his conversation is quite singular " ? Whether there is anything in such a theory or not, there can be no doubt that the great scene in which the author manages to bring the stately Mr Delvile, the builder Hobson, the vulgar little Briggs, and the vaticinatory Albany, into one room together, " each raging with a monomania of his own," as Macaulay put it, " each talking a dialect of his own, and each inflaming all the others anew every time he opens his mouth," [3] is surpassing comedy.

Between the dates of *Cecilia* and of her third novel, *Camilla*, " *Camilla* " *or a picture of youth* (1796), Fanny Burney had gone through experiences that changed her history. For several trying years she served Queen Charlotte as second mistress of the robes, and in 1793 she married General d'Arblay. Her diary went on steadily, limpid and lively as ever, in contrast to her novels, which in ease

[1] Book VII., chap. v.   [2] *Diary and Letters*, ii. 201.
    [3] *Critical and Historical Essays* : " Madame d'Arblay."

and vivacity show a gradual declension from the first of all. She was a great admirer of *Rasselas*, and of its author, who gave her advice, and has rashly been suspected of actually lending a hand in parts of her writings. A stiffness and formality in the dialogue, and more of it in the narrative prose, point, even in *Cecilia*, to the influence of the admired Johnson; in *Camilla* the trail of second-rate Johnsonian English is over everything. And yet in the unstudied entries in her diary she could mingle dialogue and story with masterly ease. Here is a bit from her colleague Colonel Goldsworthy's doleful account of how the king had worn out his equerries in a long day's hunting, and came home to Windsor without the least suspicion that they were more fatigued than he was.

"Well, after all this, fagging away like mad from eight in the morning till five or six in the afternoon, home we come, looking like so many drowned rats, with not a dry thread about us, nor a morsel within us—sore to the very bone, and forced to smile all the time! and then after all this what do you think follows?— 'Here, Goldsworthy,' cries His Majesty: so up I comes to him, bowing profoundly, and my hair dripping down to my shoes; 'Goldsworthy,' cries His Majesty. 'Sir,' says I, smiling agreeably, with the rheumatism just creeping all over me! but still, expecting something a little bit comfortable, I wait patiently to know his gracious pleasure, and then, 'Here, Goldsworthy, I say!' he cries, 'will you have a little barley water?' Barley water in such a plight as that! Fine compensation for a wet jacket, truly!—barley water! I never heard of such a thing in my life! Barley water after a whole day's hard hunting!"

"And pray did you drink it?"

"I drink it?—Drink barley water? no, no; not come to that neither! But there it was, sure enough!—in a jug fit for a sick-room; just such a thing as you put upon a hob in a chimney, for some poor miserable soul that keeps his bed! just such a thing as that!—And, 'Here, Goldsworthy,' says His Majesty, 'here's the barley water!'"

"And did the King drink it himself?"

"Yes, God bless His Majesty! But I was too humble a subject to do the same as the King!—Barley water, quoth I!— Ha! ha!—a fine treat truly! Heaven defend me! I'm not come to that, neither! bad enough too, but not so bad as that."[1]

[1] *Diary and Letters*, iii. 67-68.

Never after *Evelina* did Fanny Burney succeed in her fiction *A dull* in creating this illusion of having transferred reality, unimproved *story* and untampered with, to the printed page; very far from it in *Camilla*, in perusing which the reader marvels how the vivacious diarist could be guilty of such a rambling, dull, and amateurish performance. It is the general history of a set of young people at the marriageable age, and in particular of the way one couple, contrary to their elders' designs, fall in love with each other, and in spite of misunderstandings and other vicissitudes reach the happy goal. There is hardly anything else in it, except the common accidents, the petty troubles. In *Evelina*, the author could make the trivialities of life interesting, by quietly revealing what usually passes unnoticed. Here she labours the insignificant and relates at great length and in conscientious detail what merits no attention, until the reader is bored to death. And in place of the freshness and impromptu liveliness of *Evelina* and the diary, she writes with a forced vivacity vacant of charm, and at times with a formality and Johnsonian pedantry that benumb.

To obtain the hand of an object he so highly admired, though but lately his sole wish, appeared now an uncertain blessing, a suspicious good, since the possession of her heart was no longer to be considered her inseparable appendage. His very security of the approbation of Mr and Mrs Tyrold became a source of inquietude; and, secret from them, from her, and from all, he determined to guard his views, till he could find some opportunity of investigating her own unbiased sentiments.[1]

When love stories are written in that jargon, a lingo more *Exagger-* repellent than even Captain Aresby's, only the infatuated or those *ates her* in duty bound will read them once, and nobody twice. Towards *own* the end sundry tragic incidents are contrived and set forth in the *manner-* wildest emotional language: the prize scene in *Cecilia* is a piece *isms* of quiet narrative in comparison. Fanny Burney was always given to repeating situations and exhibitions of character. Here the same scene occurs again and again, with only minor variations. There is less of the melodrama of the Harrel chapters in *Cecilia*; but such as there is in *Camilla* she expands, dwelling on trifles, making endless fuss about nothing. Some of the characters are

[1] Chap. ii. 1-2.

pleasant enough, if they would not keep on displaying their familiar
traits : the good-hearted, optimistic, foolish old baronet, Sir Hugh
Tyrold, whose well-intended but misguided impulses lead to so
much trouble; the learned, absent-minded tutor, Dr Orkborne,
always ruminating on his great work, never alive to what goes on
around him or to his responsibilities for his pupils; the self-satisfied
bumpkin Dubster, such a nuisance to the young ladies who cannot
shake off his attentions; and the coxcomb, Sir Sedley Clarendel,
who talks like Mr Meadows:

> Pho, pho!—but why should it be so vastly horrid an incon-
> gruity that a man who, by chance, is rich, should do something for
> a woman who, by chance, is poor? How immensely impertinent
> is the prejudice that forbids so natural a use of money! Why
> should the better half of a man's actions be always under the
> dominion of some prescriptive slavery? 'Tis hideous to think of.
> And how could he more delectably spend or more ecstatically
> enjoy his fortune, than by so equitable a participation? [1]

Beautiful sentiments; but how could a lady do anything but
flee? Yet here the coxcomb is supposed to be showing his intrinsic
good nature, on an appeal to his seriousness by the accomplished
Mrs Arlbery. Half a volume, however, devoted to the history of
a ball and its train of consequences, or to a picnic or a family walk
in the park, is too much, even enlivened by the misadventures of
raw young men and the unconscious pranks of the eccentrics. As
in the previous novel, pathos is supplied by the incident of the
man nearly sent to the gallows for stealing a leg of mutton for his
starving family; it serves also to reveal Camilla's goodness of
heart to her hypercritical admirer, Edgar Mandlebert.

"*The
Wanderer*"   Fanny and her husband were in France for ten years (1802-
1812), and when she published *The Wanderer, or female difficulties*
(1814), many of the thousands who bought it at two guineas a
copy doubtless expected revelations about life there during the
war. They were disappointed, and not in this expectation only.
The prefatory letter to Dr Burney, who died later in the year,
affirms that it is a very serious work. Once she regarded the novel
as a trivial kind of writing; but she is hopeful now " that an

---

[1] Book III. 319-320.

exterior the most frivolous may enwrap illustrations of conduct that the most rigid preceptor need not deem dangerous to entrust to his pupils . . . to make pleasant the path of propriety, is snatching from evil its most alluring mode of ascendancy." After this formidable allocution, the opening chapters seem to promise better, with their lively account of the escape from the French coast of a boatload of English passengers fleeing from the Reign of Terror, and the arrival, at the instant they quit the shore, of the mysterious wanderer, taken at first to be a French lady, then for a Creole, but found presently to be as English as themselves. All this is in Fanny Burney's best style. But disenchantment is the speedy lot of whoever ventures further into this last of her tales.

What secrets of the novelist's art she revealed to Jane Austen *Some of her* it would be venturesome to particularize; but that she stands *followers* somewhere between the broad realism of Fielding and the finer portraiture of her successor, and between his rich comedy and her demure irony, is manifest. Naturally, her contemporaries learned from her a good deal, of simpler modes of telling a domestic story, and of other interests than crude sentimentalism. The one that profited most was probably Charlotte Smith, whose novels fall, however, more conveniently into the chapter following this. Soon after her first novel, there appeared a clumsy imitation, *Harcourt, a sentimental novel, in a series of letters,* " by the author of *Evelina* " (1780); and two direct imitations of *Cecilia* are recorded,[1] *Anna, or the memoirs of a Welch heiress* (1785), by Mrs Agnes Maria Bennett; and *Maria* (1785), by Eliza Blower. Both these writers were popular and by no means worthless novelists, fair at character-drawing and able to construct a story upon that basis. They were more sentimental, or at least didactic, than Fanny Burney, and more given to melodrama. Mrs Bennett's other novels were *Juvenile Indiscretions* (1786), at first ascribed to Miss Burney, *Agnes de Courci, a domestic tale* (1789), *Ellen, Countess of Castle Howel* (1794), *The Beggar Girl and her Bene-factors* (1797), said to have been done from real people at Tooting, and *Vicissitudes Abroad, or the Ghost of my Father* (1806), of which two thousand copies are reported to have been sold the day

---

[1] By Miss Husbands.

of issue—which was fortunate, if Mrs Bennett wrote to maintain a large family with no other source of income. Miss Blower also wrote *The Parsonage House* (1780), *George Bateman* (1782), and *Features from Life, or a summer visit* (1788); all her novels were translated at once into French.

CHAPTER VIII

THE GOTHIC NOVEL

MYSTERY and Wonder, Fear and Suspense, Sensation and Terror, *The com-* *ponents of* are some of the labels affixed by different historians to the romantic *ponents of* novels that traded in one or another, or in all these excitements, *Gothic* during the last few decades of the eighteenth century. The rather *fiction* absurd term " Gothic " is perhaps more convenient, and may be allowed to include both those that contented themselves with a discreet use of fear and suspense, and also those which sought the grosser sensations of terror and brutally aimed to make the flesh creep. It was a term applied first in derision to the taste for ruins and picturesque survivals, especially from the Middle Ages, which the Augustans regarded as barbarous and outlandish. Then it was amiably accepted by Walpole and others, who confessed to a fondness for what they called Gothic, little as they understood the real nature of what they admired, and grotesque as were their attempts to imitate it. In due time, it became one of those vague descriptive words, like " romantic," which offer such facilities for a useful if inexact classification. The importance of Walpole's effort in the style, *The Castle of Otranto*, entitled in the second edition " a Gothic story," is that it showed what Gothic meant and gave the name free currency.

The sources of Gothic romance were pointed out in the last *Its sources* chapter but one.[1] They are to be sought in the popular variant of the fiction of sensibility evolved by the Abbé Prévost and elaborated later on by Baculard d'Arnaud. The exciting adventures, the violent emotions, the gloomy scenes, forests and antres, castles, dungeons, and graveyards, in the abbé's novels and the plays and stories of Baculard, were to be the distinctive features of Gothic romance throughout its course. It was all a derivative of the cult of emotion ; and, the more morbid and coarse the sensibilities to

---

[1] See above, especially pp. 130-131.

be stirred, the more heady the variations and exaggerations of these stimulants. Some novelists sought only to conjure up a witching atmosphere of awe and vague apprehension; others employed the most violent shocks of physical anguish and fear. They all dabbled in the supernatural, either playing upon or playing with feelings of superstition; and, later on, those who had become acquainted with German folk-lore and its ghosts and elves and goblins found their account in satiating the greediest appetites for crime, diabolism, and nameless horrors.

Contribu-
tory
influences
But the foreign influences, from whatever point of the compass they arrived, coincided remarkably with native tendencies that have already been noted; with such curious tastes, for instance, such abnormal forms of sensibility, as appear in the literature of death and the sepulchre, which in turn gave Baculard d'Arnaud such congenial inspiration. The growing interest in the past, again, the tenderness for the hoary and decayed, the rage for the mediæval, the awakening of the historical spirit—all these nourished and were nourished by this emotional romanticism. The work of the antiquaries, the revival of the ballads and other old literature, and even the imitations and forgeries, gave it fresh sustenance. The mediæval, the antique, the picturesque, the funereal, ghostly, macabre, all were jumbled together as Gothic attributes. Such generalized Gothicism had appeared in *Ferdinand Count Fathom* (1753), that is, in a novel of picaresque adventure heavily spiced with erotic sentimentality.[1] There can be little doubt that Smollett had read Prévost, of whose works, especially *Cleveland*,[2] translations abounded, not to mention imitations and spurious continuations. So far, our attention has been chiefly directed to the results of this foreign influence in domestic realism, its effect upon Richardsonian fiction. But that was only one of the varieties of novel to which it gave new leaven. The Gothic colouring of the historical or semi-historical novel at this epoch is easily distinguished; but it is patent also in many hybrids that belong to

[1] See Volume IV. 216-220.

[2] Clara Reeve, who elsewhere alludes to the novels of " M. Prevôt," shows that editions of this favourite with English readers were so common that she did not even know who wrote it : " The life of *Cleveland*, natural son of *Oliver Cromwell*, is one of the *old Novels*, if I may be allowed the expression ; I do not certainly know the Author, nor yet the date of the first edition " (*Progress of Romance*, i. 123).

neither one class nor the other, a good proportion of them modelled on the lurid sensationalism of Baculard d'Arnaud.

Apart from a few odd instances in which events or characters from the past happened, almost by chance, to be the subject, as in some of the tales and novelettes of Deloney, Lodge, and Nashe, there had hitherto been no historical fiction in English. The genealogy of the historical novel must be sought in the same quarter as that of the novel of sensibility.[1] Gomberville and La Calprenède evolved a sort of historical romance which might as well be called romantic history, or, better still, an elaborate myth solemnly pretending to be history. They regarded their enormous chronicles as "des histoires embellies de quelque invention." Then came the anti-romantics with their realism to correct all this make-believe, Courtilz de Sandras and Count Anthony Hamilton in their romances based on fact giving precise circumstance and portraits that had to run the gauntlet of recognition and criticism.[2] So far as local colour and an adequate allowance of facts were concerned, it has been observed that Prévost's fiction is a kind of historical romance.[3] Of much the same composition is the first of the English historical romances, *Longsword, Earl of Salisbury* (1762), which might actually have been written to compete with the highly popular *Cleveland*. It was the work of an Irish clergyman, Thomas Leland, who among other historical works wrote later a *History of Ireland from the invasion of Henry II.* (1773). Whatever Leland knew of the times of that monarch, there are few facts and very little historical colouring in this story, although it is fiction in the guise of history rather than history in the guise of fiction. It gives the apocryphal career of William de Longespée, third Earl of Salisbury, the natural son of Henry II. and Fair Rosamund, who comes back to England, after a campaign in Gascony, imprisonment and many perils, to find his countess persecuted by a nephew of Hubert de Burgh, who covets his estates. Longespée discomfits his enemies, and marries the girl who had followed him as a page to her lover,

Historical fiction : "Long-sword"

---

[1] See *Le Roman historique à l'époque romantique*, par Louis Maigron (1898), especially the first two chapters : " Le Roman historique avant le romantisme, Le Courant idéaliste," and " Le Courant réaliste."
[2] See Volume III. 23-27.
[3] See above, p. 126.

the Lord of Poictiers. Several of the characters are historical; the incidents are fiction and at variance with fact.

Walpole's No one took much notice of *Longsword*; but it was very
"Castle of different when a man of letters of Horace Walpole's standing
Otranto" published a romantic novel in which similar pseudo-history of the days of knights and tourneys was fitted out with a whole apparatus of phantoms and portents, if not more terrifying, at least drawn on a larger scale and with a more matter-of-fact realism than the boldest inventions of Prévost and Baculard d'Arnaud. *The Castle of Otranto* (1764) was, like the mansion in which he wrote it, a dilettante's exploit in Gothicism, a pseudo-antique; in the one and in the other, Walpole let antiquarian taste and fantasy have free play, with less seriousness in the case of the story than he felt for his architectural hobby. Walpole relates that the tale originated in a dream, in which the hall and staircase at Strawberry Hill blended curiously with dim memories of an ancient college at Cambridge. " A gigantic hand in armour " was laid on the banister.[1] The mighty hand suggested the gigantic helmet which crushes the son of the usurping Manfred. Dreaming in his own miniature castle, he conjured up the walls of the great fortress of Otranto, and saw them thrown down by the phantom of Alfonso, " dilated to an immense magnitude," when this monstrous apparition proclaimed the boy Theodore the rightful heir. The dream pictures were the basis; the story was a piece of machinery easily contrived; and Walpole kept true to the common sense of his century in not troubling himself in the least about probability in a story obviously untrue. But the mechanism is so nakedly exposed that he fails to be impressive; our emotions are untouched. And this was the more unfortunate in that Walpole remained a sentimentalist. All the traditions, especially that of poetic justice, are strictly observed. The saturnine Manfred is marked for doom, but he is not allowed to perish until the cup of his crimes is full. All the oppressed characters, the hero above all, who is not really a peasant but of princely blood, are sustained by conscious rectitude. " My sins, thank heaven," says Theodore, " have not been numerous, nor do they exceed what might be expected of my age."

[1] See Professor O. Doughty's introductory essay to *The Castle of Otranto* (1929), xii.-xiii.

The Castle of Otranto was widely read; no doubt, it was received indulgently as a curious freak of fancy from one not much given to such eccentricities. (He had not yet written his tragedy *The Mysterious Mother*, which was to outdo Baculard again in sheer horror, and to disgust Fanny Burney, who went to Strawberry Hill on purpose to borrow it.[1]) But it did not start a new line of ghost stories, arouse a keener interest in the Middle Ages, or bring any rival historical romancers into the field.[2] In truth, no one paid it serious attention, until many years later Clara Reeve undertook to show how it ought to have been written.

Clara Reeve (1729-1807) was a sensible and very industrious writer, and well read in the history of fiction, as she showed in her conversational study *The Progress of Romance* (1785). One of the earliest tasks that she undertook was a new translation of Barclay's *Argenis*, which appeared under the new title, *The Phœnix* (1772). Thirteen years after the first edition of *The Castle of Otranto*, she was moved to write a novel, with a parallel theme and plot, recovery of his rights of primogeniture by the son of a baron brought up in ignorance of his birth, and to provide the requisite Gothic elements of awe and dread without resorting to the supernatural. Dreams and mysterious noises are the utmost that she ventures to employ. In short, her novel is carefully devised to preserve that inappropriate and ridiculous thing in romance, common sense. It aims at correctness; but the correctness is unhistorical, and the characters and manners are those of

Clara Reeve's corrective: "The Old English Baron"

---

[1] *Diary and Letters*, iii. 120-121; it is based on a revolting case of incest— the motive affected by Prévost.

[2] The usual assumption in studies of Gothic romance is that *The Castle of Otranto* inaugurated the genre which culminated in the novels of Mrs Radcliffe. But it would be more reasonable to place the starting-point either earlier or later. Prévost's novels had long been in circulation in this country and had been frequently imitated. Both Smollett's *Ferdinand Count Fathom* and Leland's *Longsword* have closer resemblances to Prévost, on the one hand, and to Radcliffian Gothicism on the other. And the later Gothic romance was not like Walpole at all. Even Clara Reeve repudiated the peculiar romanticism of his Gothic novel, and tried to correct it in *The Old English Baron*. She wrote other stories that are nearer to the Gothic formula. The great day, however, of Gothic romance was the last decade of the century, and immediate precursors of Mrs Radcliffe's novels appearing then were the sisters Harriet and Sophia Lee, who wrote novels directly inspired by Prévost and Baculard. If any single book can be said to have inaugurated the genre in this country, it is Sophia's story in the manner of *Cleveland*, the semi-historical novel called *The Recess* (1783), for which see below, p. 181.

her own time. It is a modern sentimental story in a sham-antique frame. The novel appeared first as *The Champion of Virtue, a Gothic tale* (1777); it was republished as *The Old English Baron* (1778), and this second edition was dedicated to Mrs Brigden, the daughter of Richardson. That was not unfitting, for in reducing the extravagances of Walpole's invention to sobriety and commonplace she was careful also to restore the sensibility to which he had not paid due respect. At a later date she published another historical novel, *Memoirs of Sir Roger de Clarendon* (1793), which has the lucidity and other merits of her first, but like that is dead-alive. It tells the story of the siege of Calais and the battle of Poitiers, of the deeds of the Black Prince, the founding of the Garter, and other great episodes of the age of Edward III. and Richard II. The facts are correct, she obtained them from the best authorities available; indeed her first intention was to write an historical memoir; but the romantic story into which she was lured fails to recapture the spirit and atmosphere of that distant past. Both her novels in this respect are *Longsword* all over again.

Her essays in Gothicism   More interesting as an effort in the Gothic style is her story *The Exiles, or Memoirs of the Count de Cronstadt* (1788), which was doubly based upon Baculard d'Arnaud, since it borrowed from two of his novels or novelettes, *The History of Count Gleichen*, as it was called in the English translation (1785), and the shorter *D'Almanzi, anecdote françoise* (1776), apparently never translated. Both, and of course Clara Reeve's derivative, are tragic accounts of the entanglements of a man with two women and the miseries which are the consequence. Sensibility of the regulation stamp runs full riot, and there is no lack of the terrifying incidents and the harrowing experiences that had proved so alluring to the readers of Prévost's *Doyen de Killerine*, a novel that probably gave as much of the tone and atmosphere as Baculard's two stories. Cronstadt was as good a type of despair and gloom as the earlier exemplar of romantic sensibility Patrice, and had literary off-spring in the Kruitzner [1] of Harriet Lee, a figure to be considered presently, which was the original of Byron's Werner. Miss Reeve also wrote two stories of life in her own day, *The Two*

---

[1] Cronstadt for a while takes the name of his faithful servant Albert Kreutzer; hence no doubt the name Kruitzner. See below, p. 183.

Mentors (1783) and *The School for Widows* (1791), both, characteristically, inculcating a most wholesome moral. For even when
she attempted the Gothic style her express aim was instruction,
especially moral instruction; and for this purpose she would
consent to use only " a sufficient degree of the marvellous to excite
the attention, enough of the manners of real life to give an air of
probability to the work, and enough of the pathetic to engage the
heart in its behalf."[1]

Of much more significance as pioneers were the sisters Sophia
(1750-1824) and Harriet Lee (1757-1851), whose part in the
development of the style was epoch-making, although their crafts-
manship was halting and their imagination limited. *The Recess*
(1785) by Sophia Lee was an attempt in the manner of *Cleveland,*
a sentimental novel of adventure, laid in the past, with the sombre
stage effects and displays of agitated feeling beloved of Prévost.
The gloomy retreat where the twin heroines, daughters of Mary
Queen of Scots by a clandestine marriage with the Duke of Norfolk,
are brought up in secret, is another Rumney's Hole, and the
gigantic piles of ruins by which it is environed are a heritage from
the same author which was handed on to Charlotte Smith, Mrs
Radcliffe, and countless minor romancers. The old monastery,
" half sunk in ruin, and overhung with ivy, and trees of growth
almost immemorial . . . appeared the very cell of melancholy."
Here the unfortunate sisters live, separated from their queenly
mother, and here they meet with their love adventures, for
Matilda is the unacknowledged wife of Leicester, and Ellinor goes
mad at her separation from Essex, who soon is led to execution.
The narrative is extracted, by an already time-honoured device,
from a manuscript in which the aged writer lived over again the
misfortunes of her youth. Well-known names are brought in, the
two queens, Sir Philip Sidney, Lord Brooke, Burleigh, Murray,
King James, besides the protagonists already mentioned; but the
history is the naïve version of an intelligent schoolgirl whose
imagination has been awakened, but who has nothing better to
furnish it with than the experience of her own small world and her
sentimental dreams. Ellinor's tribulations are scarce less piteous
than Amy Robsart's, her heiress presumptive, for there can be

*Sophia
and
Harriet
Lee :
"The
Recess"*

---

[1] Preface to *The Old English Baron.*

little doubt that *The Recess* gave hints for *Kenilworth*. But Leicester is admirably soft-hearted. At her telling him the melancholy story of her birth and precarious destiny, " Tears, composed of every melting sensation, seemed to fall from my eyes on his heart. Those fine eyes [evidently Leicester's] were teeming with some generous consolation, when a sudden noise obliged us to separate." Uncanny noises and terrific claps of thunder are indeed continually reverberating through the jerry-built mediæval piles and the ramshackle story, and they continued to echo in the stories that quickly followed, for the effect upon Miss Lee's readers was all that could be desired. Among others, they stirred the imagination of a young lady at Bath named Ward, a friend of Sophia Lee, who ran a thriving private school there: Miss Ward was soon to marry a gentleman named Radcliffe.[1]

"The Canterbury Tales"

Harriet Lee called *The Recess*, not inaccurately, " The first English romance that blended interesting fiction with historical events and characters, embellishing both by picturesque description. *Cleveland*, written, as I believe, by the Abbé Prevôt, had precedence of all." [2] In her own introduction, Sophia observes that the verisimilitude of the story is heightened by the marvellous nature of the incidents, since the age of Elizabeth was the age of romance. But she and her sister were able to find romance much nearer their own time. After publishing *Warbeck, a pathetic tale* (1786),[3] from Baculard's *Nouvelles historiques,* a tale very similar to *Cleveland* and in the translation made to resemble Leland's *Longsword*, Sophia co-operated with Harriet in a collection like this of Baculard's or his *Épreuves du sentiment*, also not unlike in some of its contents to Marmontel's more recent *Contes moraux* (1780). *The Canterbury Tales* (1797) were planned by Harriet, who wrote most of the stories, Sophia contributing " Pembroke " and " The Two Emilys," in which mysterious supernatural appearances are duly explained in the manner of Prévost, whose *Doyen de Killerine* was indeed the source. The stories are condensed *nouvelles* or novelettes, lacking the pith demanded of the modern short story. They deal mainly with the life of their own

[1] See *Mrs Barbauld and her Contemporaries* (1877), by the late Sir Jerom Murch, whom I have heard talk on the subject.
[2] Preface to *Canterbury Tales*.
[3] See also above, p. 136.

time and the manners and morals of society, and betray here
and there pronounced democratic feeling towards the rich and
dissolute. Some are average domestic realism; some approxi-
mate to the Gothic. "The Clergyman's Tale—Henry," or *Other*
"Pembroke" is very romantic in its scheme; but its worst *romantic*
fault is the conceited and inflated style; even the dialogue is *stories*
bombastic and unnatural. Pembroke married for love, but his
wife's pride and arrogance estranged him, and though he was
blessed with a female child he yearned to adopt a boy. One
day, in mid-Wales, he rescues a beautiful infant boy from
drowning; and, feeling that his secret desire has been fulfilled,
without making the least inquiry, he installs him in his own
house under the ill-judged pretence that it is his own bastard.
The two children are brought up together, and naturally love
each other like brother and sister, and even more. Henry reaches
manhood, and fights under Wolfe at Quebec; but he finds no
sweetness in life, although he hears that Julia steadily repulses
every suitor for her hand, even the most eligible. But the supposed father at length reveals the truth; whereupon the pair fall
into each other's arms, with the blessings of all their friends, and
are awarded still more wealth, and still more honour, by the
discovery that Henry is the long-lost scion of the house of Powys.

"Kruitzner, the German's Tale," by Harriet Lee, already *" Kruitz-*
alluded to in connexion with the Patrice of the *Doyen de Killerine*, *ner"*
is more unmistakably Gothic, and despite clumsy involutions and
obscurities of plot is not without a curious power, like the spell of
a half-intelligible nightmare. Kruitzner is the assumed name of
the young Count Siegendorf, who has disgraced the family by a
course of debauchery, and quitted Prague as an outlaw. Married
to the daughter of a great Italian savant, a misalliance but one not
too discreditable, he learns after a while that his father intends
to disinherit him and leave his wealth and honours to a Baron
Stralenheim. But the plan may be forestalled if Kruitzner, now
lurking in a town of Silesia, can make his way across the mountains
and evade the roving bands who are harrying all the country at the
end of the Thirty Years War. At the critical moment, however,
the scheming baron arrives at the castle where Kruitzner is lodged,
far from the state apartments; the baron has wind of his intentions

and is determined to thwart them. Opposing guile to guile, Kruitzner makes his way by stealth to the baron's room, is tempted by the gold he finds there, and robs him of a large sum of money. Meanwhile, his son Conrad arrives, learns with mixed feelings that his father is a thief, and being a man of action undertakes to make all safe. The next thing that transpires is that the baron has been murdered. Who is the criminal? Suspicion falls on a Hungarian soldier, and Kruitzner with his family travels unmolested to Prague. His father is dead, and he succeeds to his inheritance. But in the midst of the festivities, in the very cathedral, he catches sight of the Hungarian, who perhaps was the assassin. The Hungarian is the Cassandra of the story. His part is to taunt Count Siegendorf with the disgrace of the past, to hold over his head the fact of his theft, and at last to inform him that the adored son, who had won golden opinions by his devotion and incorruptibility, is a worse traitor and profligate than himself, and was the murderer of the baron. Conrad, banished from Prague, rejoins his old confederates, and is slain in a skirmish with the regular troops; the father dies of a broken heart. This is the story on which, with some alterations, Byron constructed his poetic tragedy *Werner*. According to Byron, Ulric, or Conrad, was to have been married to the daughter of the slaughtered baron; hence the deeper horror of the scene when the whole guilt is revealed.[1]

"The Landlady's Tale"　　Not less powerful, and not Gothic, except that analogous feelings are roused, is "The Landlady's Tale, or Mary Lawson."

---

[1] Byron read "Kruitzner" when he was thirteen, and was deeply impressed. He wrote a first act in 1815, but the extant play dates from 1821. He straightened out the perplexities, and changed the names, Kruitzner to Werner and Conrad to Ulric. He caught and deepened the tone of tragic squalor. His play is a drama of inexorable destiny. The count's father had cursed his degenerate son, who feels himself involved in a maze where he

> can only flutter
> Like the poor fly, but break it not.

He cries bitterly, "Does my father's curse descend even to my child?" And Ulric, the murderer, reproaches his father with having fixed on him by his disgrace a felon's brand. It is the Gothic idea of ineluctable fate impelling to crime, for which the wrongdoer feels shame and remorse, yet knows that it is useless to struggle against the decree : he is predestined to evil.

The connexion between Byron's play and "Kruitzner" has been carefully studied by W. Kluge (*Lord Byron's "Werner"* . . . *eine dramentechnische Untersuchung mit Inaltenstudium*, Inaug. Diss., 1913).

It is another story of nemesis, and the pathos excruciating. A young woman who was meanly betrayed by a wealthy officer finds her way to his seat in Northumberland, and by no unlikely circumstances is made nurse to the new-born child of his wife. The man tries to renew their liaison, and in her perturbation and resentment she runs off with the boy. She has formed no definite purpose; but she chances to go aboard a ship, and eventually finds herself at Weymouth. Here she lives for years, till the boy grows up, and she is at a loss how to launch him in the world. At this moment, her erstwhile seducer, now a middle-aged rake, is at Weymouth with his race-horses and grooms; and the boy makes friends with these underlings, fascinated by the free-and-easy ways of the sporting household. A theft comes to light, and the lad is suspected. The unwitting father prosecutes the boy, who is sent to Botany Bay. Too late it comes out that the supposed delinquent is his own son. Dispatches are sent to every port, to intercept the ship and convey a free pardon to the boy. He dies on the voyage, and the wretched father reaps the fruits of his ill deeds. Pathos as grim as the death sentence passed by the judge on the girl whom he had loved and ruined, in *Nature and Art*! and the radical opinions expressed are not very much removed from those of Mrs Inchbald:

"The world is divided into two classes, Mrs Dixon," said a gentleman to me one day, when we were talking together about poverty and wealth. "There are those in it who have an appetite and no dinner, and those who have a dinner, and no appetite; your rich folks are in the second class; and I doubt whether they are better off than the other."[1]

A time-worn motive will be detected in another tragic tale, *The Errors of Innocence* (1786), by Harriet Lee, of a refined lady entrapped into marriage with an unprincipled man out of pity, to make his last moments happy. The man is not really at the point of death, and the lady has given her heart to a worthy suitor, hence misery for two noble-minded beings, which is the subject of the letters in which the novel is indited. This is a novel of sensibility, but it is not Gothic. That is the term to apply, on

[1] II. 347.

*Anne
Fuller
and
James
White*

the other hand, to a couple of mediocre novels moulded upon *The Recess,* by Anne Fuller. *Alan Fitz-Oshorne* (1787) is a sanguinary and phantom-mongering story of the days of Henry III. and the Barons' Wars, and *The Son of Ethelwulf* (1789) an Ossianic tale of Saxon times. This latter came out the same year as Mrs Radcliffe's first novel, the same also as the first of James White's, a writer who dared to handle the stage properties of Gothic romance with so much playfulness and irreverence that

*A burlesque
of historical
romance*

he was reprimanded by the reviewers, who do not however seem to have suspected that he had his tongue in his cheek. In *Earl Strongbow, or the history of Richard de Clare and the beautiful Geralda* (1789), the story of the conquest of Ireland is related by the ghost of the doughty earl in a manner that would have made Peacock smile. The harangues which he rehearses are amusing hits at the oratory of White's own day in the House of Commons. There is similar burlesque in *The Adventures of John of Gaunt, Duke of Lancaster* (1790) and *The Adventures of King Richard Cœur-de-Lion* (1791), along with extravagant descriptions of gloomy scenes and the violence of nature, evidently meant for the Lees and Mrs Radcliffe. White was better-informed than the average historical romancer, and kept clear of their solecisms in spite of his farcical bent. He was determined to show life as it is, and to demonstrate " that our forefathers were as foolish as we are ourselves." So he dressed people like those of his own day in mediæval habiliments, and made them perform in the same sort of foolish comedy as he saw going on in the modern world, with its crazes, pretences, and affectations.[1] Though the critics at length perceived his humour, his more solemn colleagues the historical romancers did not stand corrected. But, with the exception of Mrs Charlotte Smith and Mrs Radcliffe, the rest of them must be passed over.[2]

[1] See "A Forgotten Humorist," by J. M. S. Tompkins (*Review of English Studies,* April 1927). White was interested in contemporary politics, and among other works wrote *Hints for Abolition of the Slove-Trade* (1788). Miss Tompkins recognizes Fox, Pitt, and Sheridan among the mouthing historical characters in *Strongbow.*

[2] Miss Knight, the author of *Dinarbas,* hardly counts among the romancers, except for one late piece, *Sir Guy de Lusignan* (1833). Her *Marcus Flaminius, or a view of the military, political, and social life of the Romans* (1792), was a series of letters " from a young patrician to his friend " conveying information in the graphic mode of *Le Jeune Anacharsis* (1788) of the Abbé Barthélémy.

Mrs Charlotte Smith (1749-1806) is not generally thought of among the exponents of Gothic romanticism, nor as one who preceded and gave useful ideas to Mrs Radcliffe. She wrote domestic fiction having a family resemblance to Richardson's, modified by what she learned from Fanny Burney. But Mrs Smith, especially after she separated from her ne'er-do-well husband and had the sole care of her dozen children, was a most industrious writer, and among her numerous novels several of the best evidently drew their romantic furnishings from Prévost, indulged in heterogeneous adventure after the same pattern, including similar mysterious and terrifying occurrences afterwards explained away, and painted sentimental landscapes in tune with the sentimental moods, in the more recent manner of Rousseau and of the *Adèle et Théodore* (1782) of Madame de Genlis.[1] This was a great stride in the direction to be taken in a short while by Mrs Radcliffe. If Mrs Smith is not a typical Gothic novelist, or not exclusively that, she was right on the border-line.

Apart from some early poems, her first published work was a translation of *Manon Lescaut* (1786). It was followed [2] by a novel, *Emmeline, the orphan of the castle* (1788), which might be summed up as of the *Cecilia* type, with reminiscences of *Clarissa*.[3] The blameless young lady is the reputed illegitimate daughter of the dead elder brother of Lord Montreville. This arrogant and ambitious nobleman, with a more arrogant and ambitious wife, might be compared with Mr Delvile, except that he turns soft-hearted in extremity, and also is not an occasion for humour. As in *Cecilia*, the eldest son, Lord Delamere (Lord, when the ambitious father becomes a marquess), falls violently in love with Emmeline, who sets propriety and an almost excessive dutifulness before self-interest and a budding attachment, and steadily repulses him. The story is complicated and leisurely. Only in the fourth volume does Emmeline discover the marriage certificate in the casket

---

[1] *Adèle et Théodore, ou lettres sur l'éducation*, was translated as *Adelaide and Theodore, or letters on education* (1783).

[2] In between appeared *The Romance of Real Life* (1787), composed of French *Causes célèbres*.

[3] As much, that is, as the same could be asserted of Susan Ferrier's novel *The Inheritance*.

proving that she is legitimate and the vast Mowbray property hers. By that time, she has a steadier and less intractable lover in Godolphin, whom she marries.

Relics of Richardson and Fanny Burney's realism
Most of the characters are aristocrats or at least very genteel. Except a few having objectionable rôles, they merit the description of " persons as respectable for their virtues as their station." One of the best is Lady Adelina, who, a very Clarissa, repulses the dissolute betrayer who is the father of her child. There is also a rejection scene boldly abridged from Sir Hargreaves Pollexfen's famous proposal to Miss Byron: Emmeline answering falteringly

That to his person there could be no objection, he goes on :
"To his fortune? "
It was undoubtedly more than situated as she was she could expect.
" To his family? "
It was a family whose alliance must confer honour.
"What then? " vehemently continued the Chevalier—" what then, charming Emmeline, occasions this long reserve, this barbarous coldness? "

So it continues, in a style often copied; even Maria Edgeworth did so in *Belinda*. The story is skilfully planned, and apart from the slowness, which was probably an asset to leisured readers, it is well narrated. Humour is alleged by the author, but must be taken for granted. Emmeline's propriety, though a general trait in heroines of her social class, is overpowering. She comes almost as near to breaking a blood-vessel as Mrs Delvile in the prize scene in *Cecilia*, when the nefarious Mr Crofts calls her a little prude and tries to snatch a kiss. Just such a gentle, shrinking, refined, and strong-minded figure of beautiful girlhood was to hold the centre of the picture and rivet the sympathies of sentimental readers in all Mrs Radcliffe's novels.

Landscape painting in "Ethelinde" and "Celestina"
But the background of harmonious landscape was as essential as the human element; Mrs Smith's successor was to accept not a single heroine failing in a proper devotion to scenery. Description is at a minimum in *Emmeline*, though there are a few seaside and woodland scenes; in the next novel, *Ethelinde, or the recluse of the lake* (1789), she took great pains, however, with her setting at Grasmere amid the lake mountains, and in *Celestina* (1791)

with the rural beauties of Provence. Here is a passage prophetic of *The Romance of the Forest* and *The Mysteries of Udolpho*:

Celestina, who was in that disposition of mind to which horrors are congenial, walked slowly on notwithstanding; but quitting the cliffs, on account of the gales of wind which blew from the sea, she went along a narrow pass, where there was a cairn or heap of stones loosely piled together, the work of the first wild natives of the country; and as that was as far as she thought it proper to venture from the house, though it was not more than eight o'clock, she leaned pensively against it, and watched with some surprise the fluctuations of the clouds that were wildly driven by the wind across the disk of the moon, and listened with a kind of chill awe, to the loud yet hollow echo of the wind among the hills, which sometimes sobbed with stormy violence for a moment and then suddenly sinking, was succeeded by a pause more terrible. It was in one of those moments of alarming silence that Celestina thought she saw the shadow of a human form for a moment on the ground, as if the person was behind her who occasioned it.[1]

In *Desmond* (1792), a contemptible husband tries to induce his wife to become the mistress of a wealthy duke. She indignantly takes flight; and, when her mother turns her away, is protected by Desmond. Both are too high-minded to take advantage of the situation. Geraldine returns and nurses her dying husband, who had thrown in his lot with a troop of bandits and been shot in a skirmish, and completes her year of mourning before she marries her lover. The novel is largely composed of letters from Desmond travelling in France, and he describes the state of things at that period. Mrs Smith's sympathies were with the revolutionaries, and neither the outspoken discussions on freedom and equality nor the strictures on the policy of the British Government met with much approval in England. Desmond, it is to be noted, is a lover of the Werther stamp; the new leaven was working and turning even the novel of sensibility towards ideas. *"Desmond" and the French Revolution*

All these diversified ingredients are combined in *The Old Manor House* (1793), which may be accepted as the type novel of Charlotte Smith. It is domestic fiction, branching off into intrigues and adventures, and exhibiting her political bias in some *"The Old Manor House"*

[1] Chap. iii. 50-51.

satire on pride of birth and in her sympathy with the other side when the young hero is sent to fight against the American revolutionaries. The rambling old mansion, with its hidden passages and stairways, haunted not by ghosts but by smugglers, the gruesome incidents of red Indian warfare and the hairbreadth escapes, along with the sentimental evocation of ominous scenery, are all features of Gothic romance. Other components are a reminder that Fanny Burney had recently been handling similar domestic problems. But Fanny Burney did not show the same consciousness that the industrial revolution was in full swing, and that the rich merchant and mill-owner were in the act of ousting the old aristocracy from their pre-eminence.

Pride of birth and snobbishness   A great house and estate, the ancient patrimony of the Raylands, are now in the hands of an aged lady, last representative of the male line. The presumptive heirs are descended from the female side; and this imperious old woman, a great lady, in spite of her prejudices and caprices, regards them as debased and adulterated by their connexion with trade, and, further, as offspring of the regicides against whom her ancestors drew their swords. It is noteworthy that the age of snobbishness is beginning, though the peculiar British snobbery of the nineteenth century, based on the inferiority complex, differing from French *snobisme* which is based on the superiority complex, is not yet in sight. It is still the insolence of birth and wealth, like the French *morgue*, scorn for natural deficiencies, jealousy of the rank which pretenders are trying to undermine. Mrs Smith is as incensed as Bage against the purse-proud grandee, and not less against the moneyed upstart, such as Stockton, who gathers round him a rabble of gamesters and debauchees, in an old castle which his huge fortune gained in commerce has enabled him to buy, who shoots all over the county, hunts down the rustic lasses, and drinks himself into the grave. Naturally, the jealous old lady hates the parvenu more virulently than even her encroaching kindred the Somerives, and any intercourse with him is sure to jeopardize their hopes of succeeding; for, although Mr Somerive is next-of-kin, she can dispose of the estate freely by will.

A Gothic story   Such is the posture of affairs. Orlando is the second son of Mr Somerive, but the eldest is a rake and a spendthrift, and has ruined his chances with Mrs Rayland. Orlando, on the contrary, is the all-too-perfect young man, the romantic hero. He wins the old lady's affections, not for mercenary reasons, but rather because he is good-natured, and still more because he is in love with Monimia, the ill-used niece of her housekeeper and confidant. The lovers meet in the secret apartments of the old fabric, and are scared by noises and mysterious sights, afterwards traced to the band of smugglers who have their storehouse in the vaults. But Orlando is given a commission, and serves in the American war. Captured by the Indians, he presently falls into the hands of the French, and a long period elapses before he escapes and at last finds himself in England again. He arrives in a destitute condition, to find his father dead, his mother and sisters in poverty, the old manor house in the hands of strangers, and Monimia vanished. The fourth and last volume deals with his feverish quest for his lost love, with the exposure of the intrigues by which a fraudulent will had been substituted for the one that left him principal heir, and with the rediscovery of Monimia. It is all fairly exciting. Mrs Smith recounts facts without realism; that was all she was competent to do. She could not draw a striking character; but she had a sound knowledge of human nature in general, and her creations act upon reasonable and well-defined motives. Her criticism of the state of society is also effective. She does not make much of the war. But her pro-American feeling causes her to exaggerate the perils of Orlando and the English troops, and the sufferings due to the rascality of contractors supplying the fleet and army. Profligate aristocrats such as the baronet who tries to capture Monimia; or the general who fails to seduce Orlando's sister, and when he prepares to marry her is cut out by his own nephew: all supply something corresponding on the one hand to the Lovelace and Pollexfen business in Richardson's novels, and on the other suiting Mrs Smith's book as a social reformer.

Her use of scenery is thoroughly romantic. The decayed *Romantic* house, set against deep woods, with a broad sheet of water in *scenery* front that looks mysterious in the moonlight, responds to the more picturesque incidents and the feelings of the harried lovers. As Orlando listens to the low wind sounding hollow through the firs and " stone pines," and faintly sighing among the reeds, he is " impressed with those feelings which inspire poetic effusions. Nature appeared to pause, and to ask the turbulent and troubled heart of man, whether his silly pursuits were worth the toil he undertook for them? Peace and tranquillity seemed here to have retired to a transient abode." He sees, " by the faint light which the old Gothic casements afforded at that hour of the evening," Monimia sitting alone. When he arrives in London, the throng of coaches, the dirt and fog, and the deafening noise, fill him with mournful reflections, and remind him that amidst these multitudes " there was not one interested for him." There are not many such set pieces, however, and no such symphonic painting of nature as those in which Mrs Radcliffe afterwards excelled; still the setting is adequately prepared, and contrasts well with the baldness of less imaginative novelists.

A later study after Rousseau   Mrs Smith returned to domestic problems and portraiture of character in *The Banished Man* (1794), and to full-blooded romance in *Montalbert* (1795). But the only one among her later novels worthy of note is *The Young Philosopher, Nature his law and God his guide* (1798), the object of which is to present " a just picture of a man so calm, as to be injured by fraud and offended by folly, and who shall yet preserve his equality of temper." Disillusioned and embittered by the ill-success of the revolutionary movement in France and of reform in England, she recounts the unfortunate career of a disciple of Rousseau, who meets with the usual fate of the idealist in a refractory world, and is driven at last to seek a better way of life in the American backwoods. Though in the main a discussion novel or a near approach thereto, this has a good deal of description of Scottish scenery; and Mrs Smith has by this time developed such a passion for nature that in footnotes she gives the botanical names of the flowers that adorn the scene. Mrs Radcliffe was to be more artistic.

Mrs Radcliffe   The name of Mrs Radcliffe has become almost a synonym for Gothic romance, and her novels do represent the best phase of the genre, before it began to degenerate into the ghastliness of " Monk Lewis " and the elaborate terrorism of Maturin. Ann Ward, afterwards Mrs Radcliffe (1764-1823), was a quiet, home-keeping lady, a good housewife, who travelled little till after she had executed her word-pictures of foreign lands; who had no adventures, and but a restricted acquaintance with the world even of ordinary affairs; and who spun her romantic inventions out of an imagination dreaming over the works of her fellow-novelists and a few books of travel. She had as much knowledge of English literature, including Shakespeare and the poets, new or resuscitated, of her own time, as the average educated woman; but there is no evidence that she had read much history, in which respect she compares poorly with the rest of her romantic colleagues. But she was well versed in the novel of sensibility, whether of home or foreign make; and her heroines, one and all, are formed in that mould. In truth, it is to the extreme development of sensibility in these refined young ladies, and particularly their acute susceptibility to the emotions of fear and awe, that is referable the dominant note of her romanticism, the sense of wonder and suspense, suspense above all.

Her first novel is negligible. *The Castles of Athlin and Dun-* Her first bayne, an Highland story (1789), was an essay in the manner of *two novels* *The Old English Baron* and *The Recess*, vaguely picturing Scotland in feudal times, with little local colour and that little erroneous. The plot centres in a missing heir, and there is the usual Gothic apparatus of secret passages and sliding panels, mysterious music, and the chill touch of a corpse in the dark, giving some foretaste of stronger sensations to come. Fuller effects are attained in her next, *A Sicilian Romance* (1790), following the same exemplars, but also levying toll upon the stagy subterranean horrors of Baculard d'Arnaud's *Euphémie, ou le triomphe de la religion* (1768), with its charnel-house in a castle dungeon, and upon other exponents of frightfulness.[1] It is a story crowded with incident, of times not long past, in which she develops her favourite plot, of a wife immured in remote parts of a huge castle, by a dissolute nobleman who has formed an alliance with a beautiful younger woman. The gentle heroine is one of his daughters, who have

[1] According to J. R. Foster (" The Abbé Prévost and the English Novel," in *Publications of the Modern Language Association of America*, xlii., 1927) she borrowed the idea of the imprisoned mother from *The Recess*, and other " tenebrous and subterranean " effects from Baculard and a tale by Madame de Genlis in *Adèle et Théodore* (1782).

no suspicion of their father's villainy. Strange sounds, alarming sights, perils from banditti, and the machinations of a hated suitor, are among the incidents of a chequered story, which comes to a happy end with the rescue of the maltreated lady, the death of her nefarious husband and his paramour, and the union of the heroine to the lover who has saved her in many dire extremities. From beginning to end, however, it is not violent scenes of action, so much as nervous apprehension, vague foreboding, subjective feelings of suspense, in short, the morbid phenomena of sensibility, that torture the heroine and those who love her, and keep sympathetic readers on tenterhooks. The novel of suspense has definitely arrived.

"The Romance of the Forest"
    The theme is further elaborated in *The Romance of the Forest* (1791), which draws upon the same and other sources,[1] Mrs Smith's *Celestina*, which had just come out, proving very serviceable. Both authoresses send their heroines on extended tours, in the course of which they pass through much impressive scenery, and this is a chief element in their emotional experiences. Mrs Smith repaid herself for part of the debt when she took Mrs Radcliffe's ruined abbey and turned it into her rambling old manor house, and put lurking smugglers instead of banditti into its dark recesses. Mrs Radcliffe's heroines show the lofty strain of their sensibility in their enthusiastic love of scenery. Even in the worst disasters, loss of an idolized parent or of a lover, or when they are in the grasp of a ruthless tyrant and in momentary dread of outrage or death, the true heroine derives untold comfort from the contemplation of forests, lakes, the sea, mountains, or a far-spreading champaign. This is only a natural result of their sensibility, and accords well with the feelings of suspense due to the precarious situation of Adeline and her pretended father La Motte, hiding in the abbey ruins, the dark secret between him and the Marquis de Montalt, and the fate hanging over her lover. Indefinable perils threaten herself; and Mrs Radcliffe plays with all these motives so as to excite the maximum of apprehension without any vulgar effusion of blood. The plot is intricate and ingenious;

---

[1] She herself refers to Guyot [or Gayot] de Pitaval, editor of *Causes célèbres*, as the source of La Motte's story. But she probably got it from Charlotte Smith's *Romance of Real Life* (see *Ann Radcliffe in relation to her time*, by C. F. McIntyre, 1920, pp. 51-58).

the main secret is well kept, and the disclosure comes with an adequate shock of surprise. But in detail it is mechanical, and improbable to the point of absurdity; the writer has neither the knowledge of life nor of history to produce more than a thin semblance of reality. Mrs Radcliffe seems to have been as ignorant of the ways of the world as her innocent heroines. Banditti are always lurking in the woods; she seems to regard them as a kind of local fauna. In themselves, the characters are null. She has no insight whatever into the mentality of her villains, who are simply dissolute, and therefore ambitious, rapacious, criminal. The good people are absurdly perfect. The heroine, here and elsewhere, is a prudish, stilted, over-refined creature, always blushing and fainting, always indelicately sensible of the proprieties; the heroine of the novel of sensibility further idealized. And the more exemplary characters of the other sex are an exact counterpart. There is the Frenchman, M. Verneuil, for instance, whose sentiments and virtues, like those of La Luc, go well with the Alpine environment near the haunts of Rousseau:

He was peculiarly susceptible of the beautiful and sublime in nature. To such a taste, Switzerland and the adjacent country was, of all others, the most interesting, and he found the scenery it exhibited infinitely surpassing all that his glowing imagination had painted; he saw with the eye of a painter, and felt with the rapture of a poet. [1]

Contemplation of the beauties of nature slides insensibly into *The* longing for the simplicity and idyllic happiness of rural life: *influence of*

In the habitation of La Luc he met with the hospitality, the *Rousseau* frankness, the simplicity, so characteristic of the country; in his venerable host he saw the strength of philosophy united with the finest tenderness of humanity: a philosophy which taught him to correct his feelings, not to annihilate them; in Clara, the bloom of beauty, with the most perfect simplicity of heart; and in Adeline all the charms of elegance and grace, with a genius deserving of the highest culture. . . . The cheerfulness and harmony that reigned within the château were delightful; but the philanthropy which, flowing from the heart of the pastor, was

[1] Chap. xviii.

diffused through the whole village, and united the inhabitants in the sweet and firm bonds of social compact, was divine. The beauty of its situation conspired with these circumstances to make Leloncourt seem almost a paradise.[1]

It reads like a quotation from " The Vicaire savoyard." Rousseau was, indeed, one of the influences that nourished and moulded the imagination of Mrs Radcliffe; but the others were still more important. The very first chapter of *The Romance of the Forest*, and a very effective opening it is, might have been written by Prévost himself: the flight of La Motte and his wife, through the " dark and tempestuous " night, their arrival after losing their way in the storm at the lonely and sinister house, and the sudden appearance of the beautiful girl, forcibly dragged along by a ruffian who locks the door, puts the key in his pocket, and pointing a pistol at La Motte, tells him,

" You are wholly in our power . . . no assistance can reach you; if you wish to save your life, swear that you will convey this girl where I may never see her more; or rather consent to take her with you, for your oath I would not believe, and I can take care you shall not find me again.—Answer quickly, you have no time to lose."

It is Prévost, again, who first devised such scenes as immediately follow, as when the beautiful girl and the other fugitives make their way into the ruined abbey:

As they approached it, Peter, who followed them, struck a light, and they entered the ruins by the flames of sticks, which he had collected. The partial gleams thrown across the fabric, seemed to make its desolation more solemn, while the obscurity of the greater part of the pile heightened its sublimity, and led fancy on to scenes of horror. Adeline who had hitherto remained in silence, now uttered an exclamation of mingled admiration and fear. A kind of pleasing dread thrilled her bosom, and filled all her soul. Tears started into her eyes:—she wished, yet feared to go on.[2]

But her finest passages of descriptive prose are evidently attempts with words on paper to rival the painters whom she

[1] Chap. xviii.   [2] Chap. ii.

most admired, Poussin, Claude, Salvator Rosa, and, especially *Deliberate* in the two later Italian romances, Guido Reni.[1] Here is Salvator *word-* Rosa blending into Claude: *painting*

Her spirits, thus weakened, the gloomy grandeur of the scenes which had so lately awakened emotions of delightful sublimity, now awed her into terror: she trembled at the sound of the torrents rolling among the cliffs and thundering in the vale below, and shrunk from the view of the precipices, which sometimes overhung the road, and at others appeared beneath it. Fatigued as she was, she frequently dismounted to climb on foot the steep flinty road, which she feared to travel on horseback. The day was now closing when they drew near a village at the foot of the Savoy Alps, and the sun in all his evening splendour, now sinking behind their summits, threw a farewell gleam athwart the landscape, so soft and glowing, as drew from Adelaide, languid as she was, an exclamation of rapture. The romantic situation of the village next attracted her notice. It stood at the foot of several stupendous mountains, which formed a chain round a lake at some little distance, and the woods, that swept from the summits, almost embosomed the village. The lake, unruffled by the lightest air, reflected the vermil tints of the horizon, with the sublime scenery on its borders, darkening every instant with the failing twilight." [2]

In *The Mysteries of Udolpho*, long tours in quest of the pictur- *"The* esque alternate with exciting melodrama, and the two are skilfully *Mysteries* harmonized by her sense of atmosphere. Some perfunctory *of* incidents are a mere pretext for the journey from Gascony into *Udolpho"* Languedoc, and her descriptions of the Pyrenees and the vast areas of forest stretching from their slopes. Those descriptions were studied from Ramond de Carbonnière's *Observations faites dans les Pyrénées* (1789),[3] which had also supplied Mrs Smith

[1] Guido was adored by that age, and Mrs Radcliffe cites him, in *The Italian*, where she depicts the melancholy nun : "Her blue eyes were raised towards Heaven, with such meek, such fervent love, such sublime enthusiasm as the heads of Guido sometimes display, and which renewed, with Ellena, all the enchanting effects of the voice she had just heard " (vol. i. 173).

[2] Chap. xvi.

[3] For her Italian scenery she drew upon Mrs Piozzi's *Observations and Reflections made in the course of a journey through France, Italy and Germany* (1789) and P. J. Grosley's *New Observations on Italy and its inhabitants* (1769). Her own journey through Holland and Germany was made whilst the proofs of *Udolpho* were in hand ; hence any idea that her Italian castle was suggested by one visited in Germany is baseless.

with landscape material for *Celestina*; but they remain vague and generalized, the effects depending on impressive adjectives used with a feeling for rhythm and sonorousness. Mrs Smith had by this time written her *Celestina*, *The Old Manor House*, and *Desmond*, all of which were helpful. Smugglers were now available to provide a change for the tedious banditti, and there were all the rest of the novels of sensibility and romances of adventure to draw upon. Mrs Radcliffe almost trespasses into the novel of personal relations, and almost achieves lifelikeness in the vulgar Madam Cheron, whose ambitions land her in such fearful disillusionment when she is married to the unscrupulous lord of Udolpho. But her genius is for something entirely different. The vast and gloomy and impossible castle frowning along the edge of a precipice in the Apennines is a magnificent stage for blood-curdling events; it reeks with terror, it thrills with suspense. Emily—that is the name of the heroine in the present novel, but there is little but the name to distinguish her from Julia or Adeline—is filled with dark foreboding when she first sets eyes on its menacing battlements; once inside, she is a prey to ever-intensified suspense. Mrs Radcliffe had as good a talent for grim interiors as for broad landscapes. Here are Emily's impressions of an evening party at Udolpho :

> Eight other guests sat round the table, who were all dressed in a uniform, and had all an expression, more or less of wild fierceness, of subtle design, or of licentious passions. As Emily timidly surveyed them, she remembered the scene of the preceding morning, and again almost fancied herself surrounded by banditti; then, looking back to the tranquillity of her early life, she felt scarcely less astonishment than grief at her present situation. The scene in which they sat assisted the illusion: it was an ancient hall, gloomy from the style of its architecture, from its great extent, and because almost the only light it received was from one large gothic window, and from a pair of folding doors, which, being open, admitted likewise a view of the west rampart, with the wild mountains of the Apennine beyond.
>
> The middle compartment of this hall rose into a vaulted roof enriched with fret-work, and supported on three sides by pillars of marble; beyond these, long colonnades retired in gloomy grandeur, till the extent was lost in twilight. The lightest footsteps of the servants, as they advanced through these, were

returned in whispering echoes, and their figures, seen at a distance imperfectly through the dusk, frequently awakened Emily's imagination. She looked alternately at Montoni, at his guests, and on the surrounding scene; and then, remembering her dear native province, her pleasant home, and the simplicity and goodness of the friends whom she had lost, grief and surprise again occupied her mind. [1]

It is easy to scoff at this staginess, and to point out that the *The story* terrible castle is built of lath and plaster [2]; that Montoni is a *melo-* villain of cardboard, and every man jack of his sinister retinue *dramatic* a stage figure, described by a single epithet, " good," " wicked," " crafty," " fond of gaiety," " frivolous," " dissolute," or " corrupt." Mrs Radcliffe's readers were as innocent as Emily, and were glad to be taken in. Happily for Emily, scenery even in her worst moments was a panacea, and in her lover Valancourt she had one who could share her enthusiasm. Even when things were at the worst, they could dismiss the thought of danger, and indulge their private sensibilities.

" I would ask," said Emily in a gentle but agitated voice, " the meaning of your words, but I perceive that the question would distress you now. Let us talk on other subjects. To-morrow, perhaps, you may be more composed. Observe those moonlight woods, and the towers which appear obscurely in the perspective. You used to be a great admirer of landscape; and I have heard you say that the faculty of deriving consolation under misfortune, from the sublime prospects which neither oppression nor poverty withholds from us, was the peculiar blessing of the innocent." Valancourt was deeply affected. " Yes," replied he; " I had once a taste for innocent and elegant delights—I had once an uncorrupted heart! " Then checking himself, he added, " Do you remember our journey together in the Pyrenees? " [3]

[1] Chap. xxiv.

[2] Her castles, monasteries, and the like, although the date may be the sixteenth century, always appear as she had seen them at the end of the eighteenth, decayed, deserted, antique. Udolpho stands a siege, but has to be hurriedly patched up to be in a state of defence, and there is some misgiving lest the cannon should bring down parts that are the worse for wear—a good test of her lack of historical imagination. Though the country is supposed to be overrun by condottieri, the castle is not kept in a state of efficiency. Anything Gothic must necessarily be in disrepair and dilapidation.

[3] Chap. xxxviii.

Suspense again   As to the more sensational excitements, they are uniformly based by Mrs Radcliffe on the device of some shock of fright, horror, or perturbing mystery, the explanation of which is withheld. Often it is merely withheld from the reader; the actors in the drama are aware of it. Such for instance is the phrase that catches Emily's eye in her father's manuscript before she burns it: the two lines of handwriting haunt her mind and shatter her peace. Long afterwards, " this tranquillity was suddenly interrupted when she recollected the words in the manuscript that had been found with this picture, and which had formerly occasioned her so much doubt and horror." Of the same kind is the incident of the black veil, which it is ultimately disclosed, hung so as to conceal, not a real corpse, but the waxen image of one in the last stages of corruption—an emblem of mortality for the penitential admonishment of an evildoer. Would Mrs Radcliffe have been more impressive had she never explained away her mysteries? Sometimes it hardly matters, oftener it matters a good deal. The music haunting the woods round the castle, the face that glares from the bed-hangings, and the strange disappearance of Ludovico, lose their sorcery and their terror when we learn that the one was produced by the lover's lute, and the others were tricks of the pirates who had their headquarters in the French château. Sometimes the reader cannot help being annoyed when she gives him an unseasonable view of the sham background and the conjurer's bag of tricks, and the world of gramarye is abruptly exchanged for that of common sense and commonplace. In this very novel there is a discussion on ghosts, and Mrs Radcliffe refuses to take sides. She gives her readers their fill of trepidation without once standing convicted of supernaturalism, at any rate, until she wrote Gaston de Blondeville.

"The Italian"   Lewis's Monk appeared two years before her next novel, The Italian, or the confessional of the Black Penitents (1797), and Mrs Radcliffe must have read it, for her crime-stained monk Schedoni is manifestly conceived in rivalry to his Ambrosio.[1]

[1] Both were no doubt indebted in varying measures to Prévost with his sinister Jesuit in Cleveland, and to the figure of Laurent in Boutet de Monvel's ghastly anti-clerical play, Les Victimes cloîtrées (1791). Monvel's plot also concerns an aristocratic mother's scheme for separating her child from the ineligible Dorval, and shutting her up in a convent with the monk Laurent as her agent.

The Italian is another full-length symphony on the same motive, a thousand obstacles and perils thrown in the way of two lovers; and the terrible suspense of the pair who escape at length from the castle of Udolpho is repeated in the flight from the Carmelite monastery in the heart of the Apennines. Again it is the unrelaxing tension of vague and inexplicable terror that is the master element, terror which as often as not arises from the terror-striking look of a place, a forest, a ruin, a mountain gorge, and by the writer's magic is wrought by a pen keeping time and tune with the incidents and the feelings into a harmony that enthralls. From the outset, the key is pitched high; the dialogue often rises into an artificial diction, as when the girl Ellena, in the terms of an enlightened Christianity, or rather of Mrs Radcliffe's militant Protestantism, exclaims against the attempt of the abbess to make her take the veil, and is haughtily answered. " 'Withdraw,' said the abbess, rising impatiently from her chair; ' your admonition, so becomingly delivered, shall not be forgotten.' " The rhetoric of the Inquisitors and their magnanimous victims in the sombre final scenes is yet more exalted; it is meant to reach the sublime.

This is the story of another virtuous orphan, Ellena di Rosalba, *Another* who is loved at first sight by Vivaldi, only son of a marquess. *elaborate* His haughty parents, especially the haughty and ruthless mother,[1] *exercise in suspense* seek to crush his wild scheme to marry her, and the lady has an apt minister in her private confessor Schedoni. This creature of hers, ambitious on his own account, contrives all manner of warnings and mysterious portents to deter Vivaldi from visiting Ellena in her secluded dwelling near the Bay of Naples. Once more, idyllic beauty blends with the intangible horror of nightmare. As a final resource, Ellena is carried off to the monastery, and almost compelled to join the order. The great abbey with its church and cloisters, its labyrinthine vaults and corridors, its chanting priests and nuns, and hordes of pilgrims, is another Udolpho, and a fit theatre for the gloomy scenes and gloomier apprehensions that Mrs Radcliffe conjures up out of her antipathy to the Roman Catholics. Aided by a soft-hearted nun and

[1] The Marchesa di Vivaldi is said to have been suggested by Madame Belcastro in Mrs Charlotte Smith's *Montalbert*.

accompanied by Vivaldi, Ellena escapes. But Schedoni tracks her down. He has her lover arrested by the Inquisition, and Ellena is carried to a desolate spot on the coast of Calabria, where the monk prepares to earn the gratitude of his patrons and high preferment in the Church by putting her away. There is a touch of Shakespeare now, and also a touch of Prévost. A base accomplice shrinking from the deed, Schedoni, like Lady Macbeth, himself takes the dagger. But when his eye falls on the sleeping girl, his passions are aroused. At that instant he sees a locket that he recognizes only too well. The monk Schedoni, once the dissipated Count di Bruno, who had contrived his brother's death and married against her will the widowed countess, believes Ellena to be his own daughter. Here, as once before, in *The Romance of the Forest*, Mrs Radcliffe came dangerously near the Prévost theme of incest.

The climax
Meanwhile Vivaldi is in the vaults of the Inquisition at Rome, charged with abetting a nun's escape from the cloister. Gloom and terror are piled up in a grandiose climax; and with praiseworthy skill the revolution in Schedoni's mind at the discovery of his supposed child, and the deliverance of the lovers whom he now befriends, are interwoven with the revelations that lead to the conviction of the arch-criminal by the Inquisition. Nothing is hurried; hopes and fears and dread of the worst calamities are balanced on the razor-edge of suspense, until justice can be dramatically executed all round.

Mrs. Radcliffe's use of atmosphere
No doubt it is all very unreal. The pictures of convent life are a caricature to those who know anything about it. And Schedoni and the malignant priest who conspires with and then betrays him are stage figures, not human beings. Mrs Radcliffe was a quiet domestic lady who never had a narrow escape in her life; and her talk of banditti and condottieri, of stilettos, pistols, and trombones, the way they are handled and the wounds they deal, is patently and absurdly a pretence. The narrative of the escape from the convent of San Stefano will not beguile the most innocent mind if it stops to reflect. The reader now must with an effort do what the reader then did with the greatest ease, enter into Ellena's panic-stricken mind, or Vivaldi's, and be plunged into the chill current of dread and premonition. He must not resist the spell of the twilit caves and dungeons, the mellifluous incantation of the

prose-poetry, the fascination of such tableaux as Schedoni's colloquy with the marchesa in the transept, or the pitiless judges and the masked agents of the Inquisition. He must submit and allow these visions to congeal the blood.[1] Mrs Radcliffe knew that fear and even repulsion may, like pathos and tears, be pleasant ingredients in a sensational dish. But probably her most lasting contribution to romance was simply this which we call atmosphere. Landscapes, seascapes, picturesque ruins, skies and storms evoke it, and make the right psychical accompaniment to the emotional drama. It was not something absolutely new in fiction, but no one had used atmosphere before as a principal element, and no one had used it so consciously. Even a souvenir can conjure it up.

His mind resembled the glass of a magician, on which the apparitions of long-buried events arise, and as they fleet away, point portentously to shapes half-hid in the distances of futurity. An unusual dread seized upon him; and a superstition, such as he had never before admitted in an equal degree, usurped his judgment. He looked up to the shadowy countenance of the stranger, and almost believed he beheld an inhabitant of the world of spirits." [2]

After a visit to Kenilworth in 1802, Mrs Radcliffe wrote a last novel, and brought a real ghost on the stage. The spectre performs in " a crucial rôle," says one critic; another sees " how completely she has failed in the management of a true spirit." What makes the book her dullest, however, is less the unfortunate ghost than the tedious historical facts which she too conscientiously worked into it. Mrs Radcliffe had to make history conform to her own preconceptions, or else leave it alone. It may have been her consciousness of this that made her refrain from publishing it, or it may have been the misgivings due to Jane Austen's pleasantries at the expense of Gothic fiction, in *Northanger Abbey*. At all events, *Gaston de Blondeville, or the Court of Henry III., resting in Ardenne* (1826), did not appear till after her death.

" Gaston de Blonde-ville "

She was the last of the novelists of sensibility; it was her

---

[1] Dr Nathan Drake, who himself dabbled in mediæval bric-à-brac and superstitious horrors, in his *Literary Hours* (1798) warmly approved Mrs Radcliffe's skill in making every nerve " vibrate with pity and terror," in appalling yet delighting the reader, etc. (" Remarks on *The Italian*," quoted by C. F. McIntyre, p. 46).
[2] Vol. iii. 118-119.

A novelist of sensibility sensibility that responded so cordially to the dual appeal of romance and of natural scenery. Her stories are all sentimental dramas; the heroines—and her heroes are all heroines—are cast in one mould, sensitive, devoted, virtuous beings, of the well-known stamp. Propriety was her watchword as it was Fanny Burney's. Remark the perfect propriety of the sentiments when the detestable marchesa, in *The Italian*, dies, in the midst of her criminal scheming: " Vivaldi, when informed of his mother's death, shed bitter tears of sorrow and remorse, for having occasioned her so much uneasiness." That is, for having fallen in love with Ellena and provided the whole occasion for Mrs Radcliffe's romance. Excellent and unexceptionable young man! For every one of her novels provides a lesson, which is received and taken to heart through the impression upon our sensibilities. At the end of *The Romance of the Forest*, it is the example of Theodore and Adeline :

> Their former lives afforded an example of trials well endured, and their present of virtues greatly rewarded; and this reward they continued to deserve—for not to themselves was their happiness contracted, but diffused to all who came within the sphere of their influence. The indigent and unhappy rejoiced in their benevolence, the virtuous and enlightened in their friendship, and their children in parents, whose example impressed upon their hearts the precepts offered to their understandings.

Nor is the conclusion of *The Mysteries of Udolpho* any less edifying :

> O ! useful may it be to have shown, that though the vicious can sometimes pour affliction upon the good, their power is transient and their punishment certain; and that innocence, though oppressed by injustice, shall, supported by patience, finally triumph over misfortune !

She was a firm believer in the sentimentalist doctrine that virtue never goes without its reward.[1]

Her imitators She had plenty of imitators during her own lifetime, especially in the decade or so after *The Mysteries of Udolpho* had enraptured a host of sentimental readers; many impudent plagiarists did not

[1] As to her natural religion—*i.e.* her deism—her strict observance of moral retribution, etc., see *Mrs Radcliffe, her relation towards Romanticism*, by Alida A. S. Wietens (Amsterdam, 1926).

scruple to put their crude sensation novels down to her discredit
by describing them as by the author of that famous book.[1] In
the romantic effusions of Sir Egerton Brydges she is actually outdone, but only in the features that lent themselves to tawdriness.[2]
She was out-sentimentalized, at any rate, in *The Children of
the Abbey* (1796) and other stories of weeping heroines, elegant
lovers, haunted castles, banditti, and the like, by Regina Maria
Roche. But the most notorious Gothic novel of the age was not
in the same tradition. Mrs Radcliffe married strangeness and
beauty; "Monk Lewis" divorced them again, and flung beauty
to the dogs, preferring the brute force of strangeness, violence,
and horror. The models he preferred, or at least the productions
he chose to vie with, were the blood-curdling German *Schauerromane*, or *Schrecksromane*, tales of terror, which were among
the most characteristic phenomena of the *Sturm und Drang*
period. So that his *Monk* [3] (1795), though confessedly inspired
by his enthusiasm for *The Mysteries of Udolpho* and the saturnine
and villainous Montoni, represents a schism, a dark heresy, in
the romantic fold, and was to offer to those who dabbled in
Gothicism an alternative pattern, to point to other attractions,
which indeed proved more appetizing to tastes now growing
cloyed.

Matthew Gregory Lewis (1775-1818) had studied German, *"Monk
in preparation for a diplomatic career, and at Weimar had met Lewis"
Goethe, whom he reverenced as author of *The Sorrows of Werther.* German
He read Schiller, was immensely impressed by his *Räuber* (1781) influences*
and the magnanimous, heaven-defying outlaw Karl Moor,[4] and
made a free adaptation of *Kabale und Liebe* in his own play *The
Minister* (1797). But it was the sensational dramas, tales, and

---

[1] One still comes across old novels in the bookshops falsely ascribed to Mrs
Radcliffe or " the author of *The Mysteries of Udolpho*." Miss Tompkins and still
more Miss Husbands have catalogued a number of quasi-historical or otherwise
Gothic novels that traded on her prestige during the period before 1800, and
a good many more appeared after that date.

[2] See above, pp. 152-153.

[3] It was first entitled *Ambrosio, or the Monk*.

[4] He afterwards constructed a play, *Adelmon the Outlaw* (produced at Drury
Lane, 1801), on the model of *The Robbers*, with borrowings from Kotzebue and
Mrs Radcliffe. *The Robbers* was Englished by A. F. Tytler, Lord Woodhouselee
(1792). There is no evidence that Mrs Radcliffe was acquainted with the work;
her banditti seem to have had a different origin.

romances of Kotzebue, Tieck, Weit Weber, Musäus, Körner, Heinse, Zschokke, Spiess, and other dealers in the uncanny, the grotesque, the horrific, the maudlin sentimental, that chiefly attracted him.[1] And he found the same sort of nutriment for a voracious appetite in such gloomy sensationalists as Baculard d'Arnaud's disciple, the anti-clerical playwright Boutet de Monvel, author of *Les Victimes cloîtrées* (1791), in which a libidinous monk keeps his prey, the young girl Eugénie, shut up in a convent. This Père Laurent stands at the head of a line of able and imperious ecclesiastics, including Lewis's Ambrosio, Mrs Radcliffe's Schedoni, and Victor Hugo's Frollo, who succumb to their passions and commit diabolical crimes.

Works based on German and similar material

Many of the tales in verse or prose which he translated more or less freely from his favourite German authors eventually went into his collections of ballads or stories in verse, *Tales of Terror* (1799) and *Tales of Wonder* (1801). Scott, who had already been fascinated by the macabre balladry of Bürger, was easily induced to collaborate; Southey also contributed. The later *Romantic Tales* (1808), in prose and verse, were of a milder brew. From the ghastly sensationalism and unmitigated supernaturalism of the German romantics came also the material for his "dramatic romance," *The Castle Spectre*, a play in which the Otranto style of Walpole was crossed with the popular melodrama of Kotzebue; it made a great hit on the degenerate taste of its day, and had a long run at Drury Lane (1797), being followed there or at Covent Garden by a whole series of dramatic pieces and operas, of similar extraction. One of the last, *Venoni, or the Novice of St Mark's*, produced at Drury Lane, 1808, was

[1] See *Der Einfluss der deutschen Litteratur auf den englischen Schauerroman*, by E. Margraf (1901). Although F. W. Stokoe's *German Influence in the English Romantic Period*, 1788-1818 (1926), is mainly concerned with influences upon Scott, Coleridge, Shelley, and Byron, it has several references to Lewis, and contains a useful list of works translated from German during the period. The largest number were from Kotzebue. Seven of his works were Englished in 1798, two of them twice; over twenty appeared next year, *Pizarro* four times over, and there were several more the year after that. Other noteworthy translations are *Popular Tales of the Germans*, by Musäus (1791), *Herman of Unna*, by Benedikte Naubert (1794), *The Black Valley*, from Weit Weber (1796), *Horrid Mysteries*, from Grosse (1797), and of course more famous works from Schiller, Goethe, Wieland, and others. The crop of translations from Bürger in 1796 are interesting from the effect they had upon Scott, as well as Lewis. Both knew German, and had a hand in the translations, Lewis especially.

an adaptation of Boutet de Monvel's *Victimes cloîtrées*, the scene transferred to Messina and the characters given Italian names. This was a subterranean play, like its original and also like Marsollier's *Camille, ou le souterrain* (1791), in which a wife is imprisoned in a cave by her jealous husband; and the audience roared with laughter at Lewis's hero and heroine declaiming alternately from adjacent cells. He soon altered that, and the play was then as successful as its predecessors.

In play, ballad, or prose story, he revelled in sheer horror. *His* The fluent doggerel (attempt to emulate the galloping rhythm of *delight* Bürger's *Lenore*) of his well-known ballad " Alonzo the Brave, *in sheer* and Fair Imogine," with which Antonia tries to soothe her *horror* enforced solitude in *The Monk*, sounds like a breakdown by a rollicking resurrectionist.

> At midnight four times in each year does her sprite,
>   When mortals in slumber are bound,
> Array'd in her bridal apparel of white,
> Appear in the hall with the Skeleton-Knight,
>   And shriek as he whirls her around.
>
> While they drink out of skulls newly torn from the grave,
>   Dancing round them the spectres are seen;
> Their liquor is blood, and this horrible stave
> They howl: " To the health of Alonzo the Brave,
>   And his consort, the False Imogine ! "

But this is very far from being a comic song. Here, as in the more repulsive incidents in *The Monk* and the rest of his work, Lewis betrays the perverted lusts of a sadist.[1] It was not merely a voracious but a morbid appetite that set him routing out the most horrifying stories of crime, Satanism, and fiendish cruelty that he could find in literature and recent collections of folk-lore. The list of his sources furnished by Lewis in the advertisement prefixed to *The Monk* is far from complete. The germ, he says, was the tale of the Santon Barsisa, in the *Guardian*[2]; the rest consisted of traditions and kindred stories from Germany, Denmark, and Spain. Addison's figure of the Santon, the venerable

---

[1] Both Lewis and Maturin take a prominent place as representing morbid tendencies in *The Romantic Agony*, by Mario Praz, trans. from the Italian (1933).
[2] No. 148.

Nourished from German sources

Mohammedan recluse who is led astray by his passion for a young girl, whom he murders, and then sells himself to the Devil, is the barest outline; it was the hero-criminals of German romance, the clerical monsters evolved by French animosity against the Roman Catholics, and such a suggestive conception as Mrs Radcliffe's Montoni, that helped Lewis to fill it out. He unquestionably borrowed something from Cazotte's little story of a supernatural temptress, *Le Diable amoureux* [1]; and features can be traced to Marlowe's *Doctor Faustus*, and probably to Greene's *Friar Bacon and Friar Bungay*, though perhaps the borrowings may have been indirect. Still more was he indebted to that congenial chamber of horrors, Joseph Glanvill's *Sadducismus Triumphatus, or a full and plain Evidence concerning Witches and Apparitions* (1666), a compendium that he read with delighted credulity. For Lewis was a stout upholder of belief in the supernatural; else he would not have written *The Monk*, which is no mere make-believe.

"The Monk"

Very far, accordingly, from following the practice of Mrs Radcliffe and attenuating the dreadful and repulsive by a meek explanation, Lewis accumulates horrors and leaves them to do their worst upon sensitive minds; his was well described as the " Golgotha " style of romancing. His realism has no art beyond

---

[1] See Praz (192). Praz also suggests (111) that Lewis took hints from the hero-villain of " the terrible German novel *Das Petermännchen*," by C. H. Spiess, the villain responsible for the death of six women. Other possible sources in foreign literature and tradition and traces of Mrs Radcliffe's novels in *The Monk* are the subject of " Studien zu M. G. Lewis' Roman ' Ambrosio, or the Monk,' " by Otto Ritter (*Archiv für das Studium der neueren Sprachen und Litteraturen*, von L. Herrig, cxi., 1903, pp. 106-121). This was soon followed by a more disturbing article, " Die eigentliche Quelle von Lewis' 'Monk,' " by Georg Herzfeld (*Ibid.*, pp. 316-323), which contended that the major part of *The Monk* was a broad translation from an anonymous tale *Die blutende Gestalt mit Dolch und Lampe, oder die Beschwörung im Schlosse bei Prag*, published at Prague before the end of the eighteenth century. Could it have been demonstrated that this appeared as early as 1792, Lewis would have been shown up as not only a wholesale plagiarist but also a shameless liar, since he claimed to have " made a full avowal of all the plagiarisms " of which he was aware (Advertisement to *The Monk*). A controversy ensued, which was finally settled by August Sauer's comparison of this story with the German translation of *The Monk*, which brought out the fact that the former was merely a rehash of the latter and appeared c.1799 (see *Grillparzers Werke*, 1909, i., Sauer's introduction to *Die Ahnfrau*, the plot of which came from *The Monk*; especially pp. l.-lxvi.). The whole controversy seems to have escaped the attention of English writers on the subject, with the exception of Dr Tompkins (see her note on p. 245), who however has not observed that Herzfeld had discovered a mare's nest and his theory was a false alarm.

that of a matter-of-fact recital; after all, Lewis was only twenty when he published *The Monk*, and he was always satisfied with the elementary way of telling a story. But the daring and frankness with which he describes his demons and putrefying corpses and his human bodies frenzied with lust or tortured with agony makes Walpole's audacity look timid; the tale of terror had made a giant stride by accepting Teutonic standards and treating reticence with contempt. His monk is a man of strong passions whose holiness is simply egotism, spiritual pride, and who is easily subdued by the wiles of a temptress, when she insinuates herself into the monastery in the guise of a novice. Remorse is followed by the stifling of conscience in renewed pleasure, and this by satiety. Lewis does not, however, spend time in showing the conflict in the monk's breast, he gets on with the story. The temptress is now in league with the Evil One; she had thus far been an unconscious instrument; Ambrosio is the object of a plot to ruin him body and soul. He is betrayed into the foulest crimes, which are described with a gluttonous fullness. He sells his soul, and then tries to make the bargain void. But the Devil outwits Ambrosio, and the wretched man is hurled into the pit. Lewis's simple, straightforward method, shrinking from no detail of horror, achieved something grandiose in the ferocity of the final scene.

"Whither have you brought me?" said the monk at length, in *The* a hollow, trembling voice. "Why am I placed in this melancholy *culminat-* scene? Bear me from it quickly! Carry me to Matilda!" *ing scene*
    The fiend replied not, but continued to gaze upon him in silence. Ambrosio could not sustain his glance; he turned away his eyes, while thus spoke the demon:
    "I have him then in my power! This model of piety! this being without reproach! this mortal who placed his puny virtues on a level with those of angels! He is mine—irrevocably, eternally mine! Companions of my suffering! denizens of hell! how grateful will be my present!"
    He paused—then addressed himself to the monk: "Carry you to Matilda!" he continued, repeating Ambrosio's words: "Wretch! you shall soon be with her! You well deserve a place near her, for hell boasts no miscreant more guilty than yourself. Hark, Ambrosio! while I unveil your crimes! You

have shed the blood of two innocents; Antonia and Elvira
perished by your hand. That Antonia whom you violated was
your sister! that Elvira—whom you murdered, gave you birth!
Tremble, abandoned hypocrite, inhuman parricide, incestuous
ravisher! Tremble at the extent of your offences! . . . Believe
you that your secret thoughts escaped me? No, no—I read them
all! You trusted that you should still have time for repentance.
I saw your artifice, knew its falsity, and rejoiced in deceiving
the deceiver! You are mine beyond reprieve; I burn to possess
my right, and alive you quit not these mountains."

During the demon's speech, Ambrosio had been stupefied by
terror and surprise. This last declaration roused him.

" Not quit these mountains alive! " he exclaimed. " Perfidious!
what mean you? Have you forgotten our contract? "

The fiend answered by a malicious laugh.

" Our contract! Have I not performed my part? What more
did I promise than to save you from your prison? Have I not
done so? Are you not safe from the Inquisition—safe from all
but from me? Fool that you were, to confide yourself to a devil!
Why did you not stipulate for life, and power, and pleasure?—
then all would have been granted: now your reflections come
too late. Miscreant! prepare for death; you have not many
hours to live! "

On hearing this sentence, dreadful were the feelings of the
devoted wretch! He sank upon his knees, and raised his hands
towards heaven.

The fiend read his intention, and prevented it. "What! " he
cried, darting at him a look of fury; " dare you still implore the
Eternal's mercy? Would you feign penitence, and again act an
hypocrite's part? Villain! resign your hopes of pardon. Thus I
secure my prey."

As he said this, darting his talons into the monk's shaven crown,
he sprang with him from the rock. The caves and mountains
rang with Ambrosio's shrieks. The demon continued to soar
aloft, till reaching a dreadful height, he released the sufferer.
Headlong fell the monk through the airy waste: the sharp point
of rock received him, and he rolled from precipice to precipice,
till, bruised and mangled, he rested on the river's banks.[1]

Lewis showed some skill in embodying a German legend
mentioned in his preface, of the Bleeding Nun whose ghost
haunts a Thuringian castle where she had slain her lover and

[1] *The Monk*, ed. E. A. Baker (1907), pp. 353-355.

met her own death, and a story not mentioned there, that of the Wandering Jew, which he may have borrowed from Schiller's *Geisterseher*.[1] The story of the lovers Agnes and Don Raymond based on this is, however, tied into the plot rather than united with it, and has very little bearing on the main theme.[2]   It is treated with the same revolting frankness.

The Monk was exceedingly popular, and went rapidly into a large number of editions, though it came under the critical bastinado for its faults of taste, and escaped legal action only when Lewis had toned down some scenes of sensual abandonment.[3] It certainly made history.   For, although feeble imitations of the Radcliffian novel continued to appear, the only examples of English Gothic that counted now followed the fashion set by Lewis.[4]   The only other work of his that need be mentioned is a minor tale in the Schiller tradition, *The Bravo of Venice* (1805), which was a much-altered version of Zschokke's story of a noble brigand, *Aballino, der grosse Bandit* (1794).   He made a Covent Garden melodrama, *Rugantino* (1805), out of it the same year. From the beginning of his literary career to the end, Lewis showed himself to be a skilful compounder of mixed and heady draughts; he was too modest to claim to be anything more.

Lewis's other works

A contemporary of his who made less noise in the Old World, but was less a borrower, and discovered lines of interest afterwards followed up by novelists in his own country, was an American; and since he contributed something to the development of fiction in English he necessarily comes into the history of the English novel.   Charles Brockden Brown (1771-1810) may or may not have read the work of Lewis.   There can be little doubt that he knew that of Mrs Radcliffe, witness the pains he took to evoke terror and then to rationalize this element by showing that everything recounted was due to natural causes.

Charles Brockden Brown

---

[1] See Alice M. Killen : *Le Roman terrifiant ou le roman noir* (1924), especially pp. 45-46, 52, and 215-216.

[2] It appeared separately as a chapbook, *Raymond and Agnes, or the Bleeding Nun of the Castle of Lindenberg* (c.1820).

[3] See Killen, 56, and Railo, 95.

[4] Praz (111-112) points out that Hoffmann drew his inspiration from *The Monk* for his *Elixiere des Teufels*, Grillparzer took from it his plot for *Die Ahnfrau*, Hugo drew upon it for his Claude Frollo and Esmeralda, Scott for the Templar and the Jewess in *Ivanhoe*, etc.

Like her too he was profuse in descriptions of scenery, though he painted landscape less because he loved it than as contributory to his aim of inspiring terror. Nor could he have been a stranger to the German terrorists, for his close friend and future biographer William Dunlap was the translator of Zschokke's *Aböllino* and the busy adapter of Kotzebue to the American stage.[1] Hence, his approximations to German terrorism could hardly have been accidental. But his chief and avowed model was Godwin, for whose *Caleb Williams* he expressed the admiration of one who despaired of rivalling it. In each of his novels, the situation of a weak and panic-stricken individual, like Caleb, in the grip of someone who is powerful and ruthless, reappears with talismanic effect. In spite of Brown's awkwardness and inability to unfold a coherent story, in the best passages the reader is held paralysed with apprehension, as if by an electric current. *Caleb Williams* is a better novel than any of Brown's, but it does not attain such a fearful intensity.

A disciple of Godwin Brown was a disciple of Godwin also in his social philosophy, and accepted the *Political Justice* as almost a sacred book. It was indeed the earnestness with which he cherished his moral ideals that made him flee from his lawyer's office; he quailed at the possibility of having to defend impartially the right and the wrong. So he turned definitely to literature, and his first writings were at any rate portentously serious. But these have none but a personal interest. Fortunately, he thought that like Godwin he could make fiction a medium for social criticism; and in his case too, not the theoretical aim, but the idiosyncrasy of the writer's imagination realized a sterling though curiously limited success. Brown was a man of poor physique, with a disposition very like Godwin's, studious, book-loving, solitary, but not sure of himself in the least. "Society was to him solitude," says Dunlap, "and in solitude he found delightful converse." He was an intellectualist out of touch with realities, dwelling with abstractions, and innocent as a child of most things in the world about him, except such as stirred his emotions. Speculating on the abnormal phenomena of the mind, and analysing every act and thought with a feverish solicitude due to his Puritan mentality,

[1] He adapted and produced at least thirteen plays of Kotzebue (A. H. Quinn, in *A History of American Literature*, ed. W. P. Trent, etc., 1918, i. 219).

he habitually reduced himself to a mass of tingling nerves, and
it was out of this almost dehumanized substance that he shaped
his imaginary figures, blanks most of them, devoid of personality,
having no concrete existence except in the racking experiences
of which their minds were the centre. Habitants of a twilight
tract, a limbo of the morbid and pathological, neighbouring the
occult, these figures were no less awe-inspiring than the ghosts
and vampires called up by the romancers. Rude though Brown's
achievements were, he was the precursor of those American
novelists, Poe, Hawthorne, Oliver Wendell Holmes, Herman
Melville, Henry James, who were to explore strange mental
cases with a more scientific or at least a surer understanding,
often with effects upon the reader very similar to those produced
by the novels of terror.[1]

All the virtue of his novels, as already indicated, lies in the "Wie-
parts; in other words, the interest is episodic. *Wieland, or the land"*
Transformation (1798), suffers from anticlimax as well as over-
strained probabilities, the explanation of the fearful occurrences
which have frozen our blood being too frivolous and inane as an
occasion for tragedy. The story was suggested by the actual
case of a religious fanatic who believed himself commanded by
heaven to destroy his idols, and who really did put his wife and
children to death. Wieland, a sober and respectable citizen of
Philadelphia, with nothing the matter with him except a touch
of religious mania, hears a mysterious voice again and again
bidding him to commit this hideous crime, and after terrible
struggles between love and a diseased conscience he obeys.
The voice is that of a ventriloquist, a man possessed by a spirit
of mischief for which he is not morally responsible. In this
" biloquist " Carwin, indeed, there is a glimpse of that kingdom
of evil pitted against mankind whose terrors were to be so powerfully set forth by Melville in *Moby Dick*. Brown's peculiar force
comes out in the distempered phases of Wieland's mind that
culminate in the dreadful deed.

In *Ormond, or the secret witness* (1799), the eponymous "Ormond"
character is a Godwinian revolutionary, except that his nature

[1] It is an interesting fact that M. Julien Green, author of *Léviathan, Le
Voyageur sur la terre*, etc., is of American origin and carries on the same American
tradition.

is warped and villainous. Brown tried to develop his ideal of pure and perfect womanhood in the much-tried Constantia Dudley, a lifeless creation that fascinated the uncritical Shelley. The ordeals through which he puts this saintly but priggish being are harrowing enough, but fail to impress through their utter implausibility and the general flimsiness of the story. In *Arthur Mervyn, or memoirs of the year 1793* (1799), Brown had grim enough personal recollections to enable him to add physical horrors to the mental tension of his more characteristic scenes. He and his family had left Philadelphia in 1793 to escape the plague, but Brown all but fell a victim to a similar visitation in New York in 1798. He was thus able to put some realistic descriptions of such an epidemic into *Ormond*, and now in *Arthur Mervyn* he wrote an account of a city devastated by pestilence that can hold its own with the classic pages on that theme by Thucydides, Boccaccio, and Defoe. The picture of a fever hospital at the height of the epidemic is appalling; but Brown's peculiar gift comes out better in his insight into the widespread and lasting demoralization due to the general breakdown of the social fabric. Mervyn is a youth of intelligence and good principle but entirely ignorant of the world, who finds himself involved in the affairs of a particularly wicked set of people, and his artless attempts to put things right produce absurd situations which the novelist handles with a ponderous seriousness. His Puritanism continually had the same ludicrous results as the propriety of the heroines of sensibility. Mervyn is Brown's Caleb, and the guilty Welbeck his Falkland; and, when Mervyn ingenuously lets out the secret incriminating that dangerous person, the paradoxical situation is closely analogous to that in Godwin's novel. But the author's peculiar touch is more evident in the scene where the sleeping lad is awakened one night by someone bending over him, and opening his eyes recognizes the face of the terrible Welbeck, whom he believed he had seen drowned.

"Arthur Mervyn"

It was as I suspected. The figure lifting in his right hand a candle, and gazing at the bed, with lineaments and attitude bespeaking fearful expectation and tormenting doubts, was now beheld. One glance communicated to my senses all the parts of this terrific vision. A sinking at my heart, as if it had been penetrated by a dagger, seized me. This was not enough: I uttered a shriek, too rueful and loud not to have startled the attention of the passengers, if any had, at that moment, been passing the street. . . . The visage and the shape had indeed preternatural attitudes, but they belonged, not to Colvill, but to—WELBECK.[1]

Edgar Huntly, or the sleep-walker (1799), also parallels *Caleb* *"Edgar Williams* in the relations between Huntly and the murderer *Huntly"* Clithero, whose crime was perpetrated in self-defence and who was under the delusion that he had killed his own benefactress. The process by which Huntly finds out the truth and his pursuit of Clithero closely resemble Godwin's story. That was written, as it were, backwards; and in this case too the antecedent events are given after the consequences, the concatenation of incidents being thus hopelessly obscure. Once more the fascination of the book is in the episodes, in which Brown secures truly romantic effects, though with a machinery very unlike that of his fellow-romancers. Here somnambulism, which at that era was as exciting a phenomenon as ventriloquism, is the agency employed, and, as was the writer's wont, it is much overworked. But he manages to infect the reader with the weird sensations and ghastly emotions of sleep-walking, and to conduct him through something like the mazes of a nightmare. Brown was a keen but untrained psychologist, studying the reflexes of characters who might be described as his patients; and he employed a Defoe-like method, noting the smallest detail, and recounting the stages of awareness, the impulses to action, and the torments of self-distrust and indecision that inhibit and paralyse at moments of crisis. In this novel, he sought romance by adventuring among " the perils of the western wilderness." He found romance; but the forbidding region which he depicts did not exist on the far slopes of the Alleghanies, where Brown had never been, but in his own inner consciousness. Nevertheless, the Indians whom he portrays from hearsay are terrible objects, and more like the real thing in all its ugliness as Bird depicted them in *Nick o' the Woods* than the idealized savages of Fenimore Cooper. For a specimen of Brown's method, take the chapters relating Edgar Huntly's escape from the cavern, the death of the panther, and his sudden encounter with a party

[1] Vol. i., chap. xxi.

of Indians on the warpath. For Brown was enough in the fashion to make this in part at least a subterranean novel.

A typical
episode

Coming to from a fit of unconsciousness, Huntly finds himself in absolute darkness and thinks he has gone blind; but groping about he becomes aware that he has fallen or been left in a cave. He is indeed in the deeper ramifications of a gigantic cavern, and for many hours he struggles desperately to find an exit, weak with hunger and thirst and repeatedly on the brink of suicide. It is only after what seem ages of convulsive effort, which infect the reader with all the terrors of claustrophobia, that he perceives the first glimmer of daylight.

My excruciating sensations for a time occupied my attention. These, in combination with other causes, gradually produced a species of delirium; I existed as it were in a wakeful dream. . . . Sometimes I imagined myself buried alive: methought I had fallen into seeming death, and my friends had consigned me to the tomb, from which a resurrection was impossible. . . . There is no standard by which time can be measured, but the succession of our thoughts, and the changes that take place in the external world: from the latter I was totally excluded; the former made the lapse of some hours appear like the tediousness of weeks and months.

Suddenly he becomes conscious of two objects visible in the surrounding gloom.

They resembled a fixed and obscure flame; they were motionless: though lustrous themselves, they created no illumination around them: this circumstance, added to others which reminded me of similar objects noted on former occasions, immediately explained the nature of what I beheld. These were the eyes of a panther.[1]

He nerves himself to the deed of violence that he hates, and hurls the tomahawk which he had found lying beside him; it hits the animal between the glowing orbs, and he is safe. But right in the exit of the cavern, he discovers four Indians sleeping, and knows that there must be one on watch outside. Huntly has the advantage of a complete surprise; but it is a feat of Defoe-like realism to convince the reader that the raw youth was able by

[1] Chap. xvi.

caution and guile, not to mention his humanitarian instincts, to
do these formidable enemies to death and make his escape. The
narrative proceeds with extreme slowness, for every minutest
thing that impinges upon the actor's consciousness or reacts
within it is recorded; yet the impression is of the swiftness of
action in moments of urgent peril. Such are numerous episodes
in these four novels. Brown wrote two love stories in letters
afterwards, but his characteristic vein had been worked out.

Brown's four novels made a deep impression on the mind of *Mrs*
Shelley,[1] who was early attracted by the German romances of *Shelley*
terror, and composed his first verse and two prose stories under
this inspiration. But, except as evidences of a phase through
which his imagination passed, his two romances of terror,
Zastrozzi (1810) and *St Irvyne, or the Rosicrucian* (1811), have
no importance.[2] It is different with his wife's *Frankenstein* (1818),
an attempt in the same style which has added a misused word to
the English language. Written by a young lady of nineteen, who
had feasted on German ghost stories, this was not likely to show
much originality; yet it had some, and what it owed to current
tradition was such a floating idea as the satanic malignity of her
monster and the ghastly tension of flight and unrelenting pursuit
which had been so tellingly exploited by her father Godwin and
his disciple Brockden Brown. The idea came to her in a dream.
Her preface tells the story of the competition proposed by Byron,
when the party were staying on Lake Leman in 1816, of which
a small fragment by him, Polidori's *Vampire*, and her own
Frankenstein were the result. Her brain was at a standstill, until
the dream gave her a starting-point; then she went straight
ahead, from the words, " it was on a dreary night of November,"
which now begin the fifth chapter. For, later on, at her husband's
suggestion, she unfortunately amplified what at first had been
" only a transcript of the grim terrors " of her dream, and
what should have been a powerful story was padded out to the
dimensions of a novel.

Frankenstein, her scientific experimenter, creates what has

---

[1] Stokoe (31) quotes Peacock's exaggerated statement of this impression.
[2] Stokoe (148-150) shows the erroneousness of Buxton Forman's theory
that these were translations or composed of translations from the German,
though they were the offspring of the *Schauerromane* (see also 145 and 158).

Franken-
stein's
monster

since been called a " Robot," and succeeds in infusing life into his handiwork; but, like the fisherman who broke open the sealed jar and released a genie, he is appalled at the result. All the forces of Gothic terror are let loose when the monster, endued with superhuman strength and stature, not merely breathes and moves, but shows himself to be in possession of individual consciousness and a will of his own, which presently is roused to indignation, fierce resentment, and thirst for revenge. The monster cannot be controlled; he runs amok, an embodiment of the spirit of evil latent in man and in him unsubdued. He must be destroyed at all costs; a terrible hunt begins that ranges all over the habitable globe, and before the hideous creature is got rid of he destroys his maker. Mrs Shelley certainly realized her longing to write a superlative ghost story: " O ! if I could only contrive one which would frighten my reader as I myself had been frightened that night ! " [1] But she works out her terrifying sequel in a manner amusingly characteristic of her parentage: her monster goes morally astray and becomes an outcast and an enemy of mankind through imbibing the doctrines of the sentimentalists and humanitarians. He learns to read, he studies history, he is impressed by *Paradise Lost*, Plutarch's *Lives*, and *The Sorrows of Werther*; his feelings of compassion and revolt from injustice are awakened by his witnessing the wrongs suffered by two unfortunate lovers. Last of all, he peruses the journal kept by Frankenstein during the process of his own creation. He becomes in fine another of the hero-villains, the prey of romantic melancholy, pessimism, the impetus to suicide. Diabolism was logically superadded. For such a being was shut out from society and marked down for hatred. " God, in pity, made man beautiful and alluring, after his own image; but my form is a filthy type of yours, more horrid even from the very resemblance. Satan had his companions, fellow-devils, to admire and encourage him; but I am solitary and abhorred." So he becomes " a malignant devil," more infernal even than the enemy of God and man, who at least " had friends and associates in his desolation." Mrs Shelley ought to have left it at that; she had provided a motive strong enough. The long account of the monster's education in

[1] Her introduction.

ethics and sociology enfeebles the tale of terror, and trenches upon absurdity.

She also wrote a protracted story of Italy in the Middle Ages. *Her other Valperga, or the life and adventures of Castruccio, Prince of Lucca novels and* (1823), and a romance of the distant future *The Last Man* (1825), *Polidori's* not to mention *Perkin Warbeck* (1830), *Lodore* (1835), a novel *pire"* about Shelley and Harriet, and *Falkner* (1837), on the lines of her father's *Caleb Williams*. The few living people who have read these agree that they are painstaking, not incorrect but devoid of historical imagination, too often grandiloquent, and generally dull. As to the other competitors, Byron's effort did not get beyond a fragment,[1] but out of this and his idea for its development Polidori constructed a prosaic story of a sinister young lord, who is killed while travelling in Greece, and reappears as a vampire, feeding on the blood of women.[2] This Lord Ruthven was suggested with other features by Lady Caroline Lamb's vengeful portrait of Byron as the fatal Ruthven Glenarvon, in her notorious but worthless novel *Glenarvon* (1816), of which she herself was of course the heroine. Polidori, perhaps at Byron's instigation, worked in much legendary lore current in Illyria about vampirism; but his is a very mild tale of terror, he was so discreet in eschewing the sensational.

The masterpiece of the school of terror did not appear till the *C. R.* end of the second decade of the nineteenth century, and was the *Maturin* most elaborate and incomparably the finest work of Charles Robert Maturin (1782-1824), a clergyman in Dublin, who wrote some plays, one of which, *Bertram, or the Castle of St Aldobrand* (1816), was a great success both on the stage and in print, though it was heavily criticized by Coleridge,[3] and several other novels besides the famous *Melmoth the Wanderer* (1820). Maturin was an odd person, whose literary ambitions and curious fopperies did not go well with his clerical profession, although he was a good preacher; he was much too fond of society and social frivolities, and yet he was given to daydreaming of a nightmarish

---

[1] Printed as App. IX. (*Letters and Journals*, ed. R. E. Prothero, 1899, 2nd ed., 1904, pp. 446-453).

[2] *The Vampire* (1819).

[3] Chap. xxiii. of the *Biographia Literaria* is devoted to a most elaborate slating, which betrays some unexplained animus.

cast. In fact, there was a good deal that was histrionic about Maturin, which probably accounts for his liking to have people in the room, and people talking, when he was engaged in literary composition. Deeply read in the English romances of terror, he made an eclectic use of his predecessors from the very beginning. In *The Fatal Revenge, or the Family of Montorio* (1807), these were Walpole and Mrs Radcliffe, who gave him his castle of Muralto; the latter's *Sicilian Romance* supplied further hints for the gloomy and mysterious background, and her monk Schedoni, in *The Italian*, was the model for the infamous Schemoli. Schemoli also embodies traits of the Wandering Jew from Godwin's *St Leon* and Lewis's *Monk*. The story is a complicated tissue of revenge, treachery, murder, parricide, suicide, black magic, and the like; it would have been too strong meat for Mrs Radcliffe, but was by no means so brutal in its scare-mongering as Lewis's book, Maturin knowing too well the superior force of suggestion in instilling terror. *The Wild Irish Boy* (1808) and *The Milesian Chief* (1812) were Irish novels that appealed to the patriotic, as Miss Edgeworth and Lady Morgan, author of *The Wild Irish Girl*, were doing at the same time. Though a Protestant and aggressively anti-Catholic, Maturin was a nationalist and an enemy of the Act of Union. In *The Milesian Chief*, the romantic events of which are bound up with the rebellion of 1798, he depicts a ruined chieftain in the west of Ireland living in a Gothic tower, like the Master of Ravenswood, and in love with a girl whose situation in regard to himself is that of Lucy Ashton; in short, this novel had the distinction of supplying Scott with the main lines of *The Bride of Lammermoor* (1819). After a spell of play-writing in which he failed to repeat the success of *Bertram*, Maturin now wrote *Women, or Pour et Contre* (1818), a novel in which there is some domestic realism, some romantic handling of sentimental predicaments without much sentimentalism, and good portraiture of the best society in Dublin and also of narrow-minded Calvinist circles. Then came *Melmoth* (1820).

"*Melmoth the Wanderer*"   Maturin was one of those geniuses who make plagiarism a fine art justified by results. He took the Faust of tradition and of Goethe and cunningly blended him with the mocking spirit of

Mephistopheles, and into the same synthesis went the fearful conception of the Wandering Jew, as it had now been fused by time out of the three legends, of St John who was supposed to have been granted the privilege of tarrying until the second coming of Christ, of Malchus or Ahasuerus who had been condemned to eternal wandering as a punishment, and of the disobedient disciple of the Buddha which came from the Far East.[1] Traces of other myths, such as that of the philosopher's stone and of the elixir of life, are also mingled into Maturin's compound, so many and so various and so skilfully transmuted that it is almost vain to look for his immediate sources in the recent tales of terror or the older repositories from which they drew. He outdoes all other Gothic romanticists in the accumulation of blood-curdling and heart-shaking effects; yet he despises alike the raw head and bloody bones of recent experts in terror and the easy legerdemain of the Radcliffe school, and by sheer psychological finesse plays upon that ineradicable susceptibility to numbing suspense and awe at mysterious contacts with the other world which is the special object of the connoisseur of terror. And he fascinated the most fastidious judges. Not only was he imitated by Victor Hugo in *Han d'Islande* (1823) and continued by Balzac in one of the *Études philosophiques*, *Melmoth reconcilié*, but he also won tributes from and left his mark upon such writers as Nodier, de Vigny, Poe, Baudelaire, Villiers de l'Isle Adam, of whom this might have been expected, and from Thackeray, Miss Mitford, Rossetti, Stevenson, and Oscar Wilde, who are less likely names to be found in such a company.

Melmoth has been wandering since the middle of the seven- *A variant* teenth century, vainly striving to persuade some wretch to relieve *of the* him of his burden of immortality. For there was a proviso in his *Wandering Jew* bargain with the Devil that he might end it and die if another *ing Jew* were willing to pay the price of immortality. To give a straightforward account of this strange being and his centuries of torment would have been beset with obvious artistic difficulties; Maturin accordingly made his book the frame for six recitals. The tortuous involution of his reported narratives inevitably makes

[1] Eino Railo, *The Haunted Castle, a study of the elements of English romanticism* (1927), gives a summary in chap. v.: " The Wandering Jew and the problem of never-ending life."

for obscurity. But, as in a nightmare the transitions are swift and inexplicable yet the horror of each successive phase is none the less vivid and overpowering, so with this.

Opening of the story

His exordium strikes the keynote of foreboding. The young John Melmoth of to-day is summoned from Trinity College, Dublin, to attend the deathbed of his uncle in County Wicklow, and finds the old man under the influence of some overmastering dread; he showed " the ghastliness of fear superadded to that of death." Sent by the miserly old man to unlock a lumber-room and fetch a bottle of Madeira, he notices a portrait on the wall, representing a man of middle age. " There was nothing remarkable in the costume, or in the countenance, but *the eyes*, John felt, were such as one feels they wish they had never seen, and feels they can never forget."[1] Looking closer, by the light of his candle he distinguishes the inscription: " Jno. Melmoth, anno 1646." His uncle questions him, what had he seen? " Only a picture, Sir." " A picture, Sir!—the original is still alive. . . . John, they say I am dying of this and that . . . but, John," and his face looked hideously ghastly, " I am dying of a fright." That night the old man died. After the funeral John finds a manuscript relating the adventures of an Englishman Stanton who had encountered the wanderer in Spain in 1676. Stanton had afterwards been put in a mental hospital, and had been visited by the terrible stranger, who offered him liberty on unspeakable terms. They had parted, and Stanton never met Melmoth again; but the manuscript ended with an illegible passage full of vague premonitions. John gazed at the portrait, which seemed to eye him menacingly. He tore it from the frame; he burnt it; and that night his bed was visited by the figure of his ancestor, whispering, " You have burned me, then; but those are flames I can survive,—I am alive,—I am beside you." In the morning he finds his wrist black and blue, as though from the recent grip of a strong hand.

The Spaniard's story

The next episode is ushered in by a tremendous storm, which recalls to everyone the tempest that shook all England on the night of Cromwell's death; and at the height of the storm a

[1] The baleful eyes are a natural attribute of these semi-supernatural beings, and a regular feature of the various presentments of the Wandering Jew (see Railo, 174-175 and *passim*).

great ship is wrecked. This scene is reminiscent of the storm and wreck in *Bertram*, which Coleridge rightly complained of as dramatically gratuitous, but which make a terrific spectacle. In trying to help the drowning crew Melmoth is nearly drowned himself. A man is saved, one Monçada, a Spaniard. He is another of those who have had dealings with the wanderer, and apart from the horrors in which he himself has been implicated he has read in a manuscript lent him by the Jew Adonijah the history of the " Indian " girl Immalee, who was found by the wanderer dwelling in solitude on a desert island, and who takes her baptismal name of Isidora again when her ill-omened lover carries her off to Spain. In Spain, another chapter of fearful transactions begins[1]; but this curt summary is enough to illustrate the complicated machinery of the novel, which thus evades the chronological difficulties, and hypnotizes the reader with its sudden breaks and enigmas even of identity, so like the fantasies of a morbid dream.

It is hard to say in which of the six main episodes Maturin *The* shows himself most powerful. In " The Tale of the Spaniard," *idyll of* in which Alonzo de Monçada recounts his sufferings at the *Immalee* hands of the Church, his imprisonment in the dungeons of the Inquisition, and his perilous escape, there is an atmosphere of horror that makes one wonder whether Maturin had seen Goya's etchings of subterranean tortures and tribunals, and also a crescendo of sensational incidents that was far beyond Godwin, from whose *St Leon* he no doubt borrowed some.[2] He beat Mrs Radcliffe on her own ground, description of scenery and natural phenomena that accord with and intensify the emotions roused by the drama. In the episode of Immalee and the wanderer, like and yet unlike the love scenes of Ferdinand and Miranda,

---

[1] The demon lover here enacts a part similar to that of the vampires imagined by sadistic story-tellers (see Praz, 118-119).

[2] See Niilo Idman : *C. R. Maturin, his life and works* (1923), especially 228. Killen (66) pointed out that there were echoes here of *La Religieuse* (1796) of Diderot. These have been worked out in detail by Mario Praz (*Review of English Studies*, vi., 1930). Diderot related what he believed to be the facts of Suzanne Simonin's forced entry into a convent, her appeal to the law, trial, and eventual escape. Alonzo de Monçada is similarly inveigled, and his story is manifestly based on that related by Diderot. But Maturin was as anti-Catholic as Diderot, and for literary reasons of his own deepened the colours and exaggerated the sufferings and perils of his hero and the malevolence of his persecutors.

there is more beauty than is often the object of Maturin's pen, but it is beauty strangely conjoined with the menace of evil and the pit. The tropical storm that heralds the stranger's return to Immalee on her island, powerfully depicted, becomes the theme of the maiden's Ossianic song " of desperation and love."

As she ended her melancholy strain, she turned from the spot where the increasing fury of the storm made it no longer possible for her to stand, and turning, met the gaze of the stranger fixed on her. A suffusion, the most rich and vivid, mantled over her from brow to bosom; she did not utter her usual exclamation of joy at his sight, but, with averted eyes and faltering step, followed him as he pointed her to seek shelter amid the ruins of the pagoda. They approached it in silence; and, amid the convulsions and fury of nature, it was singular to see two beings walk on together without exchanging a word of apprehension, or feeling a thought of danger,—the one armed by despair, the other by innocence. . . . " Danger!" said the Indian, while a bright and wild smile irradiated her features; " can there be danger when you are near me?"—" Is there, then, no danger in my presence?—few have met me without dreading, and without feeling it too!" and his countenance, as he spoke, grew darker than the heaven at which he scowled. " Immalee," he added, in a voice still deeper and more thrilling, from the unwonted operation of human emotion in its tones; " Immalee, you cannot be weak enough to believe that I have power of controlling the elements? If I had," he continued, " by the heaven that is frowning at me, the first exertion of my power should be to collect the most swift and deadly of the lightnings that are hissing around us, and transfix you where you stand!"—" Me?" repeated the trembling Indian, her cheek growing paler at his words, and the voice in which they were uttered, than at the redoubling fury of the storm, amid whose pauses she scarce heard them. " Yes—you— you—lovely as you are, and innocent, and pure, before a fire more deadly consumes your existence, and drinks your heart- blood—before you are longer exposed to a danger a thousand times more fatal than those with which the elements menace you —the danger of my accursed and miserable presence!"[1]

" *The Albi- genses* "

Maturin also wrote an historical novel, *The Albigenses* (1824), which met with considerable approval. It is a laboured attempt in the style of Scott, but ultra-romantic, weaving into the vicissi-

[1] Chap. xviii.

tudes of the war between the heretics and the crusading knights, who are depicted by the Protestant clergyman as persecutors, a complicated love story, and wild adventures with werwolves, outlaws, outraged women mad for revenge, and much more of the same sort. The heretics triumph over boastfulness and rashness in two great battles. Maturin does, however, make something of the characters of Count Raymond of Toulouse and his great opponent Simon de Montfort.

Another Irishman, the Rev. George Croly, took up the legend *Other* of the Wandering Jew again, in his high-flown romance, *Salathiel,* *tales of* *the Immortal* (1827), and the poet Moore mixed Orientalism and *terror and* Gothic terror in *The Epicurean* (1827) expanded out of his poem *of the* *burlesques* *Alciphron*; but he fell very far short of *Vathek*. Scott, both in *genre* his early poems and in many of his subsequent novels, notably in *The Monastery, Woodstock, Peveril of the Peak, A Legend of Montrose, The Bride of Lammermoor,* and *Redgauntlet,* besides several ghost stories, dealt liberally in Gothic effects. But that is a subject for later pages, together with the survival of the same element in the novels of Harrison Ainsworth, Captain Marryat, Lord Lytton, and many later novelists. This chapter cannot conclude, however, without some allusion to the satires called forth by the absurdities of the romanticists. Beckford's skits have already been mentioned, and the reader need not be reminded of *Northanger Abbey,* which Jane Austen wrote in 1797-1798 although it was not published until 1818. She had no doubt finished it when a direct satire on the school of terror appeared in the *Anti-Jacobin* (1798), in the form of four acts of a burlesque *The Rovers, or the Double Arrangement,* with introductory discourse and notes.[1]

The song chanted by Rogero, to the clang of his chains in *"The* cadence, appears in many anthologies: *Rovers"*

> Whene'er with haggard eyes I view
> This Dungeon, that I'm rotting in.

But the play is not well known. It is the wittiest of all the attacks on both the sentimentality and the terrorism of those who learned from the German schools—

[1] *Anti-Jacobin,* 4th ed., 1799, ii. 415-430 and 446-461.

The GERMAN Schools—where no dull maxims bind
The bold expansion of th'electric mind.
Fix'd to no period, circled by no space,
He leaps the flaming bounds of time and place:
Round the dark confines of the Forest raves,
With *gentle* Robbers stocks his gloomy caves;
Tells how prime MINISTERS are shocking things,
And *reigning* Dukes as bad as tyrant Kings;
How to *two* Swains *one* Nymph her vows may give,
And how *two* Damsels with *one* Lover live!

The sexual arrangements hit at by the quip in the title, with what has since been called the " divine discontent " which, in the eyes of anti-Jacobins, identified romanticists and revolutionaries —the " wild desire of undefinable latitude and extravagance "— are brilliantly caricatured. Others than the German school are bantered in the meeting of Matilda and Cecilia, the latter just alighted from a post-wagon:

Cecilia. Your countenance grows animated, my dear Madam.
Matilda. And yours too is glowing with illumination.
C. I had long been looking out for a congenial Spirit!— my heart was withered—but the beams of yours have rekindled it.
M. A sudden thought strikes me—Let us swear an eternal friendship.
C. Let us agree to live together!
M. Willingly. *(With rapidity and earnestness.)*
C. Let us embrace. *(They embrace.)*
M. Yes; I too have lov'd! You, too, like me, have been forsaken! *(Doubtingly, and as if with a desire to be informed.)*
C. Too true!
Both. Ah, these Men! These Men!

Other caricatures and extravaganzas Even Maria Edgeworth made fun of the current heroine, in *Angelina, or l'Amie inconnue,* one of her *Moral Tales* (1801). Mary Charlton, in *Rosetta, or Modern Occurrences* (1799), and Benjamin Thompson in *The Florentines* (1808) turned fatuous seriousness into farce, while Sarah Green followed the example of Mrs Lennox, in *Romance Readers and Romance Writers* (1810), describing the follies of a clergyman's daughter who has lost her common sense through reading too much fiction. The best of these extravaganzas would have been *The Heroine, or the adventures of Cherubina* (1813), by Eaton Stannard Barrett, if the writer had not carried the joke so far that he is presently flogging a dead horse. Hardly one of the novelists touched upon in this volume escapes his darts. He pokes fun at Richardson, Dr Johnson, Fanny Burney, and Rousseau, along with Mrs Radcliffe and the terrorists. Cherubina finds out that she is a heroine, and determines to live up to the character. She never speaks, without a proper sense that every syllable is destined to appear in print. She knows that certain events in

the life of every heroine are predestined, as their regular and unremitting recurrence fully proves. Of those events, the most prominent and indispensable, are: 1st. Her meeting with a hero. 2nd. Her loving him, and his loving her. 3rd. His rescuing her from peril, at a moment when she fancies him far away. 4th. Her finding every individual with whom she converses, implicated in her plot, and a friend, or a foe, or a near relation. 5th. If of mysterious origin, her being first reduced to extremities; then her discovering her family, and lastly, her attaining riches, rank, and marriage. Since, therefore, an established series of incidents are fated to befall all heroines, and since I am a heroine, it follows that I need not so much consider whether my conduct be prudent or discreet, as whether it be graceful, and fit for immortality. The grand criterion is, " how will it read? " [1]

Cherubina disowns her yeoman father, discovers that she is entitled to a loftier and more aristocratic name, and outruns the Female Quixote and all her other prototypes in absurdity. The inset piece " Il Castello di Grimgothico," memoirs of her grotesque mother, the Lady Hysterica Belamour, is a neat burlesque of the popular drama of terror.

[1] *The Heroine*, ed. Michael Sadleir (1927), 44-45.

CHAPTER IX

THE NOVEL OF DOCTRINE

The novel IT was natural and inevitable that so handy a resource as the
of purpose novel should be utilized by reformers and revolutionaries for
propaganda and polemics. The novel of purpose is the converse
of the regular novel; if it were purposive fiction and nothing else,
doctrine would be enforced and illustrated in it by an invented
version of reality. Holcroft gives the formula incidentally in
his preface to *Bryan Perdue*:

> To exemplify this doctrine [the general and adventitious
> value of human life, and the moral tendency of penal laws] it was
> necessary that the hero of the fable should offend those laws, that
> his life should be in jeopardy, and that he should possess not only
> a strong leaven of virtue, but high powers of mind, such as to
> induce the heart to shrink at the recollection that such a man
> might have been legally put to death.

Political and social writings having a strong revolutionary or
anti-revolutionary bias were nothing new in England; think of
Piers Plowman and the Elizabethan pamphleteers, of Milton's
tracts, the philosophical and yet definitely controversial writings
of Hobbes, Locke, or Hume, the polemical books and tracts and
articles of Bolingbroke and Swift, sometimes approximating to
the form and method of fiction. Even recently, Amory and
Henry Brooke had written works that could be called novels
only because there was no other category nondescript enough to
receive them. Now, as the end of the century was approaching,
with the economic and social disturbances caused by the progress
of the industrial revolution, and with the clash of ideas and the
stirrings of sedition due to the epoch-making events going on
across the Channel, a copious output of polemical fiction was
the likeliest and not the least wholesome thing to happen.

Thus a whole school of novelists can be differentiated, applying *Women* the current domestic, and even romantic and sentimental, fiction *novelists* to their own purposes. The leaders were Bage, Holcroft, and *and ideas* Godwin; they were followed by Mrs Inchbald, Mrs Opie, and others, and it has already been seen that Charlotte Smith did not dissemble her connexion with the same liberal group. Close scrutiny, in truth, would show that such theoretical tendencies were a very natural outcome of female authorship in this branch of literature. Women are sure to concentrate upon domestic fiction, and to seize the opportunities this offers for edification. The sex is more sentimental, more moralistic, more censorious, than men. Hence the insistence on fine sentiments, elegant taste, delicacy, high principle, the sense of duty, the dependence of happiness upon character and conduct. Here are the germs of the problem novel; they could be discerned in several of Charlotte Smith's stories, and even in the high-pitched novels of sensibility. They can be seen, too, in the emergence of a definite subject, idea, point of view, especially in novels by women, women having a graver sense of the issues involved, feeling their responsibility as authors more acutely, disliking the comic attitude of a Fielding, which they think flippant, though at bottom it may be more serious than their own earnest but less catholic vision. But, although there are women amongst them, the leading writers in the group now under consideration are men.

The curious novels of Dr John Moore (1729-1802) may be *Dr John* taken first, though they are not of earlier date than the others; *Moore:* but, at any rate, they show how natural was the transition *"Zeluco"* from the observation of life to theory, from fiction to criticism, doctrine, and mild propagandism. He is solely remembered now, if remembered at all, for his *Zeluco: various views of human nature taken from life and manners, foreign and domestic* (1786). Such a title renders a general description superfluous; but it does not particularize the central purpose, which is to delineate a villain. *Zeluco*, in fact, belongs to the interesting half-dozen novels embracing *Jonathan Wild, Ferdinand Count Fathom,* and that later example *Barry Lyndon.* It is not, however, an ironical portrait: Zeluco is not presented in the mock character of hero, although he is stripped of all the attributes of romance. Nor is this monster of flagitiousness, selfish, cruel, vengeful, unscrupulous though he be, represented as entirely devoid of conscience; the candour and goodness of others, especially when they have no suspicion that he does not share their feelings of humanity, do awaken his sacred sensibilities and torture him with remorse. Moore was more of a psychologist than a novelist, and he avoided one of the pitfalls of sentimental fiction. Thus the commiseration of a man who is not a complete egoist plunges Zeluco into a despairing soliloquy:

" Happy man ! " said he, with a deep sigh, " who can look back with pleasure and approbation : and forward with tranquillity and hope.—What false estimates are formed by mankind! This Bertram they will consider as an unfortunate man, yet he has never been unhappy, and has found many sources of enjoyment unknown to me. I have been reckoned remarkably fortunate, although I have never known what happiness is.—His life has been devoted to duty, and mine to enjoyment; yet it is evident he has had more enjoyment in his pursuit than I ever had in mine."

Psycho-logical pretensions   The book is the history of Zeluco; but Zeluco marries Laura, and in the intrigues by which that marriage is brought about, and still more in the troubles of their conjugal life, the book changes its character. In structure it is not by any means faultless, the old-fashioned habit of digressions and episodes giving it a loose-ness from which even the picaresque is free in Fielding's and Smollett's examples. Best of these episodes is the one centring in the two Scots, Targe and Buchanan, who respect each other so intolerantly as fellow-countrymen and fight so remorselessly over the reputation of Mary Queen of Scots, the national bone of contention. These serio-comic figures are more alive, and so are the contrasted pair Father Mulo and Father Pedro, than those on which Moore concentrates his psychological vision. On the whole, he does not go beyond the graphic portrayal of types; he conceives a general disposition of mind, and shows it acting in accordance with the general probabilities of human nature. Zeluco and his persecuted wife, her brother Seidlitz and his friend Carlostein and Signora Sforza, are reasonable enough as portraits in the rough, but hardly finished personalities. Dr Moore was a travelled man, but his ability to render national and racial traits has been overpraised. He was too easily satisfied with a mere silhouette.

His social and political criticism leads him into a detailed *Miscel-* study of slavery in America, and into some hostile sallies at *laneous* Roman Catholicism, as in the dialogue between the priest and *criticism* the soldier, who begs the former to give his dying comrade *and satire* absolution and not waste valuable time on theology.

" God love your soul, my dear father," interrupted the soldier, " give him absolution in the first place, and convince him afterwards; for, upon my conscience, if you bother him much longer, the poor creature's soul will slip through your fingers."

The priest, who was a good-natured man, did as the soldier requested.

" Now," said the soldier, when the ceremony was over, " now, my honest fellow, you may bid the devil kiss your b . . . e, for you are as sure of heaven as your master is of hell; where, as this reverend father will assure you, he must suffer to all eternity."

Moore wielded a polished, terse, and caustic style, which makes every page enjoyable as literature. He set an admirable fashion by heading each chapter with a pregnant saying from La Rochefoucauld, Shakespeare, Pope, Horace, or their peers; and those sayings are admirably illustrated by what follows. How neat, for instance, is the " Gaudet equis canibusque," for the young fellow whose inducement to enter holy orders is his fondness for hunting and shooting, and who hopes by the influence of a noble lord to " obtain a tolerable living in a hunting country " !

In *Edward : various views of human nature taken from life* " *Edward* " *and manners chiefly in England* (1796), fiction can be seen approximating more and more to the discussion novel. It is a loose-knit story, reaching its termination, only after a thousand pages, in the recognition of the foundling Edward as the lost son of aristocratic parents,[1] simultaneously with his marriage to the wealthy girl who is worthy of his perfections—a sprig of the Grandisons in a *Tom Jones* plot. The reader may easily lose his way through the supernumerary complications tacked on to the main thread, and the bewildering crowd of characters, new ones

[1] The strawberry mark of *Joseph Andrews* is changed for a mulberry.

coming in at all stages till it is difficult to distinguish one individual from the other, especially as they are all mere types of integrity or dishonesty, altruism or self-indulgence, sense or stupidity, and so on. Moore never loses a chance of girding at plutocracy. The Barnets are fair game, though the satire does not help on the story. They begin with the City clerk, later Sir Robert Barnet, who marries his master's daughter, amasses a colossal fortune, of which he loses half in a speculative attempt to double it, leaving what is left—and enough too—to George Barnet, an indolent, gluttonous skinflint, married to a wife a thousand times too good for him, who adopts the foundling, needless to say at her petition.

More criticism and reforming zeal

But the comments are better than the story. Penetrating are the remarks on real and sham benevolence, illustrated by the benevolence of the poor; admirable is the advice on self-education, which should be founded on natural tastes and one's particular bent; thoroughly enlightened the discourse on cruelty to animals, blood sports, cock-fighting, crimping salmon, skinning eels alive; and, again, on duelling, gaming, debts of honour, the state of society, particularly French immorality before the Revolution: but all this is hardly in place in a novel. He takes up such grievances as the wrongs of the military, the absurdity of regulations forcing soldiers to purchase their dress and other necessaries out of starvation pay. And, like Bage, Moore hates a lord; and when he introduces such a freak of nature paints him as cruel, base, cowardly. The satire of the medical profession, of which there was plenty also in *Zeluco*, is better founded if not more just.[1]

" Mordaunt "

At first one seems to be reading Beckford or Byron's letters of travel in *Mordaunt : sketches of life, character, and manners in various countries ; including the Memoirs of a French lady of*

---

[1] No doubt Moore kept a notebook of good stories, and had to drag some of them in by the heels. The point of the conversation with the French officer on the reason why Petrarch was never married to Laura is not in the least relevant to the matter in hand. " ' The reason that he assigned for declining the Pope's advice,' resumed Clifton, ' was lest the familiarities of the married state should abate the enthusiasm of his admiration, and the ardour of his love.' ' Parbleu ! ' exclaimed the officer, ' voilà un animal bien délicat ; it is,' added he, ' as if a man was to refuse to eat his dinner, lest it should spoil his appetite ' " (vol. ii. 246-247).

quality (1800); but later on it is clear that the literary ancestor was Grandison. Mordaunt has the virtues of a cultivated man of the world, wit, chivalry, and courage; he is the brother of a nobleman; but he has what Richardson would have deplored, easy morals with women. At Vevey, after the Reign of Terror, he has the good fortune to help a marquise to escape to England. Incidentally, he tries to profit by her apparent *tendresse* for him, but finds that she is not as the French ladies of his pre-conception, but a veritable Amelia. The rest is the story of the lovely Horatia Clifford, an English pendant to the marquise, and Mordaunt's long-deferred identification of this desirable lady with the fair unknown whom he had fallen in love with on wit-nessing an act of great charity. The sequel is the ordinary one, but it is reached after unconscionable delays.

No doubt, Moore's purpose was social criticism; hence it is unfair to object that he deals in nothing but types. Here, except the romantic figures, these are not prepossessing. Lady Deanport, the unscrupulous matchmaking mother, is not of a species unknown elsewhere in fiction; nor is the worthless rake her son; nor James Grindill, the toad-eater, who talks like a moralist, but is weak and mean, and goes to the dogs. The ugliest personage is the hypocritical, backbiting, intriguing Mrs Demure, whose machinations being detected do the lovers a service in bringing them together and confounding the evildoers. Moore's contempt for politicians—if not for the intelligent reader—vents itself too crudely in Lady Deanport's letter of advice to her creature Grindill, who is thinking of that career:

Satirical portraits

You could not employ the time better than in composing speeches, and pronouncing them before a mirror; by which you will acquire becoming gesticulation, and accustom yourself to retain a series of arguments and illustrations in your memory. You will do well to prepare harangues for both sides; because there is no knowing which party may be uppermost by the time you shall obtain your seat. And, after you have chosen your side, and shown under what banner you mean to fight, though it will be expected that you should make some kind of declaration regarding your future conduct, it will be worth your while to make yourself master of as many equivocal phrases as the English language admits, and to use general expressions, that in case of your finding it for your interest to adopt opposite measures, you may have little difficulty in explaining away the obvious sense of your former declarations.[1]

Her efforts to detach her son Lord Deanfort from Miss Clifford by hinting that the young lady was too clever for a man of his modest pretensions, are put in the same ironical shape. " I once thought of culling a few witticisms from Joe Miller," she tells a confidential friend, " and repeating them to Lord Deanport as repartees of Miss Clifford; but recollecting that his lordship was better acquainted with that book than with most others, I judged it would be safer to draw from a fountain into which he never dipped; and, having spoken of Miss Clifford as a lady of uncommon erudition and sagacity, I actually repeated two of the proverbs of Solomon as observations of hers. This had not the effect I expected; he saw nothing alarmingly sagacious in either, and said, ' If Miss Clifford can make no wiser observations than those, she runs no risk of being drowned as a witch ! ' " [2]

Wit and aphorisms   Moore lets fall many good aphorisms, along with some platitudes. " It is the business of knaves to make others believe that they are honest." " Though a man may deceive the rest of the world in that point, yet, were he as cunning as the Devil, he cannot deceive himself." Note the gibe at the opponents of the anti-slavery crusade: " If slaves are treated with what they call humanity, how are we to have sugar? "—a sentiment put in the mouth of Mrs Demure. But he was prone to forget his own maxims: " Of all the gifts of Nature to the human race, wit is the most envied, and the least forgiven "; and this implied in the sketch of Mr Proser, " who deals in nothing but sense, and that of the most solid kind; but he drew forth his commodity in such profusion, that he oppressed the whole company." [3]

---

[1] Volume ii. 167-168.   [2] *Ibid.* 286-287.

[3] The Spanish scenes are excellent. An insolent alcalde takes sides with his countryman against the Englishman who has been robbed by a muleteer, but is cowed by a dictatorial military officer, and has to send his rascally friend to gaol. Then there is the parish priest who declines to be browbeat by a fat friar for speaking to a heretic—" That is his misfortune : it would be strange for one of our cloth to refuse to speak with a man because he is unfortunate." On her arrival in England, the marquise is surprised to encounter no robbers between Portsmouth and London ; but travellers acknowledge " that the innkeepers, in a great measure, supplied the omissions of the highwaymen." Evidently it was the same in 1800 as Fielding had found it in this respect half-a-century before.

Moore, and still more his senior Robert Bage (1728-1801), in *Robert*
spite of an unfortunate discursiveness, did something to naturalize *Bage :*
the *roman philosophique* of Voltaire and his school on English soil. *the*
Bage was a paper manufacturer, whose affairs apparently went *"roman*
philo-
wrong when he was past middle age, and he sought recreation *sophique"*
and no doubt an opening for the ventilation of his discontents in
a series of novels, mostly couched in the form of letters. He was
accused of voicing personal resentment at being mulcted by the
excise on his raw materials, to help to pay for a war of which
he strongly disapproved. But he was never mercenary himself,
and branded avarice wherever he perceived it. He was a genial,
philanthropic, speculative, somewhat whimsical lover of his
species, with a turn for sentiment which he was shrewd enough
to smile at, whilst clear-sighted enough to acknowledge the good
tendencies in sentimentalism, especially as compared with the
cynical egotism of the knowing and dissolute. He delighted in
tales of paradoxical generosity and of unexpected conversions, as
well as of unbalanced natures chastened by experience of the
world and tempered to a fine humanity. In his novels, a crowd of
intimate friends exchange reports of their adventures and opinions
of the people round about them. For this, the epistolary method,
though tedious to the cursory reader, for the leisured student of
life is not inapt. He is as diffuse as Moore, and equally vivacious;
he deals in the stuff of the later discussion novel, letting his sportive
instinct have its way, even if it interferes with his more serious
intentions. He is just as prolix in his story-telling; there is no
lack of incident, or of anecdotes having a satisfactory ending and
an appropriate moral, though the bearing on the main theme is
ofttimes far to seek. His chosen young men always meet with
injustice and misfortune through their intemperate rectitude, or,
at least, the sensibility and loftiness of mind that aims high but
does not always hit the mark. He sees to it that poetic justice
shall provide them with even more than their due in the final issue.

His first novel, *Mount Henneth* (1781), is a parcel of love *" Mount*
stories loosely tied up, with a desultory story brought to a proper *Henneth"*
consummation by the lord of Henneth Castle, a mansion on the
Welsh coast where the philanthropic Foston, in his old age, gathers
round him a little utopia, or pantisocracy, or Thelema, of friends,

to whom he plays providence and dispenses wisdom as a modern Solon. Foston, like most of his heroes, appears first as an ill-tempered, impetuous young fellow; and, after a knockabout career in India, acquires tolerance and most of the other virtues. He is a merchant; Bage consistently does honour to the commercial and industrial classes. His views on social reform are set forth both by reasoning and by example. There are two stories of heart-rending pathos. That of Foston and the beautiful Cara is meant to eradicate a deep-seated prejudice. She is the daughter of a rich Persian, and was raped by native soldiers in the military operations after the Black Hole of Calcutta. Bage puts the philosophical view of her case. She complains, " In all those English books your goodness has procured for me, I find it is the leading idea : women who have suffered it must die, or be immured for ever." The novelists make out that any crime save this may be expiated. But, she pleads, " It is to be found in books, sir; and I hope, for the honour of the human intellect, little of it will be found anywhere else." The other is the story of Miss Melton, captured by an English privateer from an American, and left destitute in the hands of a brothel-keeper. The American turns out not to have been sunk and drowned; he had saved his ship and his fortune by a stratagem, and recovers his lost child in time to endow her fittingly for marriage with one of the company mustered at Mount Henneth. Four couples take part in the wedding march. The philoprogenitive Bage in this respect believed in " the more the merrier." The author's pacifist views are doubtless the motive for the many incidents of carnage, rapine, brutality, and wholesale injustice, supposed to have been perpetrated during the American War and the troubles in India.

" Barham Downs " Barham Downs (1784) is in the main a satire of individualism : " A man must either herd with his species, or hate them." It consists of garrulous, free-and-easy, readable letters, canvassing the different points of view of correspondents who are originals intellectually, if not strongly marked by anything but ideas. The prominent theme is " the vices of the herd of quality," and the person who comes in for most obloquy is a profligate Lord Winterbottom, who among other misdeeds carries off the lady beloved of the hero, and by employing hypnotic suggestion makes

her believe herself his wedded wife. There are other incidents that ought to be exciting, but are a little too well arranged. The doings of the noble villain and his pimping parasite verge on burlesque; and the other example of perversity, the surly, unsocial crank, who shuts himself up with his useless mathematical problems, indifferent to his wife and to the responsibilities of his wealth, hardly rings true, especially when in a fit of remorse and magnanimity he hands over his fortune to his ruined brother. This is one of the sudden changes from selfishness to the virtues of a saintly reformer in which the perfectibilians firmly believed. Of course, he becomes Bage's mouthpiece, like the rest of the good, that is, the middle-class, characters, in their dialectical and practical campaign against the fast set.

Bage usually has one great man in each of his books; in *Barham Downs* it is Isaac Arnold, " by birth a man, by religion a Quaker, taught to despise all titles that are not the marks of virtue." In *James Wallace* (1788) it is the Liverpool apothecary and outspoken philosopher Paracelsus Holman, connected by lineage with the sister of Roger Bacon, whence his " distilling and subliming propensities," and his unorthodox judgments and downrightness in pronouncing them. He is the most pungent of a large group of correspondents. His post, however, is simply that of mentor to Wallace, another specimen of youthful pride, " repining and discontent," joined to uprightness and generosity, who in the course of extraordinary ups and downs acquires the " firmness of mind " required of Bage's approved types of manhood. He fails as an attorney, ruining himself in the world's opinion as " a lawyer convicted of honesty." Then he is found enjoying peace of mind and freedom from care as the footman told off to the special service of Miss Lamounde, the most winning in a little cluster of marriageable heroines. The conclusion may be guessed; but it is not reached for a long while yet. Among other exciting events, Wallace finds himself in command of a ship that brilliantly repels an Algerine pirate—an incident lifted from one of Marmontel's *Contes moraux*.[1] Later he sees the inside of a Spanish gaol. But there is no more trouble when he is found to be the missing heir of a wealthy Scottish baronet.

James Wallace

[1] I.e. *La Mauvaise mère.*

*Minia-
tures of
charactery*

There are some charming vignettes; for instance, the parish priest who declines the offer of a fat living because he is sixty and will not leave the parishioners who love him as their friend and counsellor, and therefore begs the preferment for a lean curate with a wife and six children, and " every merit, save that which doubles the value of all merit—money." His sermons are simple, plain, and practical. " What can I do better, Sir Everard? " he asks his would-be benefactor; " my aim is to make my parishioners good husbands, good fathers, and good friends; not good propounders of mystery. It is true, they don't think me a very good preacher on this account; and now and then a straggler steals off to a neighbouring parish, to hear about election, reprobation, and grace; about the littleness of works, and the bigness of faith; about incarnation, atonement, with a long *et cetera*, all which I postpone explaining to my flock till I understand a little more of them myself."

*" Man as
he is "*

In *Man as he is* (1792) Bage discards the epistolary form. Sir George Paradyne, not yet twenty-one, inherits title and fortune, and to the annoyance of a frivolous, spendthrift, and querulous mother equips himself with a tutor, Mr Lindsay, who is a bit of an original, and proceeds to see the world and spend his money. Sir George falls in love with the adorable Miss Coleraine; but, unfortunately, does not offer his hand as well as his heart, and mortally wounds her. The tale, such as it is, consists of his long and desperate efforts to retrieve his folly, his backslidings among the frivolous and profligate in London and Paris, his ill-starred rencounters with the lady when he happens to be in the most compromising situations, and his long-delayed pardon. The novel of three or four volumes was now an established institution, and even a slight story had to be padded out to full dimensions.

*" Herms-
prong "*

Bage's last, and the only one that is much remembered, was a companion novel to this, his *Hermsprong, or man as he is not* (1796), which belongs to the same subversive class of fiction as the *Lettres persanes*, Voltaire's *Ingénu*, or Brooke's *Fool of Quality*. Now that the revolution in France had taken what the idealists regarded as lamentable courses, and anti-revolutionary feeling in this country was at its height, Bage shows himself

more of a radical and an idealist than ever; but, at the same
time, his common sense and his experience of men and affairs
keep him sane and practical, and a formidable critic of things as
they are. Hermsprong was brought up among North American
savages, and has been inured to simplicity of life, the practice
of virtue, muscular prowess, and, above all, sincerity and truth-
telling. He is the critical observer from another sphere, imagined
by Montesquieu and the rest, who has read Rousseau and Voltaire,
watched the course of the French Revolution, and sees through
the pretences of English conservatism and the veneer of respecta-
bility. He is a terrible and utterly fearless plain-speaker, and being
rich he has no scruples about saying what he thinks, although
he possesses the courtliness alleged to be the distinguishing
mark of the best sort of savage. He is unquestionably better-
mannered than the rakes and sycophants with whom he is thrown
in contact. For reasons that afterwards transpire, Hermsprong
buys a residence on the borders of Cornwall, under the nose of
a purse-proud nobleman, Lord Grondale, with whom he quickly
finds himself at odds. Lord Grondale's daughter loves him, but
is too high-principled to marry her father's foe, least of all when
it turns out that Hermsprong is the long-lost heir to her father's
property and title. But her scruples are smoothed away by the
opportune death of this nobleman.

It might be thought that the thrice-happy endings Bage always *The*
provides stultified his argument. But he was not foolish enough *method*
to regard a sociological novel as an argument: he was well *of Bage's*
aware that a story is not a logical demonstration, although a new *sociological*
view of the world may have drastic effects upon the receptive *fiction*
mind. His method was partly satire, and partly interpellation
and inquiry. This is a satire on the pretences of birth and riches,
an exposure of the absurdity of such claims when they run counter
to those of the body politic and are satisfied at the expense of
real worth. His plain-speaker registers many amusing hits;
he often calls to mind the " dangerous sayings " of Halifax. But
the others: the honest countryman, the candid young lady, the
debauched peer with his led parson and other hangers-on, are
only automatons galvanized by an idea, or horrid examples of
the corruption and depravity of a world gone to the bad. Only

some form of communism could have removed all the injustices of the social scheme as he envisaged it; but he never preached any such root-and-branch reconstruction: he was a thorough Englishman, who nursed his idealism, but asked for nothing more than the abolition of a host of grievances.

Thomas Holcroft   Thomas Holcroft (1745-1809), who was the son of a shoe-maker and horse-dealer, and gained an uncertain living as a strolling player, a cobbler, and in other humble situations, before he turned to the no less uncertain pursuit of literature, is another of those thinkers into whose heart the iron had entered. When he began writing novels, he had a fund of experience as realistic as that of Bage, and much more miscellaneous. Holcroft had been in the depths. Both of them knew the middle levels thoroughly; but, as to the upper, they looked at these through a glass whose distortions they never took the trouble to correct. His best book is his own *Memoirs*, which Hazlitt completed, and from it is evident the large amount of autobiography that went into two at least of his novels, *Alwyn, or the gentleman comedian* (1780), and *Hugh Trevor* (1794-1797). Holcroft, at the time French revolutionary doctrines were reacting upon the open-minded in this country, became a member of the Society for Constitutional Information; and the story is well known how he heard that his name was on a list of persons to be indicted for high treason, along with those of Horne Tooke, Thomas Hardy, and others, and offered himself for examination; how he was dismissed without trial, and ever afterwards lay under the stigma of being an "unconvicted felon."

"Alwyn" autobio- graphical   Hilkirk, in his first novel *Alwyn*, is Holcroft himself, and the autobiography obviously full of facts. The fortunes of a troop of travelling players, the writer's application to Foote for a part in his company, the very plays he rehearsed and the places where he appeared, Kendal, Dublin, Hereford, Leeds, all are particularized. The whole economy of a travelling company is displayed, with the oddities they encounter in their audiences, their temporary hosts, their critics friendly or the reverse. It is a clumsy novel, and where Holcroft invents he flouts probability; but his lively and colloquial style makes the best of an immature effort. It was a dozen years later that he published *Anna St Ives*

(1792), the best exposition of his revolutionary idealism, a
year before Godwin's *Political Justice*, which, in some sense, it
anticipates, so much more practical and moderate though it be.

Anna St Ives, like most of Bage's novels, is in letters; and "*Anna
the form proves less awkward in Holcroft's hands because his St Ives*"
experience on the stage taught him to interject a full measure of
pithy dialogue. But he did not aim at realism. As Hazlitt put it
in continuing the *Memoirs*:

> The principal characters in the novel (at least those which
> were intended by the author to be the most prominent) are not
> natural, but ideal beings. In fact, they are not so properly
> characters (that is, distinct individuals) as the vehicles of certain
> general sentiments, or machines put in action, as an experiment
> to show how these general principles would operate in particular
> situations. Frank Henley, and Anna St Ives, are the philosophical
> hero and heroine of the work.[1]

Anna, though the daughter of a baronet, is a champion of social
equality, a paragon of moral and intellectual virtue, and very
sure of herself, because she has evolved a complete social
philosophy. These are the excellences for which Frank Henley,
son of her father's estate agent, dares to love her. She responds,
but hesitates on account of their disparity of station. Then
another aspirant arrives on the scene, Coke Clifton, grandson of
a peer, a clever, caustic young fellow, a devil-may-care Lovelace,
who jeers at "the gardener's son," and is dumbfounded when
he is told by Anna to cultivate the lofty principles that actuate
his rival. Her father, too, is nonplussed by her independence, and
remonstrates with Anna. "Mr Clifton is a gentleman, both by
birth and education." "That I own, sir, may be a great disadvantage, but——" "Disadvantage, child!" After talking it
over with Henley, however, whom she owns that she loves,
Anna decides that she will do the best service to society by
accepting Clifton. Henley and she make an honest effort to win
him over to their ways of thinking, and he makes a pretence of
being persuaded. But by this time he has changed his mind
about marrying a girl with ideas, and following up the philosophic
argument tries to convert Anna to the doctrine of free love.

[1] Book IV., chap. I.

He acts the Lovelace so far as to carry her off, and tries to force her; he manages to have Frank Henley shut up in a madhouse. His letters to his henchman Fairfax at this juncture recall to the echo those of Lovelace. But the pair of young philosophers return good for evil. Henley repays his blows by telling him that there is nothing to forgive, and, though he has refused to fight a duel, vindicates his courage by saving Clifton's life. The aristocrat has to acknowledge his misdeeds and admit the superiority of the social values that he has outraged. The idealists marry, and leave him on the road to becoming a good and useful member of society.

"*Hugh* *Trevor*"

Hugh Trevor (1794-1797), the account of the making of a philosophical radical, is a more realistic performance; it is an honest if not quite an impartial study of actualities, as they appeared to Holcroft. In the picaresque earlier chapters, if not beyond, he is manifestly relating something very like his own adventures. Hugh's misfortunes after his father's bankruptcy, his being bound apprentice, his dreadful sufferings and narrow escapes in a crime-stained underworld, at once recall Holcroft's own memoirs and the darkest stories of Crabbe. After hardships on the road, and persevering attempts to get an education, punctuated by some " strange and terrible " adventures which have a Gothic tinge, the boy is adopted by his rich grandfather and sent to Oxford. But he finds that the wheedling and rascality of low life are no worse than the drinking and drabbing going on among the undergraduates or the shameless depravity of pimping tutors. Then he goes to London, and becomes secretary to a politician, only to find him a place-seeking turncoat. His introduction to a bishop and a dean is no less disenchanting; they are a pair of foul-mouthed sots, implicated in the most profligate intrigues. Trevor proposes to expose both the earl and the bishop, but is dissuaded by his wiser friend Turl: there is better work to do than to castigate vice. But his quarrels with these patrons lead to persecution on every hand; he is expelled from the university, and before long finds himself unable to earn his bread.

His conversations with the friendly and sympathetic but more experienced Turl show that Holcroft was a more sober and reasonable person than the cold-blooded Godwin, whose *Political*

Justice he thought a foolish book. There are plenty of violent *The*
jeremiads; here is a hit at our legal system :   *making*
                                                                   of a
   "Why, Mr Trevor, you imagine yourself in Turkey, telling *philo-*
your tale to a Cady, who decides according to his notions of right *sophical*
and wrong; and not pleading in the presence of a bench of English *radical*
judges, who have twice ten thousand volumes to consult as their
guides which leave them no opinion of their own. It is their duty
to pronounce sentence as the statute-books direct; or, as in the
case I have cited, according to precedent, time immemorial."
   " And this is what you call law ? "
   " Ay, and sound law too."
   " Why then, damn the——"
   " You do right to stop short, sir."

Then there are fulminating pages on such topics as getting into
Parliament, " the seduction of young orators, the influence of the
Crown, and the corruption of our glorious constitution." An
election, as it was in those days, is described, with all its accompaniments of undue influence and wholesale bribery. Even the
temperate Turl has no good word for the hereditary legislator.
" What is a peer of the realm, but a man educated in vice, nurtured
in prejudice from his earliest childhood, and daily breathing the
same infectious air he first respired ? " But Trevor learns by
experience and reflection that the moral revolution necessary to
effect a human revolution cannot be achieved in a day; and after
all his errors and violence he becomes another Frank Henley—or
another Thomas Holcroft. The writer had to admit afterwards
that he weakened his case by following the example of Bage, and
providing his hero with a long-lost uncle and a wealthy inheritance,
which enabled him to marry his Olivia. But even revolutionaries
had to conform to the circulating-library code.

   His last novel, *Memoirs of Bryan Perdue* (1805), was designed *" Bryan*
to persuade legislators " to consider the general and the adventi- *Perdue "*
tious value of human life, and the moral tendency of our penal
laws," from the incidence of which Holcroft had suffered as an
" unconvicted felon."   He denounces indiscriminate capital
punishment, and incidentally seconds the efforts of the Methodists,
and of John Howard and Elizabeth Fry, to reform the prisons.
The delinquent and victim is a man of good morals and fine

intellect, who commits an offence against the laws, but raises natural indignation " that such a man might have been legally put to death." His life is saved, providentially, and the conclusion is a picture of married bliss in Jamaica.

William Godwin William Godwin (1756-1836) became a novelist by accident, his first novel, the far-famed *Caleb Williams*,[1] if some early romances are omitted which he was glad to forget, being a sort of by-product of his huge treatise *Political Justice* (1793), and the rest called for, so he opined, to sustain the reputation which it had brought him. Godwin was a fanatical intellectualist; his spiritual home was a realm of unqualified abstractions. He was the last man in the world to be a good novelist; but by dint of a strange cold imaginative energy he produced a story which in its own bizarre way is a masterpiece. Of human life and of human beings except himself he never knew much. His mind was fed almost exclusively on books; he was a tremendous reader, in theology, philosophy, and kindred subjects, and even as a youth had the distinction of being rejected by one college for heresy. All through his preparation for the Dissenting ministry, he continued his quest for truth; and, apart from books, found guidance in that pure spirit, Joseph Fawcett, and in his friendship with Holcroft, George Dyson, and Coleridge. He was not a success as a minister, a profession which he supplemented by tutorial work. His political writing, for the Whigs, and his indefatigable reading and reflecting, debating and self-examining, led at length to the philosophical anarchism which he expounded in the *Enquiry concerning Political* *His "Political Justice"* *Justice, and its influence on general Virtue and Happiness* (1793), a book that was read by a large number of those who could afford the price, but escaped the ban on most revolutionary writings, because it was too metaphysical to affect practical politics and did not enter into competition with the inflammatory tracts of Priestley and Paine which were addressed to the man in the street. It made history in being a major influence on the mind of Shelley, Godwin's

---

[1] It impressed such a judge as Sainte-Beuve, who thought Caleb's attachment to Falkland the very counterpart of Amaury's position as adoring servitor and confidant to the Royalist Marquis de Couaën (*Volupté*, 8th ed., 1874, p. 111) : " Pour moi qui m'attachais, comme Caleb, à ses pensées, son deuil muet me sembla d'un caractère durable, indélébile, égal à celui de tout conquérant dépossédé." Note how he takes it for granted that his readers will remember " Caleb."

future son-in-law; Shelley is the only thoroughgoing expositor of Godwinism who is of the least importance.

Every one of Godwin's novels has an express purpose; they *"Caleb* all set forth his judgments on existing society in the light of his *Williams,* intellectualist philosophy, and in each case their particular object *or things* is defined at the outset. *Caleb Williams, or things as they are* *as they are"* (1794), sets it forth in the sub-title, and more definitely in the preface: "to comprehend, as far as the progressive nature of a single story would allow, a general view of the modes of domestic and unrecorded despotism by which man becomes the destroyer of man." But in constructing the story, Godwin was seized by an idea, which was more akin to those of the Gothic romancers then in fashion than to abstract sociology, the idea of terror and suspense and their extraordinary power over the mind, and it was this which proved the shaping influence throughout. There is no novel of that era in which the psychological element of suspense has fuller play or exercises more potency over the reader's imagination. Yet Godwin justified the claim of his preface; for, if the story seems to go beyond it, and a story cannot prove anything, the state of society depicted, if it rendered such a monstrous series of transactions possible, did form an adequate ground for his indictment.

Once possessed of his idea, Godwin set to work with his usual *A novel of* methodical energy to elaborate it. He says, " I invented first the *terror and* third volume of my tale, then the second, and, last of all, the first. *suspense* I bent myself to the conception of a series of adventures of flight and pursuit; the fugitive in perpetual apprehension of being overwhelmed with the worst calamities, and the pursuer, by his ingenuity and resources, keeping his victim in a state of the most fearful alarm." It is a good account of this strange story, which, in spite of the author's inability to limn a being of flesh and blood, does not fail to create the emotional impression that he designed. There are two protagonists. Falkland, from the spurious sense of honour which he has inherited, kills his boorish enemy Tyrrel to avenge an insult; his inquisitive servant Caleb unearths the secret. But, far from having Falkland in his power, Caleb now finds himself completely in the power of Falkland, who is his social superior, and can utilize all the advantages of wealth and station, and even employ the machinery of the law to hold Caleb at his mercy. Falkland has him imprisoned on a charge of theft. Wherever Caleb flees for safety, he is hounded by the emissaries of Falkland. At length, after vicissitudes of flight and pursuit, the two are brought face to face in court; but, even now, Caleb is held paralysed by the mental and moral superiority of Falkland, and breaks down miserably. This is the gist of a story which Godwin oddly described as " in some measure a paraphrase of the story of Bluebeard," in allusion to the demon of curiosity which brought Caleb to his doom.[1]

"St Leon"

Godwin was very proud of his exploit in the fiction of terror and suspense, and in the prefaces to his subsequent novels kept harping upon it, and wondering whether he would ever come across such another constructive idea. The one he developed in *St Leon, a tale of the sixteenth century* (1799), the world of troubles overwhelming a man who has gained possession of the philosopher's stone and the elixir of life, was not so fertile, although at a time when Cagliostro had but recently died it was not so hackneyed as it would be now. The story is semi-historical, and has many other features of Gothic romance. St Leon, ruined at the gaming-tables and more than half distracted, is restored to sanity by a sojourn in the Alps. Then he and his family are reduced to destitution by a terrific hailstorm, and are persecuted by the inhabitants. They migrate to the shores of Lake Constance, where they spend seven years of Arcadian bliss dedicated to " the simplicity of nature and the genuine sentiments of the heart." But one day a mysterious stranger arrives, who dies, bequeathing to St Leon the secret of the philosopher's stone. This is the end of all their happiness. It is impossible for a man with an inexhaustible supply of wealth to enjoy it without incurring the jealousy and suspicion of everyone around him or being harassed by the vigilance of the authorities. Wherever he goes St Leon is a marked man, a pariah, exposed to the fury of the mob, powerless to utilize his supernatural gift. St Leon is persecuted by the Inquisition; he goes to Hungary, and tries to put in operation a vast scheme of benevolence. Here the Gothic element comes in heavily with St Leon's formidable ally, Bethlem Gabor, " a man

---

[1] Advertisement to *Cloudesley* (1830).

of iron; though adversity pour her fiercest darts upon him, he is invulnerable; he is of too colossal a structure to be accessible to human feelings and human affections." But Bethlem Gabor turns upon St Leon, who eventually finds a partial deliverance by other means.

Having in *St Leon* endeavoured to " mix human feelings and passions with incredible situations," he turned in his next novel, *Fleetwood, or the new Man of Feeling* (1805), to " such adventures, as for the most part have occurred to at least one half of the Englishmen now existing,"[1] that is, to the trials of married life. In *Political Justice* he had discussed the question " whether marriage, as it stands described and supported in the laws of England, might not with advantage admit of certain modifications." And now he asks, " Can anything be more distinct, than such a proposition on the one hand, and a recommendation on the other that each man for himself should supersede and trample upon the institutions of the country in which he lives? A thousand things might be found excellent and salutary, if brought into general practice, which would in some cases appear ridiculous, and in others be attended with tragical consequences, if prematurely acted upon by a solitary individual."[2] Godwin was assuredly not the individualist that some critics, especially from across the Channel, have often called him.

Fleetwood is brought up among the mountains of North Wales, and delights in the magnificence of nature and the virtues of the simple life. But at Oxford he falls into dissipation, and at Paris he continues his debauchery, till the faithlessness of a mistress turns him back upon himself and his inherent integrity, and he finds solace and renewed faith in humanity through a sojourn among Swiss peasants. Then, at the age of forty-five, Godwin's reconverted Rousseauist marries the youthful daughter of a Cumberland recluse, who had been a friend of Rousseau during the latter's life in England. The worn-out roué, with his Godwinian turn for self-analysis and heavy moralization, easily becomes a prey to consuming jealousy. Once more, a grave sociological study slides into Gothicism, a lurid succession of brain-storms culminating in violent madness. Godwin was ill advised to employ the

" Fleet-
wood "

---

[1] Preface. [2] *Ibid.*

autobiographical form with a melodramatic plot. The schemes of the villain are hinted while his machinations proceed, nullifying the sense of mystery and suspense, and compelling us to ask how Fleetwood knows all this. Godwin's genuine feeling for the oppressed comes out in what is really a humanitarian digression, the intensely pathetic account of the child slaves in the silk-mills of Lyons. With bitter irony, he makes his great industrialist point out the immense service he is rendering to the community:

Our town is a perfect paradise. We are able to take them at four years of age, and in some cases sooner. Their little fingers, as soon as they have well learned the use of them, are employed for the relief of their parents, who have brought them up from the breast. They learn no bad habits; but are quiet, and orderly, and attentive, and industrious. What a prospect for their future lives! God himself must approve and bless a race who are thus early prepared to be of use to themselves and others. [1]

"*Mande-ville*"   Another introspective study of character and its moulding and marring by circumstance, gothicized by its historical setting, is his next novel, *Mandeville, a tale of the seventeenth century* (1817). It is the autobiography of a moody, resentful, violent nature, brooding over the injustices that have brought to naught his ambition to make the figure in the world which his wealth and lineage led him to expect. He ultimately works himself into monomania. There is an overplus of historical erudition in the book but a complete lack of historical imagination. Mandeville was saved from the Irish massacres of 1641, and ever after detested the Catholics. But his presbyterianism was not in favour with the masters and boys at Winchester, and he gets into hot water for his supposed anti-Royalist sentiments. Later, he encounters rebuffs when he seeks political employ, and is unjustly accused of treachery. Even the gallant young Clifford turns on him; and when this old friend, now his foe, loves and is loved by Mandeville's adored sister, the wretched man feels that his cup is full. In a murderous attack, Mandeville receives a sabre-cut in the face which blinds and disfigures him—the last straw in the misanthrope's burden of grievances against the world.

Godwin's characters seem to be born old men: they talk like

[1] Chap. xi.

disillusioned philosophers. The story is told with endless moral- *Godwin's* istic expatiation; it is often grandiloquent and bombastic, yet *factitious* not lacking in a certain appealing nobility of thought. Even the *heroes* schoolboys at Winchester are continually discussing, meditating, and criticizing the social order and themselves. It is Godwin's regular foible: too much abstraction, an almost incredible ignorance of reality.

Cloudesley (1830) is a sort of historical novel of adventure; " *Cloudes-* the autobiography of a young man, who after vicissitudes in *ley* " Russia under Peter the Great, is sent on a mission by Lord Danvers to keep watch upon the nephew, the true heir to the estates, whom he, the usurping uncle, had condemned to obscurity. Cloudesley was in the secret; he was a man who had committed crimes, yet was sound at heart and faithful; willing, nevertheless, to connive in the fraud. He loves the boy, and brings him up in Italy as his own son. Then, in a moral revulsion, he determines to effect his restoration. But Cloudesley dies, and it is left to the repentant Danvers, now bereft of his own children, to make restitution. There is something of the suspense of *Caleb Williams* in the mental plight of the false Earl Danvers when the threat of exposure is hanging over his head. But the excitement is damped by the lumbering slowness of the narrative, and nothing at all is made of the Russian horrors and the perils from bandits in Italy and Sicily. Godwin tries his hand at scenic descriptions of the Apennines, but they are thrown away.

In the preface to *Deloraine* (1833) he alludes to Scott, and even " *Delo-* has the vainglory to hint at emulation on one part or the other. *raine* " The third volume tries to repeat the thrill of *Caleb Williams*. Deloraine, a rich widower with an only daughter Catherine, marries again. The new wife had lost her lover in a shipwreck; she is another Julia de Roubigné. Deloraine suddenly finds her in the arms of the shipwrecked lover, who had escaped by swimming ashore. He shoots him, like the outraged husband in *Sidney Bidulph*, and she dies of the shock. Then the dead man's friend hunts the murderer and makes his life a hell; until the high-souled Catherine puts the case to him fairly, and he relents.

That charming young widow and lisping actress Mrs Elizabeth Inchbald (1753-1821) was one of the best-loved members of the

Mrs
Inchbald:
" A
Simple
Story "

Godwin circle, and wrote a number of comedies and two novels marked by scenes of intense pathos, warmed, too, by her own humanitarian feelings and by revolutionary sentiment in which she espoused the likes and dislikes of her friends Godwin and Holcroft. She was a devout Roman Catholic; and the finest character in *A Simple Story* (1791)[1] is the priest Dorriforth, said to be drawn from the actor Kemble, brother of Mrs Siddons, who was of the same faith. Dorriforth accepts the guardianship of a friend's daughter, Miss Milner—her other name is never revealed even in the most intimate scenes, and even after her marriage she is always spoken of as " Miss Milner " : it is one of the few old-fashioned traits in the book. Mrs Inchbald is supposed by some to have drawn this attractive but flighty and indiscreet young person from herself; but Miss Milner is only a variant of the type Manon Lescaut. She falls in love with her guardian, who having inherited an earldom and been released from his vows marries her. But, alas ! she is led astray by the vanities of fast life, and proves unfaithful; and, after some emotional scenes that pierce the reader's heart, her husband repudiates her. There is an abstinence from the gush and exaggeration of the average novel of sensibility in these scenes of tragic conflict, and an insight into the interplay of character, as, for instance, in the part of the crabbed old priest Sandford, the earl's trusted friend and a stern judge of Miss Milner's escapades, yet at bottom a generous soul, which gives this story a new distinction. Mrs Inchbald is able, and not afraid, to exhibit passion in dramatic action.

The result
of an
improper
education

But her novel falls into two parts. There is an interval of seventeen years, and now the interest centres in Miss Milner's daughter. Her goodness makes up to her embittered father for her mother's offences, and according to Mrs Inchbald's final paragraph illustrates the results of an upbringing in " the school of prudence," as contrasted with " the pernicious effects of an *improper education* " in her mother. It is true that at the beginning some readers might have been warned that Mrs Inchbald had a thesis, from her telling them that Mr Milner had " consigned his daughter to a boarding-school for Protestants "; nevertheless, they might complain of being treated unfairly when they reach the

[1] Written 1777.

last line and are informed that the whole tragedy might have been spared if " he had given to his daughter A PROPER EDUCATION."

Nature and Art (1796) is more recognizably a piece of doctrin-
aire fiction, of the *Hermsprong* kind. It is a parallel study of two
cousins, one educated in England in the orthodox way abhorred by the Rousseauist, the other brought up among African savages, his native simplicity, candour, and goodness of heart unspoiled by the foolish discipline and the cultivated affectations of the so-called civilized world. Like Hermsprong, but with more innocence, he calls things by their right names : compliments are lies ; when he mentions war and battles, he substitutes the word massacre. His frank repartees, the malice of which is, of course, Mrs Inchbald's, cause endless embarrassment when there is company. When he entered the dean's dressing-room, and saw his wig lying on the table, " Henry appeared at a loss which of the two he should bow to." " At last he gave the preference to his uncle ; but, afterwards, bowed reverently to the wig."

He had a contempt for all finery ; and had called even his aunt's jewels, when they were first shown to him, " trumpery," asking " what they were good for ? " But being corrected in this disrespect, and informed of their high value, he, like a good convert, gave up his reason to his faith ; and becoming, like all converts, over-zealous, he now believed there was great worth in all gaudy appearances, and even respected the ear-rings of Lady Clementina almost as much as he respected herself.[1]

His cousin William, who reads law, becomes a successful barrister, and in due course a judge, in his youth seduced a village girl and deserted her, leaving his child to be saved from want by Henry. His old sweetheart falls to the lowest depths, and is brought before William on a charge of forgery. It is a scene as carefully prepared for as the one on which Fanny Burney plumed herself in *Cecilia*, and it was probably the model for the scene in Lytton's *Paul Clifford* in which a father condemns his own son.

When every witness on the part of the prosecutor had been examined, the judge addressed himself to her :
" What defence have you to make ? "
It was William spoke to Alice ! The sound was sweet ; the

[1] Chap. xii.

voice was mild, was soft, compassionate, encouraging! It almost charmed her to a love of life!—not such a voice as when William last addressed her, when he left her undone and pregnant, vowing never to see or speak to her more.

She could have hung upon his words for ever! She did not call to mind that this gentleness was the effect of practice, the art of his occupation; which, at times, is but a copy, by the unfeeling, from his benevolent brethren of the bench. In the present judge, tenderness was not designed for the consolation of the culprit, but for the approbation of the auditors. . . .

But when William placed the fatal velvet on his head, and rose to pronounce her sentence, she started with a kind of convulsive motion; retreated a step or two back, and, lifting up her hands, with a scream exclaimed:

" Oh, not from you ! " . . .

Serene and dignified, as if no such exclamation had been uttered, William delivered the fatal speech, ending with, " Dead, dead, dead."

She fainted as he closed the period, and was carried back to prison in a swoon; while he adjourned the court to go to dinner.[1]

Novels by Mary Wollstone-craft, Mrs Opie, and Thomas Day

Another of the Godwin circle, Mrs Opie, was a novelist and a writer of story-books for children; and Godwin's wife, Mary Wollstonecraft, most famous for her *Vindication of the Rights of Women*, also wrote a moving story, partly of her own life, *Mary, a fiction* (1788), which would have been still more moving perhaps had she not conformed to the prevailing taste for analysis of sensibility. Mrs Opie's *Adeline Mowbray, or mother and daughter* (1804), on the other hand, satirizes the female revolutionist, and, without actually taking liberties with the facts of her career, paints just such another as Mary Wollstonecroft, in the vein of travesty. They were all people of strong views on education, and alongside Mrs Inchbald and Mrs Opie may, in that sense, be placed the great educationist Thomas Day, with his *Sandford and Merton*. Sandford is another *ingénu*, like Henry in *Nature and Art*, who confounds the sophisticated with his natural wisdom and invincible common sense; whilst Tommy Merton is the delicate, fretful, and ill-conditioned product of luxury and refinement. The pair represent a favourite contrast at that day; and the tutor, the Rev. Mr Barlow, typifies the philosophy of education derived

[1] Chap. xl.

from *Emile*, with his tales of Laplanders, Greenlanders, High-landers, Scythians, and other exponents of fortitude, simplicity of life, and skill in all natural pursuits.

A vehement outbreak of what may now be called the modern spirit, in arms against the repressions of philistine surroundings and a purblind morality, came from still another woman who had learned from Godwin and his school, the semi-autobiographical *Memoirs of Emma Courtney* (1796) by Mary Hays. Though she was later the author also of another novel of revolt, *The Victim of Prejudice* (1799), she must not be understood in either case as being an undiscriminating rebel: her point is that the morbid state of mind and the clash with the forces of environment are alike " the natural and odious result of a distempered and un-natural civilization."[1] Emma pours out her mental tribulations for the benefit of the son of the man whom she loved and who repulsed her, and tells him, " Be not the slave of your passions, neither dream of eradicating them." It is an indiscreet and perhaps a dangerous thing to do, for a person who confesses to " a morbid excess of distempered imagination." That is Emma; but Miss Hays describes even herself in the preface as " loving virtue but enslaved by passion," and the directness of her story was bound to arouse incomprehension and violent protest.

Mary Hays : " Memoirs of Emma Courtney "

Emma cries out against the common restraints by which the respectable would preserve the decencies. She demands freedom for herself, and for her sex. She tries by sheer force of argument to persuade the young man whom she has singled out as the only possible mate for one of her superior nature to marry her or even take her for his mistress. Coldly repulsed, she takes another without loving him, and then has the supreme anguish of tending the beloved in his last moments after a fatal accident, violent recriminations from the jealous husband being the natural but as she thinks the most outrageous consequence. The insoluble problem is submitted as the result of an unnatural and hypocritical state of society. That may be; but Miss Hays was unwise to select a case of morbid hysteria as her illustration.

Elizabeth Hamilton, in *Memoirs of Modern Philosophers* (1800),

---

[1] She is really much less intransigent than her contemporary, William Blake.

Elizabeth seized rather upon Mary Hays in particular than the whole school
Hamilton's in general as a subject calling for burlesque. Mrs Hamilton (she
burlesque never married, but assumed the matronly style in her riper years)
was an earlier and milder Peacock, in her satire of current social
philosophies and programmes of life. She shoots from two angles,
ridicule and refutation by reasoning and example. Whole slices
from *Political Justice* are served up in the speeches of her pseudo-
philosophers; but her foremost heroine, Bridgetina Botherim,
and the imaginative Glib, who is carried away by gusts of
enthusiasm when a new project inflames his irrational soul, are
mainly digs at Mary Hays and the dialectic she had so badly
learned from others and employed with such tactlessness.

" And do you think," cries Bridgetina, " I am now *at liberty*
to remain here? I wonder, mamma, how you can speak so
ridiculously. Have I not told you again and again, that I am
under *the necessity* of preferring the motive that is most preferable?
The company, if they are not very ignorant indeed, must know
that my going instantly to Mr Glib's is a link in the glorious chain
of causation, generated in eternity, and which binds me now to
act exactly as I do."
So saying, she put her arm in Mr Glib's, and hurried off as
fast as the shortness of her legs would permit.[1]

Unfortunately for the purpose of the satire, the characters
never act sensibly; they would have been fools under any dis-
pensation. And the horseplay, the savage and dirty jokes at their
expense, are a still cruder method of carrying conviction than the
rebuttal of the doctrinaires by process of argumentation.

Satire of   The tragic method is used in the case of the other victim of
Rousseau enthusiasm. Her name is Julia, and other allusions to the *Nouvelle
Héloïse*, not to mention the Swiss name of Valloton for a scurrilous
caricature of Rousseau, show beyond all possibility of mistake
what is the butt. In short, this is another *Julie*, assimilated to
Clarissa. This well-meaning but entirely irrational young woman
is led astray and comes to sorrow through the activities of Valloton.
At the crisis of her fate, she contemplates herself as resisting a
father who attempts, " with all the cruelty of all the Harlowes,"
to force her to a hateful union; and in her suitor she recognizes

[1] Volume i. 28-29.

another Solmes, in herself a heroine fighting the good fight of her sex.[1] At the end, those people who retain a measure of common sense are rewarded or put in the way of reformation; the rest are too far gone in absurdity to be converted even by the arguments of the wise or the visible results of folly.

[1] Volume iii. 265.

SELECT READING AND REFERENCE LIST

GENERAL

BAKER, ERNEST A., and PACKMAN, JAMES. *A Guide to the Best Fiction, English and American, including Translations from Foreign Languages.* Third edition. 1932.

BERNBAUM, ERNEST. *Guide through the Romantic Movement.* 1930.

BRÉMOND, HENRI. *Pour le romantisme.* 1923.

CHARLANNE, LOUIS. *L'Influence française en Angleterre au XVIIᵉ siècle.* 1906.

COLLINS, A. S. *Authorship in the Age of Johnson, being a Study of the Relation between Author, Patron, Publisher and Public (1726-1780).* 1927.
> "The Growth of the Reading Public in the Eighteenth Century" (*Review of English Studies,* July-October, 1926).
> *The Profession of Letters: a Study of the Relation of Author to Patron, Publisher and Public (1780-1832).* 1928.

ELTON, OLIVER. *A Survey of English Literature, 1780-1830.* 2 vols. 1912.

GOSSE, EDMUND. *A History of Eighteenth Century Literature (1660-1780).* 1889.

GRAHAM, WALTER. *English Literary Periodicals.* 1930.

HORNER, JOYCE. "Women Novelists, 1688-1797" (*Smith College Studies in Modern Languages,* XI., Nos. 1-3).

MORE, PAUL ELMER. *The Drift of Romanticism.* 1913.

REEVE, CLARA. *The Progress of Romance, through Times, Countries, and Manners, with Remarks on the Good and Bad Effects of it, on them respectively; in a Course of Evening Conversations.* 1785.

REYNAUD, LOUIS. *Le Romantisme: ses origines anglo-germaniques.* 1926.

RICHTER, HELENE. *Geschichte der englischen Romantik.* 4 vols. 1911.

SCOTT, SIR WALTER. *Lives of Eminent Novelists and Dramatists.* 1825.

STEPHEN, SIR LESLIE. *English Literature and Society in the Eighteenth Century* (Ford Lectures, 1903). 1904.
A History of English Thought in the Eighteenth Century. 2 vols. 1876.

SWANN, GEORGE R. *Philosophical Parallelisms in Six English Novelists.* 1903.

TOMPKINS, J. M. S. *The Popular Novel in England* (1770-1800). 1932.

TURBERVILLE, A. S. *English Men and Manners in the Eighteenth Century: an illustrated narrative.* 1926.

WARD, A. W., and WALLER, A. R. (ed.). *The Cambridge History of English Literature.* 15 vols. 1907-1927.
Especially vols. ix.–xi., dealing with the later eighteenth century.

CHAPTERS II.-IV.—MINOR CONTEMPORARIES, ORIENTAL NOVEL, ETC.

BECKFORD, WILLIAM. *The Episodes of Vathek.* Translated by Sir F. T. Marzials. With introduction by Lewis Melville. 1912.

BLACK, WILLIAM. *Goldsmith.* (English Men of Letters.) 1879.

CONANT, MARTHA PIKE. *The Oriental Tale in England in the Eighteenth Century.* 1908.

GOLDSMITH, OLIVER. *Letters.* Edited by Katharine C. Balderston. 1928.
   The Vicar of Wakefield. Edited, with introduction, by Oswald Doughty. 1928.

GRAVES, RICHARD. *The Spiritual Quixote.* Edited by Charles Whibley. 1926.

JOHNSON, SAMUEL. *Rasselas.* Edited by R. W. Chapman. 1927.

MAY, MARCEL. *La Jeunesse de William Beckford et la génèse de son " Vathek."* 1928.

SELLS, ARTHUR LYTTON. *Les Sources françaises de Goldsmith.* 1924.

SMITH, HAMILTON JEWETT. *Oliver Goldsmith's " The Citizen of the World."* (Yale Studies in English.) 1926.

SMITHERS, L. C. (ed.). *The Thousand and One Quarters of an Hour (Tartarian Tales).* 1893.
   A modern translation from T. S. Gueullette.

STEPHEN, SIR LESLIE. *Samuel Johnson.* (English Men of Letters.) 1891.

CHAPTERS V.-VII.—SENTIMENT AND SENSIBILITY

BERNBAUM, ERNEST. *The Drama of Sensibility : a sketch of the history of English sentimental comedy and tragedy, 1696-1780.* (Harvard Studies in English, 3.) 1915.

BROOKE, FRANCES. *Lady Julia Mandeville.* With introduction by E. Phillips Poole. 1930.

BURNEY, FANNY (MADAME D'ARBLAY). *The Early Diary (1768-1778).* Edited by A. R. Ellis. 2 vols. 1913.
   Diary and Letters (1778-1840). Edited by Austin Dobson. 6 vols. 1904-1905.

DOBSON, AUSTIN. *Eighteenth-Century Vignettes.* Three series. 1892-1896.
   Fanny Burney. (English Men of Letters.) 1903.

ÉTIENNE, SERVAIS. *Le Genre romanesque en France depuis l'apparition de la " Nouvelle Héloïse " jusqu'aux approches de la révolution.* 1922.

FAIRCHILD, HOXIE NEALE. *The Noble Savage : a study in romantic naturalism.* 1928.

FOSTER, JAMES R. " The Abbé Prévost and the English Novel " (*Publications of the Modern Language Association of America*, xlii., pp. 443-464). 1927.

HAZARD, PAUL. *L'Abbé Prévost et l'Angleterre : étude critique sur " Manon Lescaut."* 1929.

INKLAAR, D. *François-Thomas de Baculard d'Arnaud : ses imitateurs en Hollande et dans d'autres pays.* 1925.

LARROUMET, GUSTAVE. *Marivaux, sa vie et ses œuvres.* Nouvelle edition. 1894.

LASSERRE, PIERRE. *Le Romantisme français : essai sur la révolution dans les sentiments et dans les idées au XIXᵉ siècle.* 1919.
Nouvelle édition augmentée d'une préface.

LE BRETON, ANDRÉ. *Histoire du roman français au XVIIIᵉ siècle.* 1898.

MACKENZIE, HENRY. *Anecdotes and Egotisms.* Edited by H. W. Thompson. 1927.

PRÉVOST, ABBÉ. *Adventures of a Man of Quality.* Translated by M. E. I. Robertson. 1930.
Mémoires d'un homme de qualité. 1927.

SINGER, GODFREY FRANK. *The Epistolary Novel : its origin, development, decline and residuary influence.* 1933.

TEXTE, J. *Rousseau et les origines du cosmopolitisme littéraire.* 1895.

THOMPSON, HAROLD WILLIAM. *A Scottish Man of Feeling : being some account of Henry Mackenzie and of the Golden Age of Burns and Scott.* 1931.

TRAHARD, PIERRE. *Les Maîtres de la sensibilité française au XVIIIᵉ siècle.* 2 vols. 1931-1932.

Van Tieghem, Paul. *Le Mouvement romantique* (1912). New edition. 1923.

    Le Préromantisme. 2 vols. 1924-1930.

    " Les Droits de l'amour et l'union libre dans le roman français et allemand, 1760-1790 " (*Neophilologos*, 1927, pp. 96-103).

CHAPTER VIII.—THE GOTHIC NOVEL

Barrett, Eaton Stannard. *The Heroine.* With introduction by Michael Sadleir. 1927.

Birkhead, Edith. *The Tale of Terror : a study of the Gothic romance.* 1921.

Brauchli, Jakob. *Der englische Schauerroman um 1800 unter Berücsichtung der unbekannten Bücher.* 1928.

This contains the fullest list of Gothic or semi-Gothic novels in English from *The Castle of Otranto* onwards. By 1802 about 140 had appeared, by 1818 about 180 more, and from 1819 to 1830 another 180, making a total of some 500.

Idman, Niilo. *Charles Robert Maturin : his life and works.* 1923.

Killen, Alice M. *Le Roman terrifiant ou roman noir de Walpole à Anne Radcliffe et son influence sur la littérature française jusqu' en 1840.* 1924.

McIntyre, Clara Frances. *Ann Radcliffe in relation to her time.* 1920.

Maigron, Louis. *Le Roman historique à l'époque romantique : essai sur l'influence de Walter Scott.* 1898.

Mehrotra, K. K. *Horace Walpole and the English Novel : a study of the influence of " The Castle of Otranto," 1764-1820.* 1934.

The author thinks that Gothic romance was an affair of Walpole's influence.

Praz, Mario. *The Romantic Agony.* Translated. 1933.

Railo, Eino. *The Haunted Castle : a study of the elements of English romanticism.* 1927.

SCHNEIDER, RUDOLF. *Der Mönch in der englischen Dichtung auf Lewis's "Monk,"* 1795. (*Palæstra,* 155. 1928.)

STOKOE, F. W. *German Influence in the English Romantic Period* (1788-1818). 1926.

STUART, DOROTHY MARGARET. *Horace Walpole.* (English Men of Letters.) 1927.

TRENT, W. P., etc. (ed.). *A History of American Literature,* vol. i. 1918.

VAN DOREN, CARL. *The American Novel.* 1921.

WALPOLE, HORACE. *The Castle of Otranto.* Edited, with introduction, by Oswald Doughty. 1929.
> *The Castle of Otranto; and The Mysterious Mother.* Edited by Montague Summers. 1924.

WALZEL, OSKAR. *Deutsche Romantik.* 2 vols. 1918.
> *German Romanticism.* Translated by A. E. Lussky. 1932.

WIETENS, ALIDA ALBERTINE SIBBELLINA. *Mrs Radcliffe: her relation towards Romanticism; with appendix on novels falsely ascribed to her.* 1926.

CHAPTER IX.—THE NOVEL OF DOCTRINE

GREGORY, ALLENE. *The French Revolution and the English Novel.* 1915.

HANCOCK, A. E. *The French Revolution and the English Poets.* 1899.

HOLCROFT, THOMAS. *Life.* Edited by Elbridge Colley. 2 vols. 1925.

INDEX

INDEX

A

Hutcheson, Francis, influence on Mackenzie, 35, note
Hutton, James, the Moravian, perhaps the original of Fanny
    Burney's Albany, 169

I

IDMAN, NIILO, on C. R. Maturin, 223, note
Imaginary voyages. *See* Utopias
Incest, Prévost's *Cleveland*, 107, 108, 128
— *Sally Sable*, 93
— Walpole's *Mysterious Mother*, 179, note
Inchbald, Elizabeth, 229, 249-252
— *Nature and Art*, 69, 251-252
— — compared with Harriet Lee's *Landlady's Tale*, 185
— plays, 29
— *A Simple Story*, 250
Industrial revolution in Charlotte Smith's novels, 190, 192

J

JAMES, HENRY, 213
Jenner, Charles, *The Placid Man*, 88
Jesuits libelled in a novel, 51, note
Johnson, Dr Samuel, antithetic style reproduced by Mackenzie,
    103
— anti-sentimentalist, 77-78
— as anti-sentimentalist as Fanny Burney, 155
— colleague with William Guthrie, 91
— did he write part of *The Female Quixote*? 41 and note
— dissatisfied with *The Vicar of Wakefield*, 81, note
— Fanny Burney's Albany a favourite character, 169
— Fanny Burney's Mr Smith his favourite character, 163
— John Wesley nearer Johnson than to Mackenzie or Brooke, 119
— liked Mrs Lennox's *Harriot Stuart*, 39
— moral views shared by Mackenzie, 112
— on didacticism in fiction, 20, 23, 36
— on *Sidney Bidulph*, 21, 141
— Oriental tales, 60

Q

R